Hard-Boiled
Masculinities

Hard-Boiled Masculinities

Christopher Breu

University of Minnesota Press
Minneapolis • London

Chapter 2 originally appeared as "Going Blood-Simple in Poisonville: Hard-Boiled Masculinity in Dashiell Hammett's *Red Harvest*," *Men and Masculinities* 7, no. 1 (2004): 52–76; copyright 2004; reprinted by permission of Sage Publications. Chapter 5 originally appeared as "Freudian Knot or Gordian Knot? The Contradictions of Racialized Masculinity in Chester Himes' *If He Hollers Let Him Go*," special issue "Black Literary Masculinities," *Callaloo: A Journal of African Diaspora Arts and Letters* 26, no. 3 (2003): 766–95; reprinted with permission.

Published by the University of Minnesota Press
111 Third Avenue South, Suite 290
Minneapolis, MN 55401-2520
http://www.upress.umn.edu

Library of Congress Cataloging-in-Publication Data

Breu, Christopher.
Hard-boiled masculinities / Christopher Breu.
    p. cm.
Includes bibliographical references and index.
ISBN 0-8166-4433-0 (acid-free paper) — ISBN 0-8166-4434-9 (pbk. : acid-free paper)
    1. American fiction—20th century—History and criticism. 2. Masculinity in literature. 3. Detective and mystery stories, American—History and criticism. 4. American fiction—Male authors—History and criticism. 5. Modernism (Literature)—United States. 6. Sex role in literature. 7. Men in literature. I. Title.
PS374.M37B74 2005
813'.509353—dc22

                                                      2005016728

Printed in the United States of America on acid-free paper

The University of Minnesota is an equal-opportunity educator and employer.

12 11 10 09 08 07 06   10 9 8 7 6 5 4 3 2 1

For Elizabeth, my partner in crime

Contents

Introduction
Hard-Boiled Masculinity and the Work of Cultural Fantasy

> If we want to go on believing in categories like social
> class, then we are going to have to dig for them in the
> insubstantial, bottomless realm of cultural and
> collective fantasy.
> —*Fredric Jameson, "Reification and Utopia in Mass Culture"*

Hard-Boiled Fantasies

This book is enmeshed in fantasy. It takes as its central subject one of the
dominant ways in which masculinity was fantasized in the interwar years.
Hard-boiled masculinity had its avatars in both fiction and everyday life
but remained, beyond the confines of both, a cultural fantasy.

The fictional hard-boiled male first emerged in the pulp magazines of
the nineteen twenties and thirties and quickly became an icon of modern
American masculinity. Initially linked to a specific genre, the hard-boiled
detective story, the conception of masculinity represented by this fictional tough guy quickly spread to other sites within American culture:
first to the ostensibly high-cultural writings of American modernists and
then, after the beginning of World War II, to the silver screen, yielding
the tough guy of film noir.

As the name suggests, the hard-boiled male was characterized by a
tough, shell-like exterior,[1] a prophylactic toughness that was organized
around the rigorous suppression of affect and was mirrored by his detached, laconic utterances and his instrumentalized, seemingly amoral
actions.[2] The suppression of affect central to this conception of masculinity was structured by the dynamic of projection, in which the forms of
affective and libidinal investment foreclosed from representation within
the subjectivity of the hard-boiled male returned and were punished in
various gendered, sexual, and racial others. This affective displacement
was paired with a commitment to autonomy that at times indicated, as

1

Erin Smith has demonstrated, an expression of residual solidarity with the nineteenth-century working-class ideal of the autonomous artisan-laborer and at other times manifested itself as a fully pathological version of American individualism, one that repudiated connection and community at every turn.[3] A primarily, though not exclusively, white conception of male identity, hard-boiled masculinity was surreptitiously modeled on an understanding of black masculinity, as vitally and violently primitive. Hard-boiled masculinity, in its externalization of masculinity as a prophylactic toughness, its investment in moral detachment, and its secret borrowing from the iconography of black masculinity, thus emerged as a modernist and class-inflected rejection of the Victorian conception of middle-class white manliness, which was structured around a conception of manhood as an internal moral quality, one that was defined as the civilized opposite of the "primitive" forms of male identity ostensibly embodied by African Americans and other racialized groups.

The central argument of *Hard-Boiled Masculinities* is that the form of manhood that I have just described, what I term hard-boiled masculinity, emerged in the period from 1920 to 1945 as an iconic conception of male identity, one that found approximations in both fiction and life—but which remained, beyond the confines of either, a collective fantasy. In the pages that follow, I focus primarily on the distillation and elaboration of this fantasy in fiction, yet I also suggest that this fantasy had its avatars in everyday life between the wars. Indeed, a central focus of the analysis will be the dialectical relationship between fiction and life, a relationship, I argue, that is mediated through the workings of cultural fantasy. Thus I move from the analysis of the singular fantasy of hard-boiled masculinity to its multiple embodiments—or from hard-boiled masculinity to hard-boiled *masculinities*.[4]

In the remainder of this introduction, then, I will more fully detail the historical emergence of the singular fantasy and the multiple embodiments of hard-boiled masculinity in fiction and in everyday life, sketch out the literary conventions attendant on the representation of hard-boiled masculinity, theorize the workings of cultural fantasy, and conclude by summarizing the different approaches to the cultural fantasy of hard-boiled masculinity taken in the chapters that follow.

Representing Hard-Boiled Masculinity

An account of what I am terming hard-boiled masculinity has of course been posited by film theorists for some time now. Frank Krutnick, in his groundbreaking study of the representation of masculinity in post–World

War II film noir, *In a Lonely Street*, theorizes the emergence of the noir tough guy as part of a shoring up of the "phallic order" in reaction to a postwar crisis in masculinity precipitated by the growth of the female workforce during the war and the challenges of adjustment for men returning home from the front.[5] Similarly, in his recent work on constructions of masculinity during the cold war, Robert Corber situates the popularity of the noir or hard-boiled tough guy as a reaction against the implicit threat to hegemonic conceptions of masculinity represented by the growth of white-collar work and corporate capitalism in the full transition to a Fordist political economy after World War II. While theorizing a wider range of postwar films than the classic cycle of noir analyzed by Krutnick and Corber, theorists such as Kaja Silverman and Stephen Cohan repeat this historical account of noir and other genres preoccupied with masculinity as a response to the postwar "crisis" in male identity.[6]

More recently, the last few years have seen a spate of new readings of hard-boiled and noir fiction that have offered an invaluable corrective to the film studies narrative of noir and its representation of masculinity as an entirely postwar phenomenon. Thus Greg Forter has intensively explored the psychoanalytic dynamics of the representation of male violence in hard-boiled and crime fiction in his *Murdering Masculinities*, while Sean McCann and Erin Smith have differently traced the rhetoric of masculinity in hard-boiled fiction in relationship to changing constructions of American liberalism in the former case and working-class identity in the latter.[7]

Drawing on the groundbreaking work of these scholars, even as it challenges some of the specifics of each of their narratives, *Hard-Boiled Masculinities* attempts to provide a fully theorized account of the emergence of hard-boiled masculinity as a social and a literary phenomenon, one that theorizes the subjective and the socioeconomic with equal attentiveness. In this way it works to overcome the antinomy between psychoanalytic and social accounts of hard-boiled fiction that has formed in this recent criticism, with Forter providing incisive but dehistoricized accounts of the workings of subjectivity in the hard-boiled novel and McCann and Smith providing rich attention to the social context out of which hard-boiled fiction emerged while not theorizing the ways in which this social context intersects with a specific set of subjective dynamics. It is this work of fully theorizing the intersection of the social, or socioeconomic, with the subjective in the formation of hard-boiled masculinity that this book undertakes.[8]

Hard-Boiled Masculinities also undertakes the work of revising the narrative of the midcentury crisis of masculinity that has been codified in film studies and more generally within the emergent field of masculinity studies. As Bryce Traister has incisively noted, too much work in masculinity studies structures itself around a notion of "crisis."[9] This has the unfortunate effect of masking the very forms of male power that this nascent field is ostensibly designed to interrogate. This tendency is exacerbated by a specific (mis)reading of queer theory and social constructionist approaches to gender as producing an understanding of masculinity (which in this context functions as synonymous with white, straight, male identity) as inherently insecure and continuously under siege. Rather than indicating the ways in which gender and gender identities are both variable and structured by unequal forms of power that systematically privilege (those who are marked as) men in U.S. culture, these theoretical appropriations seem designed to evade fully confronting the materiality of male power and privilege.

As its title suggests, *Hard-Boiled Masculinities* can be situated within the broad rubric of masculinity studies, but it also works to overcome the analytical limitations that Traister rightly attributes to the field. While I borrow from the invaluable work done by queer and gender theory to denaturalize cultural understandings of gender and sexuality, I also ground my analysis in a psychoanalytic understanding of subjectivity that emphasizes the ways in which the iterations of fantasy shape, and place initial limits upon the malleability of, gender identity. In this schema gender is neither a performance nor an essence, but a set of phantasmatic deposits and cathexes that shape psychical and bodily constitution of gender and overdetermine the subject's conscious relationship to gender's social meanings. I combine this psychoanalytic account of gender formation with a materialist analysis of the forms of gendered, racial, economic, and sexual inequality that organized everyday life in the early- and mid-twentieth-century United States. I thus examine the phantasmatic and material constitution of hard-boiled masculinity as a twentieth-century form of what Dana Nelson has aptly named "national manhood," which she defines as a hegemonic conception of manhood in the United States that inscribed gender and racial hierarchy in order to manage the destabilizing and exploitative effects of the nation's commitment to capitalism.[10] As I will address more fully in chapter 1, hard-boiled masculinity must also be historicized in relationship to a set of more oppositional meanings that it inherited from nineteenth- and early-twentieth-century conceptions of criminality and social banditry. These meanings posed a challenge to the hegemony effected by this twentieth-century version of national manhood. Yet even these more oppositional meanings tended to leave unquestioned structural forms of male privilege.

My attention to the material and phantasmatic coordinates of male privilege thus enables a different approach to the historiography of masculinity than has been current in masculinity and film studies. This difference can be highlighted by contrasting my own position to the historiographical narrative provided by Robert Corber in *Homosexuality in Cold War America*. I choose Corber's narrative not only because it can be situated at the intersection of masculinity studies and film theory but also because it provides the most compelling and effectively historicized version of the crisis thesis.

For Corber, the film noir tough guy represents the dialectical negation of the organization man: in place of the latter's other-directedness, malleability, and respect for hierarchy, the noir tough guy remains obdurately self-directed, inflexible, and rebellious.[11] While I agree with Corber's reading of hard-boiled or noir masculinity as a reaction to the growth of corporate capitalism, I want to suggest that this reaction and the emergence of corporate capitalism itself must be situated farther back in the history of the twentieth century. It is only by ignoring the emergence and popularity of hard-boiled masculinity in the pulp fiction and modernism of the twenties and thirties that it can be located as a specifically postwar phenomenon. Similarly, the equation of corporate capitalism with high Fordism obscures the way in which, as Martin Sklar demonstrates, the transition from entrepreneurial capitalism to corporate—or monopoly—capitalism began as far back as the 1870s and reached an apotheosis in its initial development in the 1920s, the decade, uncoincidentally, that saw the initial emergence of hard-boiled and noir fiction.[12]

Situating the emergence of hard-boiled masculinity in the interwar period reveals the way in which the fantasy represented an adaptation to, as well as a reaction against, the workings of corporate capitalism. This understanding of hard-boiled masculinity as adaptive as well as reactive also challenges the crisis narrative that underpins Corber's account. It suggests that hard-boiled masculinity represents an aggressive reformulation of male hegemony as much as a defensive reaction to what might have been perceived as a set of economic and social threats to this hegemony.[13]

The hard-boiled male embodied a thoroughly modernized conception of masculinity, one as seemingly instrumentalized and efficient as the corporatized landscape in which he operated. Yet while conforming to this landscape, he also resisted it in precisely the ways that Corber describes: by maintaining a rigorously individualist stance, by being self-directed, and by rebelling against all forms of authority and social connection. Thus hard-boiled masculinity represented a reformulation, rather than the capitulation, of older fantasies of masculine individualism and worker autonomy to the collectivized world of corporate capitalism. By homeopathically incorporating the instrumentalized logic of corporate capitalism into the very structure of his personality, the hard-boiled male was able to adapt older notions of masculine individualism and autonomy to a newly collectivized world.[14] The emergence of hard-boiled masculinity thus needs to be understood as a retrenchment of cultural conceptions of masculinity as well as a reconfiguration of the meaning of male identity in the face of new socioeconomic circumstances. It is to the continuities and transformations of cultural notions of manhood represented by hard-boiled masculinity that I turn next.

Hard-Boiled Masculinity in Everyday Life

The shifts in the literary representation of masculinity paralleled broader shifts in the cultural construction of manhood. As the historians of masculinity Gail Bederman and Michael Kimmel have argued, nineteenth-century discourses of "manliness" in the United States were predicated on a Victorian conception of "civilization" that emphasized physical restraint and conscious sexual renunciation and that produced its phantasmatic double in the unrestrained sexualized "masculinity" of the black rapist or savage.[15] This discourse of manliness also emphasized a largely interiorized conception of male identity as one in which white middle-class men were seen as the intellectual and moral centers of the joint projects of evolution and civilization. The turn of the century marked a gradual but decisive shift in the cultural ideology of what constituted a valorized male identity, moving from the older discourse of manliness to a newer celebration of an active, exteriorized, and more violent conception of masculinity, one that was associated more readily with working-class men. Manhood was no longer a moral quality but a physical attribute; it was to be proven on the playing field, in the bar, in the bedroom, in the streets, and on the factory floor. Following in the long tradition of white fantasies of "going native" and paralleling the emergence of primitivism in the arts, this new conception of white, primarily working-class masculinity borrowed in ambiguous and disavowed ways from the iconography of black masculinity that was explicitly repudiated by earlier conceptions of manhood.

The ambivalent embrace of both the modern and the primitive in this emergent conception of manhood echoes the same mix of modernist and antimodernist impulses that structure the literary representation of hard-boiled masculinity.[16] Indeed, the literary representation of hard-boiled masculinity can be seen as one of the privileged sites of expression of this new conception of manhood, one which shaped this conception, even as it was shaped by it.

A sense of the cultural ubiquity and appeal of this newly muscle-bound and primitivized conception of masculinity can be gleaned from looking at the advertisements and illustrations in the pulp magazines in which hard-boiled fiction first appeared. The iconographic representation of manhood on *Black Mask* covers, to take just one example, shifted from a still-Victorian-influenced representation in the very early 1920s, featuring covers with men in top hats and mustaches, to a much more overtly violent and muscular depiction by the middle of the decade, culminating in the December 1927 cover, which, under the heading "The He Man's Magazine," featured an image of a shirtless and tattooed hulk of a man who holds a knife and is backed against the wall (see Figures 1 and 2).

A similar conception of masculinity was advanced by Charles Atlas and Earle Liederman's body-building correspondence courses, which were long-standing advertisers in the pages of *Black Mask* and other detective pulp magazines. As Erin Smith has pointed out, the regular appearance of such advertisements over a period of twenty-plus years suggests that they were successful in reaching their targeted consumers (45). One of the techniques used by both Liederman and Atlas was to suggest correspondences between the muscular heroes of the fiction contained in the magazine and the form of masculinity the reader could achieve by taking their courses. For example, in the June 1, 1923, issue of *Black Mask*, the same issue that saw the publication of the first hard-boiled story, Carroll John Daly's "The Knights of the Open Palm," the Liederman correspondence course ran an advertisement that posed the question "What is a Bootlegger?" and went on to argue: "He is nothing but a common lawbreaker who exacts unreasonable prices from the public because of the chances he takes. But how many of us are almost as bad? We daily break the laws of Nature and think nothing of the terrible chances or consequences" (see Figure 3).[17]

The nature in question here is that of masculinity, which is defined in explicitly muscle-bound and primitivist terms: "Get wise to yourself. Get back to Nature's laws and be a real He-man. Pull in your belt and throw out your chest" (3). What is striking in this ad is not only the valorization of the emergent conception of manhood that I am terming hard-boiled masculinity but the way in which the text of the advertisement echoes the language and iconography of the fiction in *Black Mask* to make its pitch.

Figure 1. *Black Mask* cover in 1920: an iconography of manhood still Victorian-influenced.

Figure 2. *Black Mask* cover in 1927: hard-boiled masculinity fully formed.

What Is a Bootlegger?

HE is nothing but a common lawbreaker who exacts unreasonable prices from the public because of the chances he takes. But how many of us are almost as bad? We daily break the laws of Nature and think nothing of the terrible chances or consequences.

Do You Know the Law?

To look at the average man you would swear he never knew the laws of Nature or else he is just plumb crazy. He goes on stuffing any kind of food into his stomach till it sticks out like a loose meal sack, while his chest looks so flat you would think a steam roller had run over it. He stays out most of the night and then abuses his body most of the day. He never gives his lungs half a chance while his arms swing like pieces of rope with knots on the end.

Freedom

Cut it out, fellows. Get wise to yourself. If Adam had looked like some of you, Eve would have fed him poison ivy instead of apples. This foolishness will never get you anywhere but the graveyard. Get back to Nature's laws and be a real Heman. Pull in your belt and throw out your chest. Give your lungs a treat with that good pure oxygen that is all about you and you will get a better kick than you could get out of a whole case of whiskey.

90 Days

Will you turn your body over to me for just 90 days? That's all it takes—and I guarantee to give you a physique to be really proud of. Understand, I don't promise this—I guarantee it. In 30 days I will increase your arm one full inch, and your chest two inches in the same length of time. And then, just watch 'em grow. From then on you will feel the pep in your old backbone. You will amaze yourself and your friends as well. Do you crave this new life—these new joys—this abounding health and strength? If you do

EARLE E. LIEDERMAN
The Acme of Physical Perfection

Send for My New 64-Page Book
"MUSCULAR DEVELOPMENT"

It contains forty-three full-page photographs of myself and some of the many prize-winning pupils I have trained. Some of these came to me as pitiful weaklings, imploring me to help them. Look them over now and you will marvel at their present physiques. This book will prove an impetus and a real inspiration to you. It will thrill you through and through. All I ask is 10 cents to cover the cost of wrapping and mailing and it is yours to keep. This will not obligate you at all, but for the sake of your future health and happiness, do not put it off. Send today—right now, before you turn this page.

EARLE E. LIEDERMAN
Dept. 1706, 305 Broadway, New York City

Figure 3. Hard-boiled masculinity: it's the law. Advertisement for Earle E. Liederman body building, June 1, 1923, page 3.

Both Daly's story and the ad in that June 1923 issue drew on the language of an earlier genre of prohibition-era crime fiction that had been appearing in the pages of *Black Mask* from 1920 forward. Interestingly, the ad, like Daly's story, represented a mutation in the logic of reader-identification encouraged by the earlier fiction. The earlier fiction often featured criminal protagonists, such as bootleggers, of a resolutely unheroic nature who were pitted against the equally unappealing and corrupt forces of law and order, leaving the reader suspended without a clear locus of identification. Both the ad and the story define their version of the muscle-bound and newly heroic hard-boiled tough guy explicitly against criminality: bootleggers in the ad and an explicitly criminal chapter of the Ku Klux Klan in Daly's first hard-boiled story. Yet both borrow from the criminal idiom employed by the earlier fiction. Daly's story is rife with prohibition-era criminal argot, and the ad, in its invocation to "get wise," employs it as well. The name of Daly's protagonist, "Race Williams," and his initial enemies, the Ku Klux Klan, also suggest the disavowed form of racial borrowing that structures hard-boiled masculinity.

What emerges from this complex set of relays between ad and story, fictional characters and "real-life" masculine ideals, then, is a fantasy of correspondence, in which fiction and everyday life are presented as inextricably bound together, meanings from the one shaping and reformulating those from the other and vice versa. This fantasy of correspondence was encouraged by the pulp magazines themselves. Many of them featured columns or headers arguing that their stories were adapted from "real life" knowledge or situations. Many of them also published true-crime stories and lessons in police work, such as the "Ready for the Rackets" column that appeared regularly in *Dime Detective* or the fingerprinting column that appeared briefly in *Black Mask* in the early 1920s. The style and tone of these true-crime and police-work narratives were all but indistinguishable from those of hard-boiled fiction with which they rubbed shoulders in the table of contents.

Readers of the pulp magazines often affirmed this connection between fiction and everyday life. The ostensible "realness" of a story in its depiction of everyday life represented one of the major evaluative criteria that readers used in their letters to editors of magazines like *Black Mask* and *Clues*. What emerged from this intentional blurring of fiction with everyday life was a cultural fantasy of the "realness" of hard-boiled masculinity, a fantasy that, in eliding its very status as fantasy, encouraged a conflation of the forms of masculinity imagined in fiction with those enacted in daily life.

Tracking the Trajectory of a Mobile Fantasy

In the chapters that follow, I attend to this conflation of fiction and everyday life, tracing the emergence of hard-boiled masculinity in the literature and popular culture of the early and mid-twentieth century and suggesting how this emergence was bound up with, and helped initiate, these transformations in the broader cultural constructions of male identity. In charting the hard-boiled male's literary trajectory, I follow him as he crosses and recrosses the great divide between high and popular culture, attending to the changes that each crossing produces to the construction of specific masculine identities.[18] In attending to this movement back and forth between popular and high culture, *Hard-Boiled Masculinities* provides a different account of the relationship between these two spheres of cultural production than has been posited by the most recent work in modernist studies. Andreas Huyssen's and Fredric Jameson's different accounts of the negative dialectical relationship between the two spheres, by challenging earlier modernist critical dismissals of popular culture and its relationship to modernism, have provided much of the terrain for current approaches to this question.[19] Much of the new work in modernist studies has suggested that Huyssen's and Jameson's accounts, by maintaining a negative, if mutually constitutive, relationship between the two spheres, has not gone far enough in positing the interpenetration of and parallels between modernism and popular culture. This most recent work, evident in such essay collections as *Marketing Modernisms* and *Rereading the New*, has been salutary, demonstrating the ways in which modernist works do not function at a remove from the market or from the world of mass culture.[20] Yet this work, in turn, runs the risk of erasing any of the material differences in production, marketing, and consumption between the two spheres.

In its approach to theorizing the relationship between modernism and popular culture, *Hard-Boiled Masculinities* draws on the insights of Huyssen's and Jameson's accounts as well as the revisionist work done under the rubric of the "new modernist studies," while positing a relationship between the two spheres that differs in certain ways from each of these perspectives. I see modernism and popular culture as mutually constitutive and partially overlapping spheres that are in a positive as well as a negative dialectical relationship to each other, yet which are marked by material difference—by distinct forms of production, marketing, and reception. On a stylistic or conceptual level, this dialectic is not only present between works but can be seen to work within a given text, such as when Dashiell Hammett employs modernist forms of parataxis to construct forms of epistemological uncertainty, or William Faulkner draws on pulp materials for his modernist meditations on questions of causality. This combinatory approach also shapes my theoretical approach to theorizing the commodity form and its relationship to both moderism and popular culture. In the pages that follow, I draw in equal measure from the Frankfurt School and cultural studies, theoretical approaches that are conventionally seen as opposed. Combining these two approaches enables me to theorize the powerful cultural work differently done by both the modernist and the popular cultural text, without losing sight of the parameters set on the former by its limited circulation and class-bound address and on the latter by its very status as a commodity.[21]

Just as I trace his movements back and forth across the great divide between modernism and mass culture, I trace the hard-boiled male's movement across the racial divide, attending to the ways in which the different racializations of the hard-boiled male produce discrete masculinities. In theorizing this movement back and forth across the color line, I draw on much recent work in critical race theory and whiteness studies that suggests the ways in which cultural understanding and definitions of whiteness and blackness are interdependent and mutually constitutive.[22] However, while much of this recent work has focused on the discursive construction of racial difference, following the lead of the groundbreaking work of Eric Lott, I want to theorize the specifically *phantasmatic* dimensions of racial definition in its relationship to the construction of male subjectivity. Thus, as with its account of gender, *Hard-Boiled Masculinities* provides an account of race in which it is neither simply a performance nor an essence but rather a set of phantasmatic deposits and cathexes that shape psychical and bodily meanings and overdetermine the subject's conscious relationship to the dynamics of racial formation.

The Coordinates of Hard-Boiled Fiction

The hard-boiled story is typically structured around a core set of narrative elements and oppositions. The hard-boiled protagonist is usually presented as doing one of two things: observing or acting. The former activity situates him as the subject of the gaze, implicitly controlling that which he observes, a positionality that is reinforced by the first-person narrative voice. The story also requires that the hard-boiled male be in motion. He becomes an early-twentieth-century American descendent of Benjamin's flaneur, gaining agency as he moves knowingly through seemingly opaque urban spaces.[23] But whereas the flaneur's activity was an avocation, the hard-boiled male's is a vocation, and as such it is represented as instrumentalized—merely a means to an end. While this movement around the city is certainly action, it does not qualify as such in the hard-boiled narrative. The term is reserved for the kinds of violent action that were the stock-in-trade of most pulp magazines (one of the pulp magazines that published hard-boiled stories was entitled *Action Detective*, assuring potential buyers that the tough guy found within was no armchair sleuth). Action usually comes in quick bursts in the hard-boiled narrative and is represented as chaotic and potentially disorienting. Indeed, it is presented as somewhat akin to modern warfare: the trenches have been replaced by speakeasies, road houses, or the streets and apartments of the modern city, but the battle is just as chaotic and confusing, the weapons are just as deadly, and the struggle is as potentially pointless. The action, in fact, often exceeds any relationship to the solution of the mystery or resolution of the narrative.

Instead, the action is organized around the fantasy oppositions that structure the hard-boiled narrative. These oppositions structure the protagonist's complex relationship to gender, race, class, and sexuality. The class fantasies enacted by the hard-boiled narrative are especially ambivalent and turn, as I demonstrate in chapter 1, on a reformulation of a more rigorously negative and oppositional stance taken by the forms of noir and crime fiction that immediately predated the appearance of hard-boiled fiction in the pages of *Black Mask*. This earlier fiction, which I argue represents the first flowering of noir and which itself was a descendent of nineteenth-century true-crime and dime-novel narratives, allegorizes class relations in purely negative terms. The criminal classes, literary descendents of the more heroic working-class outlaws of the dime novel, are rigorously opposed to the forces of law and order, which are figured as petit-bourgeois defenders of the social order. Neither position is positivized as a stable site of reader identification. The hard-boiled narrative enacts a phantasmatic resolution of this opposition, combining the class associations and social meanings of both positions and positivizing them into a newly composite figure, the hard-boiled detective. Yet the more negative and oppositional meanings of early noir fiction resurface from time to time in the hard-boiled narrative, making the class associations and class positioning of the latter particularly complex and ambivalent.

The sexual, gendered, and racial organization of the hard-boiled narrative is equally complex, although at times less ambivalent. As I demonstrate in chapters 2 and 3, the hard-boiled narrative is conventionally organized along both homosocial and heterosexual axes. The relationships that fall along the homosocial axis alternate between collusion and competition, with an emphasis on the latter. The hard-boiled male's relationship to other men is generally antagonistic, forming the locus of much of the narrative's violent action. This antagonism between men can cross racial lines, as the criminals are often racialized in implicit and explicit ways. The racial opposition can also function in the other direction. As I have asserted, white hard-boiled masculinity borrows in disavowed ways from the iconography of black masculinity in order to define itself against both older forms of Victorian manhood and the larger social order of which it is a part. My readings of *Light in August* in chapter 4 and *If He Hollers Let Him Go* in chapter 5 demonstrate how this racial borrowing can be literalized as well, opening up a space for the production of black hard-boiled masculinity.

The heterosexual axis is organized around the opposition between the hard-boiled male and the femme fatale. The relationships along this axis also alternate between collusion and competition, but in this case they are explicitly eroticized as attraction and repudiation. As I explain in chapters 1 and 2, the femme fatale allegorizes all the forms of connection—national, racial, sexual, and economic—that the hard-boiled male both desires and repudiates. The ambivalence of the hard-boiled male's relationship to the femme fatale becomes the other site of violent action in the narrative. But whereas the violent action between men is represented as public and impersonal, the violence associated with the femme fatale, whether she is the perpetrator or the victim, is figured as both secretive and libidinally charged—a dark secret which the tough-guy protagonist both participates in and disavows. However, if the violence (whether imagined or real) crosses the color line from black to white, this secrecy becomes paradoxically public: the relationship between the hard-boiled male and the femme fatale becomes transformed into the relationship between the black rapist and the virtuous white woman.

It is the argument of *Hard-Boiled Masculinities* that all the oppositions I have just enumerated are fundamentally phantasmatic ones. The relationship of hard-boiled masculinity to larger cultural oppositions around race, gender, class, and sexuality and to political and economic change is structured by the workings of cultural fantasy. It is to theorizing this concept that I turn next.

Theorizing Cultural Fantasy

The concept of cultural fantasy rests at the center of this book, forming its key theoretical postulate. The category provides a link between psychoanalytic theories of subjectivity and materialist theories of culture and political economy. As such my use of it can be located broadly within the tradition of post-Althusserian psychoanalytic Marxism, that Robert Miklitsch has humorously but trenchantly entitled "psycho-Marxism." Psycho-Marxism, then, provides the overall theoretical frame for *Hard-Boiled Masculinities*, with cultural fantasy functioning as its central analytical category.

As an interpretive category, fantasy, like much in psychoanalytic theory, occupies a space between materialism and idealism. On the one hand, fantasy can be described as a specific kind of discourse, one that produces a "scene in which the subject is a protagonist, representing the fulfillment of a wish (in the last analysis, an unconscious wish) in a manner that is distorted to a greater or lesser extent by defensive processes."[24] On the other hand, this form of discourse is intricately bound up with material processes: from the production of bodily affect, through the working through of trauma (which is either bodily to begin with or becomes embodied), to its complex and often contradictory relationship to action. Similarly, as Jean Laplanche argues, fantasy can have its genesis in either material or purely symbolic intersubjective acts.[25] Thus fantasy is neither purely a matter of representation and discourse nor is it simply a matter of material processes and drives. It is, instead, one of the privileged ligatures between the two.

As such, it is parallel to the status of ideology in Marxist theory. While Marx's early definitions of ideology equated it roughly with false consciousness, presenting it as the idealized representation of society and of the relations of production formed by the ruling class that become "in every epoch the ruling ideas," his later specialized definition of it in relationship to the commodity form, what he terms "commodity fetishism," emphasizes the intertwining of the material and the ideal.[26] Describing the transformation of a table into a commodity, Marx articulates this mixing of the material and the ideal:

> Nevertheless the table continues to be wood, an ordinary, sensuous thing. But as soon as it emerges as a commodity, it changes into a thing that transcends sensuousness. It not only stands with its feet on the ground, but, in relation to all other commodities, it stands on its head and evolves out of its wooden brain grotesque ideas, far more wonderful than if it were to begin dancing of its own free will.[27]

While Marx describes the "transcendence" of the material form produced by commodity fetishism, it is quite clear that this transcendence is dependent on the material form of the table itself. It is only because the table has a sensuous existence that its idealization in the form of a commodity is ideological. On one level, this conception of ideology seems relatively continuous with Marx's earlier definitions—for what we have here is a description of the idealization of the material even as it marks the centrality of the material to such an idealization. However, the ideological effect of the commodity is also dependent on a dynamic of materialization in which the "commodity reflects the social characteristics of men's own labour as objective characteristics of the products of labor themselves, as the socio-natural properties of these things" (164–65). Thus ideology works in the mature Marx not just through a process of idealization but through a process of materialization.

The parallels between ideology and fantasy as ligatures between the material and the ideal suggest that the two can be productively thought through in relationship to each other. The category of cultural fantasy represents my attempt to do just this by rethinking the two in terms of a single category. While this hybrid approach runs the risk of losing the analytical specificity of each term, it enables me to think beyond the ideological divide between the sociological and the psychological that is one of the defining characteristics of the modernist era. As I argue in chapter 2, it is precisely this divide that needs to be theorized in the analysis of hard-boiled masculinity. The detached, affectless narration of the hard-boiled protagonist constructs a fantasy of sociological objectivity and disavows and projects onto others all forms of affect that could be categorized as psychological. In order to demystify the ideology of the hard-boiled form, I must undo the division between the psychological and the sociological. The category of cultural fantasy provides the tools to undertake such a demystification.[28]

In order to be effective in this undertaking, however, the category of fantasy has to be unmoored from an orthodox psychoanalytic framework and transformed into a category for historical analysis. In positing the idea of a "political unconscious," Fredric Jameson provides an important model for rethinking psychoanalytic categories in relationship to historically specific political and economic formations. Jameson posits the production of literary and cultural narratives as a privileged site of cultural mediation, in which the political and economic contradictions that organize the social field find resolution in the production of narrative. Combining a Marxist conception of contradiction with a psychoanalytic conception of affective investment, Jameson views the production of narrative as libidinally charged with the desires of a political unconscious. Narratives both contain and potentially release cultural energies of transformation—energies that attempt to overcome the divisions produced by socioeconomic contradiction. Jameson describes the movement between containment and release as the dialectic between ideology and utopia.[29]

Jameson's model provides the basic framework through which I construct my understanding of the historical and social dimensions of cultural fantasy. While employing this framework, however, I alter it in a number of significant ways. First and most importantly, I transform the category of narrative in Jameson's analysis into the category of cultural fantasy. I define cultural fantasy as an imaginary scenario produced by the intersubjective and collective forms of libidinal investment that shape the relationships of individuals and groups to the social field, which I understand broadly as encompassing both the cultural and the political-economic.[30] These scenarios function as the stuff of fantasy in the psychoanalytic sense but also the stuff of ideology in the Marxist sense: they are daydreams, reveries, dreams, and repressed scenes, but also the doxa that informs political, literary, and cultural production. I thus view narrative and other forms of literary production as linguistic embodiments of the scenarios of cultural fantasy.

Second, my emphasis on fantasy and its relationship to individual and collective subjectivity attempts to add a fully developed theory of subjectivity to Jameson's primarily sociological and economic analysis. I thus restore to Jameson's psychoanalytically inflected Marxist account of the relationship between social antagonism and social desire the whole complex web of the psychoanalytic theory of subjectivity. This addition seems necessary for reasons both theoretical and political. The positing of a psychoanalytic subject in relationship to the workings of the political unconscious restores the complex causality articulated by psychoanalytic theory—with its condensations and displacements, its projections and inversions, its repetitions and workings through—to any understanding of the relationship between individual and collective agents and forms of cultural representation and political struggle. Similarly, I would suggest that genuine political transformation is impossible without a transformation in forms of individual and collective affect and fantasy. Such a transformation involves a working through of the phantasmatic investments that animate forms of representation and social action as well as a transformation of representation and action themselves.

Third, I see fantasy as productive of material, cultural, economic, and political relationships and contradictions as much as such relationships and contradictions are productive of fantasy. While Jameson importantly adds a theory of desire to the Marxian model of the social, he basically leaves intact the orthodox Marxist account of the dependence of culture and ideology on the material conditions of economic and cultural production. However, as we saw with Marx's definition of commodity fetishism, ideology involves a process of materialization fully as much as one of idealization. I would assert that the same is true for the workings of cultural fantasy. As Slavoj Žižek points out, fantasies often preexist their objects.[31] Thus the relationship of fantasy to the material conditions of every day life is one of materialization as well as idealization. Fantasies are productive of processes of materialization fully as much as they are libidinal transmutations and abstractions of the material contradictions that organize social relations. Thus my understanding of cultural fantasy is Žižekian as well as Jamesonian.

Finally, by slightly reworking Jameson's salutary definition of narrative as "a socially symbolic act," I argue that narrative also forms a crucial site of social symbolization, one that exists in a dialectical relationship to both social action and the workings of cultural fantasy (*Political* 1). Drawing on the twin psychoanalytic distinctions between symbolization and acting out and repetition and working through, I view narrative and other forms of cultural production as crucial loci of symbolization, ones that allow the materials of cultural fantasy to be represented and thus potentially worked through, rather than merely repeated and acted out.[32] This theory thus sees potential value in even the most seemingly retrograde forms of cultural representation. For to the degree that they serve as an objectification of the materials of cultural fantasy, they hold out the possibility for an individual and collective process of working through, one that may run counter to the hegemonic work done by such forms.

The Permutations of Hard-Boiled Masculinity

It is this understanding of cultural fantasy that informs my analysis of the genesis of the hard-boiled form and my readings of novels by Dashiell Hammett, Ernest Hemingway, William Faulkner, and Chester Himes. In chapter 1, I examine a forgotten strain of crime fiction that appeared in the pages of *Black Mask* prior to the celebrated birth of hard-boiled fiction in the magazine. I argue that this fiction, written by writers both forgotten, such as Julian Kilman, Harvey Wickham, and Harold Ward, and famous, such as Dashiell Hammett and Carroll John Daly (the creators of the hard-boiled story), represents the first flowering of the noir aesthetic. The chapter thus inverts the chronology that is usually associated with hard-boiled fiction and noir. Rather than the former preceding and providing the template for the latter, it is noir that precedes hard-boiled fiction and provides it with its most radically negative elements. The chapter also historicizes the emergence of the rigorous negativity of noir in relationship to the advent of corporate capitalism and to the form's transformation and condensation of various types of social negativity associated with nineteenth-century popular forms such as the dime-novel bandit narrative and the gothic true-crime narrative. The chapter concludes by charting the emergence of hard-boiled fiction and hard-boiled masculinity out of this earlier noir fiction.

In chapter 2, I address the workings of cultural fantasy in Dashiell Hammett's brutal allegory of American violence, *Red Harvest*. Written at the close of the decade that saw the emergence of hard-boiled fiction, *Red Harvest* can be read as the genre's first autocritique. Hammett draws on the negative presence of noir in the hard-boiled form in order to expose the violence produced by the protagonist's ethic of objectivity and moral detachment. Yet the self-reflexive dimensions of Hammett's novel do not extend to its formal narration of masculinity. The inability of the novel to reflect upon its representation of masculinity derives, I argue, from its ideological separation of politics from gender, which manifests itself as a separation between content and form. Although, at the level of content, Hammett's novel criticizes the social effects of instrumental rationality, at the level of gendered affect and narrative form, it reproduces this rationality on another level.

Chapter 3 on Ernest Hemingway's *The Sun Also Rises* chronicles the transformations that take place when the hard-boiled male and the cultural fantasies he embodies travel from the mean streets of the American city to the bars and cafés of Paris and Pamplona. In charting the fantasy work enabled by this geographical shift, I analyze what I term the novel's spatial staging of the historical transformation from nineteenth-century conceptions of manliness to the twentieth-century dictates of hard-boiled masculinity. I suggest that this transformation of space into time is produced through the touristic gaze of the novel's narrator, Jake Barnes, who, like Hammett's Op, views the landscape in which he moves through the lens of male fantasy. In Jake's eyes, the spatio-temporal opposition between Paris and Pamplona becomes organized by a quest narrative. Disturbed by the threats and temptations that the emergent figures of the new woman and the urban homosexual represent to his conception of masculinity, Jake travels to the Basque country to revitalize his sense of manhood by coming into contact with an avatar of primitive virility, the bullfighter Pedro Romero. However, rather than locating the fantasized source of masculine regeneration in Pedro, Jake instead finds that Pedro occupies the same fallen world that he does. In representing this failed journey, the novel both valorizes the primitivism that forms a constitutive part of hard-boiled masculinity and opens up a space for its critique.

The racial imaginary that underlies Jake's ambivalent embrace of the primitive and forms an implicit but important part of the Op's subjectivity becomes the central focus of the next two chapters. My revisionist interpretation of one of the most celebrated works of American modernism, William Faulkner's *Light in August*, enables me to address the racial borrowing that implicitly underpins the hard-boiled form. My analysis focuses on the racially ambiguous Joe Christmas. In contrast to conventional accounts of the novel, which situate Joe in relationship to interwar constructions of black or miscegenated masculinity, I argue that he must also be read in relation to contemporaneous fantasies about white masculinity. By reading Joe in this twofold manner, I demonstrate the interdependent relationship of fantasy figures that usually are seen as distinct: the hard-boiled male and the primitivized figure of the black rapist. My strategy of reading Joe Christmas in relation to these twin fantasies highlights two key aspects of hard-boiled masculinity: the defining role of racist cultural iconography in its formulation, and racism's constitutive presence in the gendered violence that the hard-boiled male practices and legitimates. The dependence of white hard-boiled masculinity on fantasies of black masculinity reveals a distinctly racialized set of meanings attaching to the negative dimension of the aptly named noir aesthetic.

My analysis of Chester Himes's hard-boiled excoriation of American racism *If He Hollers Let Him Go* in chapter 5 further explores the explosive relationship between fantasies of race and fantasies of gendered violence. By first literalizing, then challenging the genre's racist iconography, Himes, the first African American hard-boiled writer, interrogates the ways in which the discourse of white supremacy in the United States has promulgated a systematic conflation of the distinction between fantasy and action. Himes's protagonist, Bob Jones, finds himself enmeshed within the lethal dream logic of white supremacy's favorite fantasy: the black man's rape of a white woman and his subsequent punishment by white male avengers. Rather than acting out the fantasy scenario in which he finds himself situated, he comes to recognize that representation and action are not necessarily complicitous and can function in opposition to each other. By symbolizing the fantasy on a conscious level, Bob is able to resist its violent repetition on the level of action. This symbolization thus becomes what in psychoanalytic terms can be a described as a process of "working through." The possibilities for agency that this process suggests are ironically undercut by the novel's conclusion: Bob is accused of the very crime he has abstained from committing. I read this conclusion as Himes's sardonic commentary on the limitation of individual agency in relation to a systemic erasure of the distinction between fantasy and action. However, Himes's novelistic practice stands in partial opposition to the pessimism of this conclusion. By tapping into both the racialized and critical dimensions of the noir aesthetic latent within the hard-boiled form, Himes structures the novel around negative representation, forcing readers to confront and symbolize their relationship to the forms of racist exploitation and violence that organize social and economic life in the United States of the 1940s and that continue to haunt our present society.

Himes's insistence on the distinction between symbolization and action and the politicization of reading that his novel performs are taken up again in my conclusion. There I attempt to reconstruct the reading communities that formed around pulp magazines such as *Black Mask* and *Clues*, by examining their letters to the editor pages. Two different reading communities formed around the fiction in the magazines—those who read the stories as diversions or literary games and those who read them as indexes of everyday life. These two models of reading in different ways deprivileged the act of reading itself: the first by dismissing it as a game, the second by seeing stories and their meanings as transparently referential. The relationship of fantasy to reading remained largely unexplored. A recognition of the importance of fantasy to the act of reading, to the ethical and political constitution of subjective meanings, might have eventually led readers to construct different masculinities in everyday life, ones that did not need to echo the misogynist and often racist versions they encountered in the hard-boiled fiction they read. The suggestion of such an alternate reading practice can point productively toward the politics of reading mass cultural texts for the possibilities for cultural transformation in our own era. The relationship of the politics of reading to the process of "working through" gendered fantasies, especially when reconceived as a collective rather than an individual form of praxis, can help us rethink contemporary masculinity and its relationship to political-economic struggle.

1
Wearing the Black Mask

> The "blank," the staying out of imaginary
> identification, is constitutive for the [noir] subject.
> —*Slavoj Žižek,* Enjoy Your Symptom!

Noir as Negativity

Negativity is an elusive thing. This is every bit as true of social forms of negativity as it is of its philosophical manifestations. Whether one conceives of social negativity in a Lacanian register, as that which renders the hole in the symbolic or the arbitrariness of the phallus visible, or, in Marxist terms, as the forms of contradiction inherent within the capitalist political economy that pushes toward a different social and economic logic, the negative remains a slippery concept.[1] As soon as one begins to positivize it, to name and examine it, one runs the danger of losing sight of it altogether. At best, one can perhaps, in Slavoj Žižek's terms, tarry with it as long as possible.

The aim of this chapter is to tarry with the forms of social negativity embedded in the hard-boiled form, negativity that at various points and by theorists of various media has been termed noir. Like negativity, noir is a notoriously slippery concept. I want to argue that the elusiveness of the two terms is less than coincidental. As the film theorist Marc Vernet has demonstrated, attempts to positivize noir into a generic category in film studies have repeatedly failed. Literary theorists such as William Marling and Christopher Metress, while nicely detailing the pervasiveness of the thing we call noir in midcentury fiction, have fared little better in defining it as a positive category. When it is talked about as a genre in fiction, its redundancy with both hard-boiled fiction and crime fiction, genres that are more clearly delineated, becomes evident.[2]

I want to suggest instead that noir is best characterized as a resolutely negative cultural fantasy, one that finds expression in a wide range of twentieth-century literary and filmic texts and that functions as both a condensation of and a catalyst for various forms of social negativity that are distinct to the era of corporate capitalism. In defining noir as a historically specific cultural fantasy, I am both synthesizing and reworking earlier definitions of noir that tend to categorize it as either a historical expression distinctive to the thirties, forties, or fifties and/or as a specific fantasy structure that obsessively replays a set of psychoanalytic and social meanings. On the one hand, for historically minded critics such as E. Ann Kaplan, Alain Sliver, Frank Krutnick, Robert Corber, Paula Rabinowitz, William Marling, and David Reid and Jayne L. Walker, noir is theorized as either an expression of post–World War II malaise or as a coded form of Depression-era social protest.[3] On the other hand, for strictly psychoanalytic theorists such as Slavoj Žižek, Joan Copjec, and Elizabeth Cowie, noir is theorized as narrativizing a specific cultural, ontological, or critical fantasy structure.[4]

In constructing my own account of noir as a historically specific negative cultural fantasy, I draw on the psycho-Marxist theoretical paradigm I elucidated in the introduction, to both historicize the rather ahistorical formulations of the psychoanalytic critics and to reveal the phantasmatic and economic underpinnings of the accounts provided by the historicist critics. This chapter thus shows the importance of both sides of the psycho-Marxist dyad for understanding the thing that we call noir. Noir must be understood as both a fantasy and a historical phenomenon, if both its subjective and socioeconomic resonances are to be given their full due.

For the sake of shorthand, I will at points in what follows refer to noir as a "form." However, as my discussion of noir as a negative cultural fantasy suggests, I see it less as a form than as a phantasmatic deformation or volatilization of other forms such as the crime or hard-boiled story. While, in keeping with the historicist critics, I locate noir as a twentieth-century phenomenon, I am much less interested in fixing the coordinates of noir as a specific genre or form than with attending to the ways in which it animates and volatizes the negativity present in other genres.

This chapter revises the accounts of the historicist critics on historical grounds as well. Historicizing the emergence of noir as either a postwar phenomenon or, as the more recent revisionist accounts of Rabinowitz, Marling, and Reid and Walker suggest, as a response to the economic devastation of the Depression misses the way in which the history of this form stretches back further into the history of the twentieth century. I locate the origin of the fantasy we call noir in the forgotten crime narratives that appeared in *Black Mask* in the years just prior to the advent of hard-boiled fiction in the magazine. *Black Mask*'s crime fiction was written by authors who were famous, including the two figures credited with inventing hard-boiled fiction, Dashiell Hammett and Carroll John Daly, and others who have been largely forgotten.[5] The fiction resembled in almost every way the later noir fiction of writers such as James M. Cain, Cornell Woolrich, Edward Anderson, Horace McCoy, Kenneth Fearing, Patricia Highsmith, Dorothy Hughes, David Goodis, and Jim Thompson, as well as the narrative structures of the films from the forties and fifties that we term noir. As we will see more fully below, the fiction even predicts the division manifest in these later forms of cultural production: between noir that is primarily organized around a sociological fantasy of negativity and noir that is primarily organized around fantasies of psychological or intersubjective negativity. It is the presence of these parallels that enables me to describe this fiction as the first efflorescence of noir.

The definition of noir as enacting a fantasy of the subject's negative relationship to the law is, of course, central to psychoanalytic accounts of noir by Slavoj Žižek and Joan Copjec. But whereas they stage this fantasy as a quasi-metaphysical or ontological one that is central to the transhistorical construction of subjectivity itself, I want to situate it as a specific phantasmatic response to the changes inaugurated by the advent of corporate capitalism in the United States. This is not to deny that the ontological meanings that Žižek and Copjec ascribe to noir may also be present in the negative fantasy enacted by the form. It is rather to argue that the appearance of noir at a specific historical conjunction, the 1920s, when the transition from entrepreneurial capitalism to corporate capitalism was relatively complete and the workplace revolutions of Taylorism and, more incipiently, Fordism were underway, and its disappearance—or at least its mutation into a kind of nostalgic neo-noir—with the advent of late capitalism in the 1960s and 1970s, suggests that the negative fantasy enacted by the noir narrative does a certain kind of historically situated and locatable work.[6] This work, one of several phantasmatic cultural responses to corporate capitalism in the era, manifests itself most concretely in the fantasy of the subject's negative relationship to the law. This fantasy radicalizes the negative figuration of the relationship between forces of criminality and those of law and order present in earlier nineteenth-century forms such as the dime-novel bandit or detective narrative and gothic true-crime narratives, presenting a modernist allegory in which neither the position of the criminal nor the

position of the law functions as a stable or comfortable site of identification but instead both are posed as radically negating of each other
and of themselves.[7] Thus in place of the collective forms of identification
and resistance that, as Michael Denning has shown, are allegorized by
the dime-novel bandit story and city mystery, and in place of the legal or
moral resolution (albeit ambivalent) promised by the gothic fictional or
true-crime narrative, the noir narrative refuses both identification and
comfortable resolution.[8]

This resolutely negative recasting of fantasies of earlier popular genres is at the heart of my reading of noir as a response to the advent of
corporate capitalism. The refusal of identification and of a collective
narrative of resistance in noir suggests the ways in which the rhetoric of
collectivity itself had become appropriated by the forces of management
and the ideologues of corporate capitalism in the 1920s.[9] The Taylorist
reorganization of work in the early twentieth century, with its deskilling
of manual labor and its appropriation of the intellectual dimension of
work as the sole province of the emerging profession of management,
opposed the kinds of individualism and autonomy central to the earlier
artisanal and republican rhetoric of workers within entrepreneurial capitalism to a new image of the worker as part of the collective machine.[10]
Within the context of this appropriation of collectivism, even the idea of
collectivity in the service of worker resistance and struggle seemed like
too much of a concession to the logic of the emerging order. The idea
of collectivity also cut against the way in which "white" wage labor articulated itself in the nineteenth century, as David Roediger and Dana
Nelson have differently demonstrated, within a rhetoric of "free labor"
and republicanism that conservatively situated the white worker against
the worker of color (both slave and free) and located the male worker as
the citizen-head of the household.[11]

It is only with a generation more fully adapted to the collective organization of corporate capitalism and with the economic devastation wreaked
by the Great Depression that a new form of collective representation,
proletarian fiction, emerged as a response to the depredations of corporate capitalism. And noir regularly recurred throughout the first sixty
years of the twentieth century as a negative cancellation of both the economic and political structure of the present and of the failed promises
represented by more affirmatively political forms of representation such
as proletarian fiction.

Noir must be read within this larger historical context. Its refusals of
positive representation function as a negation of the shift to corporate
capitalism with all that it entailed for both the reorganization of work

and the challenge to earlier republican and artisanal visions of white male identity. Both of these politically contradictory negations are manifest within the fantasy of the negative relationship between the subject and the law that the noir narrative enacts.

In one version, the negative relationship between the subject and the law encodes the refusal to adhere to the new regime of work. While it may not allegorize a collective resistance to this regime, its very negativity cancels individual identity as much as collective identity. Like Adorno's account of modernism from the same era, noir holds out the possibility for a utopian resolution of the contradictions of the present in its very refusal to resolve them within the frame of the narrative.[12] Of course, the logic of negation in noir, as a mode of popular fiction, functions differently from the formal negations of high modernism privileged by Adorno. Noir functions through the logic of reader transference in relationship to the cultural fantasies allegorized by the text. Yet the negation of the present and surreptitious longing for a transformative future is common to both noir and high modernism. This is the fantasy structure that is central to the sociological noir narrative.

In another version of the noir narrative, the resistance to the transformation of gender and racial relations threatened by the transformation of work relations becomes narrated as a fantasy of gendered and racial transgression. In this case, the white male protagonist of the noir narrative draws implicitly on the racist iconography of black masculinity in order to construct a more fully transgressive version of male identity. This transgressive identity is ratified by a narrative of sexual violence, violence that is usually both enacted and blamed on a female other. This is the fantasy structure that is central to the psychological noir narrative. Both forms of noir become partially postivized in the hard-boiled narrative.

Detecting the Historical Roots of Noir

In the cultural dream work of the early twentieth century, noir appears as a specific condensation, one that reconverts and catalyzes the negative energies of a number of cultural forms that precede it.[13] Within the logic of the noir aesthetic a whole range of earlier cultural forms can be detected: from what Eric Hobsbawm and Michael Denning have described as oral and dime-novel stories of social banditry; to the gothic narrative structure that Karen Halttunen has described as central to popular narratives of crime in the early nineteenth century and that Teresa Goddu has suggested lends a specific racial cast to much nineteenth-century American literature; to the popular city mysteries of the criminal underworld that were set in Philadelphia, New York, Paris, and other nineteenth-century cities; to the tradition of salacious urban guidebooks and city exposés that were popular throughout the century; to the racial melodramas of writers like Thomas Dixon, who presented an eroticized as well as exoticized representation of black criminality; to what Shelley Streeby has described as the popular literature of (intracontinental) empire, which helped to determine the often mutually antagonistic yet deeply imbricated structure of nineteenth-century race and class formation; to the celebrated realisms and naturalisms of the nineteenth and early twentieth centuries.[14] The phantasmatic coordinates of these earlier forms persist in the noir aesthetic, shaping the specific forms of negativity present in the text.

Bandit stories are perhaps the earliest precursor to the noir aesthetic. Initially rooted in oral tradition, these stories narrate the feats of a virtuous criminal or "bandit" who becomes a folk hero for a dispossessed or disenfranchised rural population. As theorized by Hobsbawm, such stories and the acts of banditry they describe are a specifically agrarian expression of counterhegemonic resistance to state power and the encroachments of metropolitan markets and can, in special circumstances, help lay the groundwork for revolution. Bandit stories typically emerge when a largely pre- or noncapitalist region becomes subordinated to the logic of the capitalist market and the concomitant forms of state power (whether this power takes the form of explicit imperialist occupation or merely the restructuring and incorporation of local governmental entities into a larger market logic) or when a region shifts from one stage or form of capitalist production to another (e.g., the shift from agrarian to industrial capitalism) (Hobsbawm 7–62).

In the context of capitalist and imperialist expansion of the United States, the bandit story has appeared in a range of different forms, from the *corridos* that protested the annexation of Mexican territories by the United States, to slave rebellion narratives (the most famous being, of course, that of Nat Turner), to the tales of the Molly Maguires and other outlaw labor organizations, to Western outlaws such as Jesse James and Billy the Kid, to their twentieth-century descendents such as Bonnie and Clyde.[15] As this list suggests, bandits in these stories were often defined in racial or class terms that were set in opposition to the dominant order, and their outlaw status seemingly derived as much from this as from any actual criminal activities in which they engaged. Indeed, as Richard Slotkin has demonstrated, these bandit stories can be seen as forming a countertradition that defines itself both against and within the dominant cultural mythos of the frontier hero (125–55). Whereas the frontier hero is celebrated for his justified—indeed regenerative—use of violence in the service of a conquering imperial order (to which he has an ambiguous relationship) and for his rugged individualism, linking him to a republican and artisanal version of what Dana Nelson has termed white "national manhood," the transgressive violence of the bandit challenges the conquering order and is constructed in terms that are usually more collective and racially and ethnically marked (1–28). As Marcus Klein has demonstrated, this opposition structures one of the foundational ur-texts of hard-boiled fiction: James McParlan's first-person account of his infiltration of the Molly Maguires. Klein reads the hard-boiled hero as a straightforward descendent of the type of amoral professionalism embodied by McParlan, one derived in part from, though—as an ostensible representative of the law—also crucially distinct from, the kinds of social banditry embodied by the Molly Maguires. Indeed, the cultural fantasy of hard-boiled masculinity, as I will demonstrate more fully below, can be read as producing an imaginary resolution to the opposition between the frontier, or law-and-order, hero and the bandit, yoking the cultural negativity embodied in the latter to the former's more acceptable visage and pedigree. It is in the hard-boiled tradition's inheritance from noir that the forms of cultural negativity embodied by the bandit story are still evident.[16]

While both the setting and the image of the outlaw hero have clearly been transformed, the outline of the bandit story is still discernible within the negative logic of noir. In order to trace these transformations of hero and setting, we need to turn to two other genres that influenced the formulation of the cultural fantasy we term noir. The sensationalist city mysteries and the urban guidebooks of the mid- and late nineteenth century shifted the representation of crime from the imperial frontier or agrarian hinterland to the teeming metropolis. Both forms functioned via the logic of the exposé in which the corruptions of the era's exponentially expanding cities were both hyperbolically decried and voyeuristically enjoyed, often in the same sentence. This heady combination of private vice and public virtue was not merely a cynical gesture of obligatory fealty to nineteenth-century notions of morality with their emphasis on the public presentation of a "civilized" demeanor and ethical stance. Instead, it reflected a genuine ambivalence, one derived in part from the ways in which these forms represented an urban reworking of the tradition of the bandit story. For even as the settings of these stories shifted from rural agrarian life to the industrial metropolis, the critical vantage associated with the former, a perspective that was suspicious of cosmopolitan power as a threat to the agrarian values of the Jeffersonian republic, persisted in the new setting. This was made explicit in the urban guidebooks and exposés, which often constructed their audience as tourists and new arrivals to the city and were written in a style that played on traditional agrarian condemnations of the city as a modern-day Babylon even as they were careful to provide specific street addresses and supposed "insider information" for those who might want to see this Babylon up close.

Both forms gleefully and repeatedly transgressed the line between fiction and nonfiction, providing an urban correlate to the intentional blending of history and myth in bandit stories. As David S. Reynolds and Stephen Knight have differently demonstrated, city mysteries such as George Lippard's *Quaker City* and guidebooks such as the multiply authored *Darkness and Daylight; or, Lights and Shadows of New York Life* and *The Spider and the Fly, or Tricks, Traps, and Pitfalls of City Life* derived their models from various fictional and nonfictional European sources, from Eugene François Vidocq's *Memoires*, to Eugene Sue's *The Mysteries of Paris* and G. M. W. Reynolds's *The Mysteries of London*, to the gothic-influenced, urban realism of Balzac and Dickens. They also found domestic precursors in the literature of anti-Catholic and anti-Masonic paranoia.[17] In both the city mystery and the urban guidebook or exposé the representation of the agrarian bandit or outlaw collective was transformed into the urban criminal or syndicate. Individual criminals were usually presented as either morally ambiguous outlaws from the lower orders or depraved and thoroughly corrupt representatives of the upper classes. In both cases the social negativity and implicit class critique articulated by the bandit story are still palpable. Collective criminals were presented as either an amorphous and unlocatable menace or as representatives of an alternate, and in many ways more organic and just, social order.

Noir derives not only its urban setting but also its ambivalent representation of both law and order and criminality from these stories. The urban criminal in noir is both a manifestation of corruption, part of the spreading stain of iniquity that infects life in the modern metropolis, and a class warrior manqué who represents in condensed form the desires of an unjustly dispossessed urban proletariat. Similarly, the law is both the last line of defense against the depredations of modern corruption and an oppressive apparatus designed to maintain an unjust social order. Indeed, the resolute negativity of noir, in which neither the position of the law nor the position of the criminal function as stable or unconflicted sites of identification, derives in no small part from its inherited ambivalence from the city mystery and the urban guidebook/exposé.

It also emerges out of another generic precursor to noir, one that shaped many of the gendered and racialized meanings taken up in the latter's phantasmatic logic. This genre is the gothic true-crime narrative that, as Karen Halttunen has demonstrated, formed one of the central ways in which crime was narrated in the late-eighteenth- and early-nineteenth-century United States. Gothic true-crime narratives represented a radical reworking of both the form and the cultural logic of the seventeenth- and eighteenth-century execution sermon. The gothic true-crime narrative replaced a sacred narrative that constructed murder and other crimes as merely an extension of the general sinfulness of the community as a whole with a secular, Enlightenment narrative that represented murder as a monstrous and finally incomprehensible crime against reason. These gothic true-crime narratives, like the novels from which they draw their name, represented the dark underside of Enlightenment notions of absolute reason and the essential goodness of human nature.[18] The refusal to give a positive account of the genesis and meaning of crime in the gothic narrative finds its echo in the noir narrative's rigorous refusal of positivity. Similarly, the noir narrative, in its coding of its protagonist and of crime as darkly transgressive, draws on (even as it transmutes) the iconography of the criminal as unknowable monster that is part of this tradition.

The image of the victim in noir is also shaped by aspects of this tradition. A specific subset of the gothic true-crime narrative, what Halttunen aptly describes as "sexual murder stories," deflected attention away from the monstrous aspects of the generally male murderer and toward the gendered monstrosity of, in this case, the always female victim (172–207). These stories thus projected the monstrosity associated with the criminal onto the female victim, implying that the sexual and gynecological monstrosity of femininity was the root cause of male violence. This projective dynamic famously returns in noir and becomes codified in the hard-boiled narrative in the twin figures of the hard-boiled male and the femme fatale. As I demonstrate in my reading of *Red Harvest* in the next chapter, the affect that is purged from the consciousness and voice of the hard-boiled protagonist finds its projective return in the figure of the femme fatale.

Halttunen theorizes the emergence of the sexual murder story in relation to the confluence of a range of transformations that took place in the late eighteenth and early nineteenth centuries. The scientific rationality of the Enlightenment, a rationality that was coded as masculine, combined with the emerging cult of romantic love, the new cult of domestic womanhood, and the relative disappearance of pain and violence from public life to produce the pornographic structure of the sexual murder story. In such stories, the dark side of romantic passions, passions that were defined against a valorized and dispassionately rational conception of male subjectivity and public life, were projected onto a newly privatized conception of femininity and linked with the forms of pain and violence that had also been purged from the public sphere. If the sexual murder story appears at the beginning of these changes, the noir story appears near their end, when women decisively, if unevenly, gain access to the public sphere. Over the same span of time, male identity shifts from an interiorized notion of rationality to a more externalized one, paralleling the way in which shifts in management practices produced by Taylorism removed decision making and control from the individual laborer and replaced it with larger systemized forms of rationality of which the workers' newly rationalized external actions were merely a part.

To this substrate of gendered meanings that the noir form inherits from the gothic true-crime narrative, we need to add a set of racialized meanings as well. Halttunen notes: "By the early nineteenth century, rape-murder had entered the literature. Some of the earliest of these cases involved, significantly, African American men accused of assaulting white girls" (175). While Halttunen only notes this "significant" fact in passing, these explicit moments of racialization link the tradition of the gothic true-crime story to the larger set of meanings associated with the construction of race and gender in the United States, with its central cultural fantasy of the rape of white women by black men, a fantasy that displaces the material history of the rape of black women by white men both during and after slavery. It also participates in the broader dynamics of the racialization of criminality (and the criminalization of race) that Shelly Streeby argues form central ideological features of the popular literature of U.S. imperialism (38–77, 251–90). That these stories appear at the outset of the sexual murder genre suggests that they form the phantasmatic template out of which the genre evolved. Within this larger phantasmatic context, then, even stories that do not explicitly feature racially marked perpetrators have the potential to carry an implicit set of racialized meanings.

This possibility is also reinforced by the larger set of racial meanings accruing to the gothic form. As much recent writing on the gothic form and specifically on Poe suggests, this form, once thought ahistorical, carries within its fantastic and horrific effects a whole range of historical meanings about the cultural resonances of race.[19] Teresa Goddu has demonstrated, for example, the ways in which gothic narratives such as Poe's *Narrative of Arthur Gordon Pym* alternate between fantasies of racial convertibility (the exchanging of white identity for black and vice versa) and contrasting fantasies about the ontological fixity of race (73–93). In dramatizing such fantasies the gothic novel participated in a larger set of cultural practices, such as blackface minstrelsy, that were organized around similar notions of racial conversion and its opposite. As Eric Lott has demonstrated, blackface minstrelsy and other practices of racial imposture were structured by a logic of racial borrowing, in which white, working-class, male identity was defined by simultaneously drawing on and defining itself against a phantasmatic notion of black manhood.[20] This dynamic of disavowed borrowing had a sexual dimension. Not only was the relationship between black and white masculinity imagined in resolutely homosocial and almost explicitly homoerotic terms in the minstrel show but, in donning the mask of blackness, white masculinity defined itself in relationship to a whole range of sexual and social fantasy figures associated with black virility and its opposition to the dominant order, such as the figures of the rebellious slave and the sexually potent black male.

The association of black masculinity with both social and sexual transgression became codified in the fantasy figure of the black rapist. While this figuration had its roots in the antebellum representations of gothic criminality and minstrel performance that I have just described, it became an increasingly central part of post-Reconstruction figurations of race, forming the central fantasy image employed to justify the regime of Jim Crow and the practices of racial terror that underpinned it. By the turn of the century, the fantasy figure of the black rapist, as an iconic representation of the sexual and cultural dangers represented by enfranchised and unsubordinated forms of black masculinity, was central to a whole range of cultural expressions from the white supremacist writings of Thomas Dixon, to D. W. Griffith's cinematic watershed, *The Birth of a Nation* (which was adapted from Dixon's *The Clansmen*), to Philip Alexander Bruce's study *The Plantation Negro as a Freeman*, to Charles Carroll's polygeneticist popular-science volume, *The Negro as Beast, or In the Image of God*.[21]

It is in the context of this larger trajectory of cultural fantasies about racial borrowing and gendered violence that the racial resonances of the gothic true-crime and fictional narrative become manifest. This set of fantasies reaches one apotheosis in Poe's midcentury stories of sexualized violence, which form a key generic precursor to noir. While much has been made of the invention of the detective story by Poe and of the way in which his gothic racial imaginings form a template for, as Toni Morrison put it, the disavowed "Africanist" presence in classic American literature, less attention has been paid to the intertwining of racial and gendered fantasies in Poe's horror fiction and the ways in which these stories, in their cultural condensations and borrowings from nonfictional forms such as the true-crime narrative, lay the groundwork for a whole range of nineteenth- and twentieth-century popular forms (Morrison 1–60). Thus, in stories like "Bernice" and "The Fall of the House of Usher," Poe's white (or at least racially unmarked) protagonist finds himself possessed by an unnamable and obsessive "blackness" of the soul that drives him to murder or otherwise violate the woman he loves. The phantasmatic logic of these stories, in which the unacceptable and disavowed aspects of white male identity are projected onto a blackness that returns to haunt and take possession of the narrator's psyche, causing him to act out the misogynist fantasies he has banished from his consciousness, reveals in metaphorical terms the way in which the central fantasy of the race/gender system in the United States is structured by a logic of projection and disavowal. In the context of this fantasy, blackness, either metaphorical or embodied, becomes an alibi for the misogyny that is central to the construction of white masculinity. Yet the fantasy also reveals how white masculinity is modeled on and troubled by a fantasized black masculinity in ways that challenge the very constitution of racial difference.

This fantasy and its incoherence become central to the logic of both noir and the hard-boiled narrative. Indeed, the two forms can be seen as both situated between and partially replaying the opposition between the representation of blackness in Poe's gothic stories, where it haunts, disrupts, and finally possesses whiteness, and its representation in Poe's first detective story, "The Murders in the Rue Morgue," in which it is represented as so radically distinct from the whiteness embodied by C. August Dupin as to be embodied in an inhuman beast that must be killed. Yet even in the latter narrativization, one that points toward the codification of animalistic imagery in the figuration of the black rapist in texts such as Carroll's *The Negro as Beast*, the dynamic of projection that is at the heart of noir and hard-boiled constructions of (white) masculinity is evident. The beastlike black rapist clearly stems from within the white male subject, even if it is punished in various external manifestations.

The ways in which noir condenses a whole range of larger cultural meanings about the entanglement of race with fantasies of gendered violence and socioeconomic transgression is suggested symptomatically in the retrospective naming of the genre itself. In coining the term "film noir," Nino Frank fortuitously called attention to the "blackness" of the texts he was discussing, a blackness, as the genealogy just traced indicates, that carries racial as well as metaphysical meanings. And indeed, as James Naremore has demonstrated, the connection between the racial and metaphysical meanings of "noir" was very much in the minds of the French intellectuals who pioneered the use of the term.[22] While Frank is generally credited with coining the term for film studies, it was already being used to market American hard-boiled and crime fiction in France under the Gallimard *Série Noire* imprint. French intellectuals such as Jean-Paul Sartre and Boris Vian saw the novels of Hammett and Cain (along with, later, Chester Himes's hard-boiled "Harlem domestic" novels) published in the series as relatively continuous with social realist novels of black protest and black criminality such as *Native Son*, and, more ambiguously, *Light in August*, a fact made explicit by the publication in the series of Boris Vian's *J'irai cracher sur vos tombes* (*I Spit on Your Graves*), which claimed to be a translation of a banned crime novel by an African American writer. Vian's novel is narrated from the point of view of a light-skinned black man who can pass as white and who revenges the racist killing of his brother by raping and then killing white women. A more perfect distillation of the racial fantasy narrative at the heart of noir, with its intertwining of social protest and gendered violence, can hardly be imagined.

The racial dimensions of noir are also symptomatically suggested by the name of the magazine in which the first noir and hard-boiled stories appeared: *Black Mask*. The magazine initially published classical detective fiction, ghost stories, and horror stories, along with the early noir fiction that I examine in the next section of this chapter. While this diversity of genres might initially seem to argue against the symptomatic naming of the magazine, as I have already suggested, both the horror story and the classical detective story have direct relationships to the constellation of racial meanings that coalesce in noir. Moreover, the noir crime stories that were featured in the magazine appeared almost from the magazine's inception, suggesting that they fit with its initial conception. Within this context, the image of the black mask suggested the mask worn by a criminal, one that was also metaphorically donned, the title suggested, by both the writers and the readers of the magazine. Here to write about criminality or horror was to metaphorically take on a black visage, one that suggests the conflation of criminality with a blackness that is at once metaphysical, social (i.e., as a locus of social negativity), and racial.

The surreptitious racial borrowing, or implicit blackface performance, central to the cultural dream work of noir and hard-boiled fiction is suggested by other similarly symptomatic displacements, such as the presence of racial meanings in the naming of two of the early hard-boiled protagonists, Race Williams and Sam Spade, and the birth of hard-boiled fiction in the special Ku Klux Klan issue of *Black Mask*. This special issue, which appeared on June 1, 1923, featured a range of articles and stories that debated/demonstrated the relative merits, or lack thereof, of the infamous and, in the early twenties, increasingly popular vigilante society. Daly's story, the first to feature Race Williams, was one of the anti-Klan entries. The story, entitled "Knights of the Open Palm," pitted Williams against the Klan, which is revealed, against its rhetoric of antimodernist moral purity, to be a corrupt "racket" just like any big-city criminal organization. As Sean McCann has pointed out, the hard-boiled detective, in his inception, is thus defined in opposition to the racist and antimodernist morality of the Klan.[23] This opposition also suggests the ways in which the hard-boiled male, and the figure of the noir criminal before him, borrowed in implicit ways from the iconography of black masculinity. He defined himself against a Victorian morality that constructed white middle-class manliness in virtuous opposition to the figure of the black savage or rapist. Here the hard-boiled male, as a version of twentieth-century working-class masculinity, finds its shadowy double in the figure of the transgressive and primitivized black male.

The transgression associated with black masculinity thus lends a specifically racialized set of meanings to the transgressive "blackness" of noir, one that inflects the forms of social negativity condensed and catalyzed by the form. If, as I've suggested, the negativity of noir can be read as a response to the advent of corporate capitalism, then this negativity is organized in relationship to the white borrowing from the image of racialized blackness as an outlaw or transgressive social identity, one that is defined both against Victorian notions of morality and, crucially, against the increasingly collectivized (and almost exclusively white and male, due to the racist prohibitions produced by the AFL and other craft-based unions in this period) factory workforce that was the target of Taylorist and Fordist reform. The emergence of corporate capitalism thus cannot be theorized separately from the codification of the color line in the same era.[24] The fantasies produced by both become visible in the logic of noir and in the hard-boiled form that emerges out of it. In its implicit borrowing from the figure of the black criminal, the forms of social rebellion encoded by what I term sociological noir and the forms of sexualized transgression and violence enacted by psychological noir become conflated: the black male criminal, as a model for the construction of white masculinity, becomes a figure of both social rebellion and sexual violence, giving a masculinist cast to sociological noir narratives and a sociopolitical resonance to psychological noir stories. This combination of sexual and social transgression becomes part of the dual inheritance of the hard-boiled form from the forms of noir narrative that preceded it in the pages of *Black Mask*. It is to those narratives and the emergence of the hard-boiled form that I now turn.

Unmasking Early Noir

The traces of all the forms I have just outlined are visible in the early hard-boiled fiction that appeared in *Black Mask* and in the forgotten genre of prohibition-era crime fiction from which it evolved. This crime fiction, none of which has been republished since its initial appearance in the pulp magazines, was the immediate precursor to hard-boiled fiction in the pages of *Black Mask*, and the latter drew much of its negative energy from the earlier genre.

As a genre, hard-boiled fiction can be seen as a partial positivizing of the more negative currents of this earlier crime fiction, which represents the first flowering of the noir aesthetic. In the remainder of this chapter, I explore the noir elements of this early crime fiction, attending to the negative cultural energies that the fiction condenses, and trace the complex emergence of hard-boiled fiction out of the context of this earlier fiction. I focus exclusively on fiction published in *Black Mask* because the pulp magazine is the location of the hard-boiled and the noir aesthetic's first emergence; in doing so, however, I do not want this exclusive focus to obscure the larger cultural resonances of this fiction. This is why I have described these fictions as cultural condensations, the manifest content of the larger workings of cultural fantasy, and why I have traced the long gestation of the negative energies of the noir aesthetic in the previous section of this chapter. In this regard, it is also important to keep in mind the larger influence of the fiction published in *Black Mask* on interwar culture. Not only did hard-boiled fiction quickly become a staple in the pulp market, appearing in a range of pulp magazines from *Dime Detective* to *Action Detective* to *Clues*, but the hard-boiled and noir fiction that appeared in the pages of *Black Mask* shared aesthetic and some ideological affinities with a wide range of cultural production in the twenties and thirties: crime, gangster, and urban fiction by the likes of W. R. Burnett, Damon Runyon, Ring Lardner, and Jack Lait; the gangster films of the early 1930s; the tough-guy journalism of writers like Walter Noble Burns and H. L. Mencken; the noir fiction of writers like James M. Cain, Horace McCoy, and Kenneth Fearing; and the writings of modernists such as Ernest Hemingway and William Faulkner.[25] So in examining the genesis of noir and hard-boiled fiction in the pages of *Black Mask*, I am focusing on only one part, though a privileged and germinal one, of a larger web of cultural meanings and practices.

In tracing the emergence of the hard-boiled aesthetic from the earlier strain of noir fiction, I demonstrate that the noir aesthetic has always been an aspect, indeed one of the original ingredients, of hard-boiled fiction. This genealogy reveals the negative cultural work done by the hard-boiled form, locating the most radical and critical elements of the hard-boiled text in the negativity it inherits from noir.

Before Carroll John Daly published "Knights of the Open Palm" in the June 1, 1923, issue of *Black Mask*, a variety of writings appeared in the pages of the magazine: classical and "golden era"–style detective fiction; stories that mixed romance and suspense; horror and supernatural fiction; various noir crime stories. Even after hard-boiled detective fiction became an overnight sensation, with the magazine publishing stories by Daly and Hammett as quickly as they could dash them off, the magazine continued to publish a diverse range of material in addition to the hard-boiled detective fiction that was its most popular staple. However, by the final years of the decade, *Black Mask* had become almost synonymous with hard-boiled fiction, representing not only the birthplace of the new medium but also the genre's most celebrated and critically recognized venue, publishing, among others, Hammett, Daly, Erle Stanley Gardner, Raul Whitfield, Paul Cain, and in the 1930s, Frank Nebel and Raymond Chandler. It was, as Erin Smith argues, a pulp with pretensions, claiming to be the rare pulp that published material equal to or superior to the fiction that was being published in "slick" and literary magazines of the period (23–26). *Black Mask* thus functioned as a kind of cultural ambassador for the emergent genre of hard-boiled fiction, establishing its reputation not only with its regular readership, which consisted primarily of working-class men, but also with representatives of what Pierre Bourdieu has sardonically termed "legitimate" culture.[26]

This association of *Black Mask* with both hard-boiled fiction and "legitimate culture," which served to grant it a kind of cultural capital that was largely denied other popular writings and venues, has lasted to the present moment.[27] Most histories of the hard-boiled form provide a heroic origin story in which this uniquely "literary" form of popular culture emerged wholesale from the genius of two men, Dashiell Hammett and, to a lesser extent (since his fiction is harder to reconcile with conventional notions of the literary), Carroll John Daly. It was nurtured, the story goes, by *Black Mask* and its discerning editor of the late twenties and early thirties, Captain Joseph Shaw, who, by his commitment to literary value as well as profit, enabled the full abilities of Hammett and that most celebrated and atypical of hard-boiled writers, Raymond Chandler, to flourish within the pages of the magazine.[28] What this narrative obscures is not only the diversity of writings and writers that were associated with the moniker "hard-boiled" and the range of venues in which this writing appeared but also the much more complex history of the emergence of the hard-boiled form and its indebtedness to a distinctive vein of noir crime writing that was appearing in *Black Mask* long before Joseph Shaw ever assumed its editorship.

Written by a host of forgotten writers such as Ashton Crowell, Julian Kilman, Elizabeth Dudley, Arthur Seymour Witt, C. S. Montayne, Walter Deffenbaugh, Harvey Wickham, John Baer, R. W. Milnor, and Harold Ward (who also wrote under the pseudonyms "Ward Sterling" and "H. W. Starr"), as well as by the soon-to-be inventors of hard-boiled fiction, Daly and Hammett, this noir fiction appeared in the pages of *Black Mask* from 1920 to 1923, just prior to the emergence of hard-boiled fiction in the magazine. Indeed, the hard-boiled stories of Daly and Hammett seem to have replaced this earlier fiction in the pages of the magazine, suggesting that the phantasmatic cultural work done by the hard-boiled story effectively reworked and replaced that done by the earlier genre.

Sociological Noir

Like the city mysteries and urban guidebooks of the nineteenth century, these noir crime stories narrated the life in the mean streets, back alleys, and teeming slums of the modern city. Take, for example, the following description from C. S. Montayne's "The Plan That Was Outlined by Monahan," which appeared in the January 1921 edition of *Black Mask*:

> The door was opened by a small boy who had freckles and red hair.
> The boy munched a piece of rye bread decorated with a slab of cheese.
> Malone looked over the boy's head. The room inside was squalid and
> miserable. Paper hung from the walls in tatters. A mantle of dust had
> sifted over chairs, desk, tall wooden filing cabinet and ancient lounge.
> A broken window had been stuffed with newspapers. (54)

This description, with its representation of an orphan boy living in squalor, could have come from urban exposés such as George C. Needham's *Street Arabs and Gutter Snipes,* which first appeared in 1887, or from George Lippard's earlier *Quaker City,* except that the language of the passage, with its clipped sentences, detached description, and deflationary humor (the bread "decorated" with the slab of cheese) situates it as the immediate precursor to hard-boiled fiction. Indeed, many features of the hard-boiled style are already present in these stories. In addition to their use of a clipped, usually affectless parataxis and deflationary, and often ironic, humor, these noir stories also employ the criminal argot associated with hard-boiled fiction. They are rife with terms like "soup" (safe cracker), "wire man" (dynamiter), "yegg" (criminal), "dopin'" (putting someone on), "cheese" (loot), "can" (safe), and many other examples of thieves' lingo.

By combining the descriptions of urban squalor and corruption characteristic of the city mystery and urban guidebooks with the detachment and humor characteristic of hard-boiled narration, these stories transform the reformist impulse present (if ambivalently so) in the earlier genres into a picture of underclass and underworld life that is at once more bleak and more pedestrian. Gone are the implicit agrarian vantage of these earlier forms and their explicit rhetoric of exposé, with its shocking and titillating revelations about how the other half lives, and along with them has vanished any positive sentimental or progressive impulse toward reform. Left in its place is a more fully negative form of representation in which the grim aspects of underworld life are not contrasted to any more positive site of cultural renewal.

As the criminal argot employed by these stories suggests, many of the stories featured protagonists who were part of the criminal underworld. "The Recoil" by Arthur Seymour Witt, which appeared in the March 1921 edition of the magazine, featured a main character by the name of "Duffy the Soup," who is described in the following manner: "Reared in the evil atmosphere of Chicago's West Side 'Valley' he early in youth graduated from the poolrooms and drifted quite naturally into the lush-toucher and leather-snitching class; then he became a stick-up and from there pushed his way into crookdom proper by becoming a full-fledged yegg. Can after can he ripped asunder and always dodged the pollies" (67). Other stories such as "The Second Safe" by Walter Deffenbaugh, John Baer's "The Hole in the Alibi," and "Playing a Hunch" by Julian Kilman, to name just a few, feature similar "yeggs" as main characters.

In contrast to the resolutely first-person narration of most hard-boiled fiction, these stories were almost always narrated in the third person, formalizing the distance between the reader and the story's ostensible protagonist (indeed the term "central character" is perhaps more accurate than "protagonist," with its implication of readerly identification). This distance was also inscribed by the resolutely unheroic characteristics of the main characters and the often miserable or ironic position in which they find themselves at the end of the story. For example, Duffy the Soup winds up breaking into his own safe and stealing his own diamonds, of which he is promptly divested by his associates. Similarly unheroic or darkly ironic endings conclude "At the Expense of James Cathew" by J. Burton Loftus, "The Hole in the Alibi," by Baer, and Charles S. Wolfe's "Unlucky Friday."

While this fiction may bear a resemblance to the gangster fiction of the interwar years, it also differs from it in important respects. Unlike the gangster narratives, there is nothing affirmative about the portrayal of the criminals in this noir crime fiction. As David E. Ruth has demonstrated, the gangster narratives of writers such as W. R. Burnett, Charles Francis Coe, and Jack Lait engaged in a whole range of positive, as well as negative, forms of ideological work (1–36). The representation of the gangster as a glamorous and fashionably dressed individual, whose violent amorality was both clearly reprehensible and secretly appealing, worked simultaneously to instill and critique the values of the emerging secular, consumer-oriented culture of the modernized city. Similarly, the collective dimensions of the gangster narrative, in which the protagonist is imagined as part of a vast criminal enterprise, worked to reconcile readers to the new corporate and Taylorist structure of work, while also suggesting that the new business culture of the 1920s was indistinguishable from the illegal and amoral activities of the criminal syndicate.

The noir crime narratives that appeared in *Black Mask* in the early twenties differed from the gangster narratives in both these regards (while sharing their critique of Taylorism and corporate capitalism). The protagonists of the crime stories were far from glamorous and their narrative trajectories were resolutely individualist. Moreover, unlike the hard-boiled fiction that emerged out of these stories, the law is not presented as even an equivocal site of identification for the protagonist. Instead it is presented as both arbitrary and unremittingly hostile.

The negative representation of both criminality and the law lies at the heart of most of the stories and lends them much of their power. Take, for example, "Playing a Hunch" by Julian Kilman, which appeared alongside C. S. Montayne's "The Plan That Was Outlined by Monahan" in the January 1921 issue of *Black Mask* (41–49). The story focuses on a criminal named Dave Lacey, "the best 'soup' man in the business," who has just been released from prison at the beginning of the story (45). He hops a train and travels to a town called Brookville. Lacey's first stop in town is to a house to beg for food, where he is turned down and told disdainfully to "get a job" by a man we later learn is named Edsall and is vice president of the town bank. The next day, Lacey mockingly asks

Edsall for a job and is summarily refused. Lacey takes a job at a bowling alley and pool hall across the way instead. After working there, Lacey wonders why he has remained in this two-bit town so long and then realizes he has been playing a hunch—that Edsall is actually a crook. And Lacey realizes who Edsall is: a criminal named the Denver Ringer. He shadows Edsall as the latter embezzles $38,000, tracking him to Buffalo. He confronts Edsall in his hotel room, beats him, and takes his money. When Edsall begs for some of the money, Lacey brutally kicks him three times in the head. Lacey then walks down to the lobby of the hotel, where he is immediately apprehended with the money and accused of Edsall's crime by a cop who has followed him from the train station.

The story turns on a set of ironic reversals. Lacey, after seemingly going straight, is arrested for a crime that someone else initiated. Moreover, the perpetrator of this crime is the story's seeming representative of respectability and the status quo, the bank vice president, Edsall. Edsall's profession is not incidental to the critical work undertaken by the story's negativity. Like the corrupt representatives of capitalist law and order who populated the dime-novel stories of justified outlaws and social bandits of the late nineteenth century, Edsall is a figure for banking and other forms of capitalist accumulation as legalized thievery and criminality on a grand scale. His identity as the Denver Ringer should thus be taken as metaphorical as well as literal: read through the "mechanic accents" that Michael Denning has theorized as shaping a collective class-based understanding of dime-novel narratives (and which, as I've suggested, continued to shape the cultural interpretation of noir fiction), Edsall becomes an embodiment of Bertolt Brecht's ironic query in *The Three-Penny Opera*, "What's breaking into a bank compared with founding a bank?"[29] This point is further underscored by the way in which Edsall becomes the mouthpiece for the conventional bourgeois rejoinder to the figure of the tramp or drifter: "Get a job." The fatuous and hypocritical nature of this rejoinder is revealed when Edsall denies Lacey the possibility of a job.

In his actions, Lacey embodies a modern composite of two different heroes conventional to the dime novels: the tramp, who was celebrated for the ways in which he eluded institutions of industrial control, and the detective, valued for his embodiment of an artisanal work ethic and his hermeneutic facility in comprehending the elaborate workings of the capitalist economy. However, in both these embodiments he proves less than heroic. As the tramp, he quickly adheres to the dictates of the contemporary regime of labor (even as this is in part a cover), and as a detective, while he effectively discovers the criminal activities of Edsall, he is outdone in this activity by the anonymous police detective who has followed him.

While we might initially be inclined to interpret the story as an allegory about the ways in which crime doesn't pay, the structural similarities between the role of Lacey and that of the nameless police detective, as well as the purely perfunctory appearance of the latter, suggest the arbitrary qualities of the law. Indeed, Lacey seems to have performed the job of the police detective in everything but name and his relationship to the crime that he is arrested for is at best ancillary.

In this story, then, there is no conventional protagonist, moral, or stable locus of reader identification. This negativity is conventional to these early noir stories. What emerges from these narratives, then, is a resolutely negative fantasy space, in which the reader has no stable site of identification and in which no larger social collectivity or unproblematic social or moral position can be imagined. It is the presence of this phantasmatic negativity, and the forms of negative cultural energy it condenses, that lead me to describe these stories as the first efflorescence of noir. In them, the negative energy of noir deforms the generic contours of the crime or gangster narrative, opening it up to the possibility of a range of more resolutely critical meanings. These narratives have the potential to function in much the same way that Theodor Adorno posits the resolutely negative modernism of, say, Arnold Schoenberg or Samuel Beckett as functioning: as a negation of the present economic and social order and, in their very refusal of any positive resolution or affirmative meaning, as an index of a utopian order to come. The difference between the kinds of negativity embodied by these popular stories and the negativity of the modernist texts celebrated by Adorno is that the negativity of the noir narrative inheres more in the kinds of fantasy staged by the form and the deformation of various generic conventions that this produces rather than in the resolutely abstract and formal negativity of modernism. Thus, while the negativity of these stories seems on one level to shut down the possibility of any larger allegorical or politically redemptive meaning, it also opens up a range of critical possibilities, possibilities that are encoded in what Adorno terms the work of art's opposition to the "empirical world" that functions to preserve in its very negativity the possibility of a utopian world to come (1).

The critical work enabled by this negativity is nowhere more visible than in J. Burton Loftus's "At the Expense of James Cathew," which appeared in the February 1922 issue of *Black Mask*, and Ashton Crowell's "The Prison Clock Nine," which appeared in the May 1920 issue. Loftus's story was what the magazine called a "short-short," consisting of only two pages. The story's concision adds to its impact; a more fully fleshed out narrative only would have diluted the starkly allegorical negativity etched by the almost anonymous narrative. It begins with the title character turning himself in to the police, along with the money he took, for a bank job he pulled five years ago. He does so because he is convinced that he has been trailed the whole time even as he has fled to various parts of the globe. Cathew feels certain that one person in particular is a police detective. The man turns up at many of the same locations to which Cathew travels and strikes up conversations with him. When Cathew finally breaks down and returns the money, the head of the detective bureau informs him that they weren't trailing him and that they had given up five years ago. It turns out that the man who seemed to be trailing Cathew merely liked talking to him (101–2).

The story enacts a negative allegory of interpellation.[30] It is not the real police who trail Cathew but a more effective and ubiquitous phantasmatic police force. Moreover, given that the primary readership for the pulps was working-class and given the "mechanic accents" that structured the address of this fiction, this allegory of interpellation would be more than a generalized representation of modern systems of social control but would have specific resonances with the Taylorist transformation of work in the early twentieth century. The transfer of decision-making power and the intellectual aspects of labor from worker to manager and the institutionalization of a system of managerial control produce a specific form of interpellation for workers, in which the internalized voice and figure of the manager takes on a super-egoic, policing function, thereby helping to reproduce the conditions of production on the factory floor. These resonances become stronger given the genealogical relationship between the representation of the criminal in noir and the representation of the social bandit in dime novels and earlier narratives. The criminal as a coded working-class rebel or hero becomes allegorically charged with the force of class resistance.

In the context of this story, then, this resistance is radically undone by the internalization of a fantasized police force, indicating the ways in which the new Taylorist regime of work limits the forms of alliance and organized resistance that are central to class struggle. This is the negative allegory enacted by this story: rather than being organized around a hero who stands as a figure for collective resistance, the story enacts the failure of such a figure, as well as the failure of the law to which he is opposed. In this way, it inscribes its political meaning, like Adorno's modernism, only in the negative. The story's attention to the dynamics of fantasy is also worth noting. It is Cathew's relationship to fantasy that determines his fate. This attention to the phantasmatic emphasizes not only the importance of collective fantasy as a social and political category but also the ways in which the commodity form embodied by the story itself can function as a phantasmatic lure or fetish, in Marx's terms, that was increasingly central to everyday life in the early twentieth century and which threatened to replace collective political resistance with an ethos of individual consumerism.

The story shares this metacritical dimension, in which it interrogates the very commodity form that is integral to its production, with Ashton Crowell's "The Prison Clock Strikes Nine." On one level Crowell's story is merely a rewriting and slight radicalization of Ambrose Bierce's "An Occurrence at Owl Creek Bridge," but on another level it is a radical reworking and metacritique of crime fiction as a genre. The story's central character is a largely anonymous and resolutely small-time hood named Puggy Mullane. The story opens with this small-time "yegg" on death row, minutes before his execution. Employing limited third-person narration that shifts between the prison guard and the prisoner, the story recounts Mullane's miraculous escape. He manages to break out of his cell and escape from the prison right as the prison clock strikes nine, the time scheduled for his execution. We then follow him as he flees to a nearby town and begins to take on a new—equally nondescript—identity. He attends a boxing match in the town in which one of the boxers takes sick and backs out of the fight. Mullane, who we learn was a boxer in his former life, volunteers to replace the sick boxer. The match begins, and Mullane fights like he has never fought before. Just when he is about to knock the other boxer out, however, the wooden rafters at the top of the building in which the fight takes place catch fire and fall on Mullane, killing him. The scene switches back to the prison and to the guard's perspective, recounting the execution of Mullane by electric chair. The reader realizes that the preceding events of the story were merely an escapist fantasy.

At first glance, the story may seem a rather conventional, if somewhat adventurous, popular narrative, right down to the denouement that throws into question everything that has come before. However, within the context of the noir genre, this story not only challenges the emerging crime-fiction aesthetic, which was organized around a gritty, naturalistic representation of everyday criminal life, but also interrogates the very forms of fantasy that invest this aesthetic with the trappings of reality. By complicating the line between the narrative construction of fantasy and reality, the story challenges the reader to reflect metacritically on the forms of fantasy that invest the crime-fiction text with a seeming verisimilitude, a verisimilitude that is, of course, predicated on not only the reader's experience of the world but, even more fundamentally, his or her fantasy of the world and the kinds of criminality that inhabit it.

This metacritical reflection is enabled in part by the aesthetics of negativity that animate noir fiction. Denied any simple identification with either the criminal protagonist or the forces of law and order, the reader is suspended in negative space. This negativity works to challenge reader understandings of the mechanics of the popular story itself. Within this context, the story can be seen as enacting an allegory about the consumption of popular forms, one which reflects metacritically on the ideological fantasy that structures the relationship between consumer and commodity. The fantasy, which has all the trappings of everyday life yet is a fundamental misrecognition of the material coordinates of this "reality," is not only the experience of Puggy Mullane but more fundamentally the experience of the consumer within a capitalist economy. It is precisely such a phantasmatic misrecognition that Slavoj Žižek in *The Sublime Object of Ideology* has described as central to Marx's conception of commodity fetishism (16–26). The brilliance of Crowell's narrative is that it not only leaves the mass cultural reading community in suspension, casting around for a point of identification, but also challenges them to reflect upon the material determinants of the forms of fantasy in which they indulge.

Psychological Noir

The emphases on both collective and individual forms of fantasy and on the "protagonist's" subjectivity in Ashton Crowell's story become more pronounced as the early noir crime fiction edges closer to hard-boiled fiction. This movement is discernible in the shift from third-person to first-person narration in the noir stories just before the advent of hard-boiled fiction. This shift in voice marks a parallel shift from a more purely sociological emphasis to a more psychological one. The difference between these two manifestations of noir is picked up again by later noir writers. Thus the noir narratives of Horace McCoy, Edward Anderson, and James M. Cain have a more sociological emphasis on criminality and the lives of working-class drifters, while those of Jim Thompson, Dorothy Hughes, Cornell Woolrich, and Patricia Highsmith plumb the depths of criminal psychology, with the fictions of Kenneth Fearing and David Goodis splitting the difference. This division is also manifested as one of the central tensions in the hard-boiled narrative, which attempts to bridge the gap between the sociological and the psychological (as we will see more fully in chapters 2 and 5) by welding a detached first-person narration with a mapping of socioeconomic space.

The shift from the sociological to the psychological in the early noir fiction is enacted by way of a return to the gothic. While the third-person noir stories discussed in the previous section find their roots primarily in dime-novel social-bandit narratives and city mysteries and guidebooks, the more psychologically oriented noir stories reflect the legacy of the gothic true-crime and fiction narratives, with their pre-occupation with the psychologically aberrant figures of the monstrous, either implicitly or explicitly racialized criminal and the sexually debased and debasing woman.

It is in its inheritance from psychological noir, with its roots in the gothic, that hard-boiled fiction takes on many of its characteristic racial and gendered meanings. While a set of racialized and gendered meanings inhere in the sociological noir as well, these meanings are more muted and, I want to suggest, less determining. Although the sociological crime stories I've just been examining are resolutely male-centered, little is made of this gendering. In this relative lack of attention to gender, these stories differ radically from hard-boiled fiction with its obsessive preoccupation with masculine toughness and feminine entrapment. On one level, the lack of attention to gender combined with the resolutely male-centered focus of the stories suggests that the ideological workings of cultural fantasy are more seamless and more fully effective in the sociological noir stories than in the much more symptomatic representation of gender in hard-boiled fiction. And indeed, I don't want to obscure the way in which this fiction inherits from its dime-novel precursors an ideology that conflates the val-orized male identity of the heroic artisan, frontier hero, or bandit with the public sphere and the space of labor *tout court* (whether this labor is criminal or otherwise). However, to focus exclusively on this inheritance is to miss the ways in which the negative fantasy enacted by these stories tends to complicate the effectiveness of any positive ideological content. Thus, while the allegories of artisanal class resistance enacted by the most radical of the dime novels were transformed into the resistant negativity of the noir narrative, the utopianism of the narratives thus shifting from the explicit to the implicit, the gendered meaning of these stories was, in a similar fashion, partially divested of positive content.

This emptying out of positive content is the kind of generic defor-mation that I argue is central to the negative fantasy work undertaken by noir. The genres of the city mystery, the bandit story, and the urban guidebooks are deformed in the sociological noir stories, emptied of their positive allegorical meanings and charged with a new negativity.

A similar dynamic structures the construction of race in these stories. The most immediate precursor to the representation of race in the sociological noir stories that appeared in the pages of *Black Mask* in the early 1920s, however, was the construction of white masculinity in the dime-novel stories of social banditry. White working-class identity, in these stories, in contrast to middle-class definitions of manhood in the same period, was structured around a dynamic of racial borrowing, in which white working-class radicalism drew on the iconography of the racialized bandit collective and the phantasmatic transgression associated with blackface to construct an iconography for collective action. This borrowing mixed with the explicit racialization and ethnicization of crime in criminological discourses of the turn of the century to produce the form of whiteness represented in the sociological noir stories in *Black Mask*. The criminals in these stories were often marked explicitly as ethnic, as the prevalence of Irish names suggests, and were implicitly racialized. This racialization drew on the generic inheritances from the dime novel and criminological literature; it also drew on the ways in which ethnicities like Irish and Italian were only imperfectly associated with whiteness in the 1920s.

Yet as with the gendered meanings inhering in the stories, these racial meanings are complicated by the negativity that structures these noir narratives. While criminality is ethnically marked and implicitly racialized in the sociological noir stories, the line between criminality and the law is represented as entirely arbitrary. Indeed, as I have already demonstrated, characters associated with the law are often represented as even more corrupt than the criminals they pursue. Moreover, the reader is denied any real identification with the figure of the criminal, who is often presented as inept and resolutely small-time. In this context, the racialization of criminality does not take on its full significance; it remains a relatively inert but potentially potent set of cultural codings that awaits a more positive set of cultural meanings to fully activate their phantasmatic charge.

These meanings emerge in the psychological noir that directly precedes the advent of hard-boiled fiction in the pages of *Black Mask*. These psychological noir stories borrow from the legacy of gothic forms such as the true-crime narrative and the stories of Poe to produce a first-person confessional narrative that turns on the twin gothic tropes of monstrous (male) violence and dangerous (female) sexuality. While it doesn't evidence all these traits, "The Passing of Bloody Dan" by Ward Sterling (a.k.a. Harold Ward), which appeared in the February 1922 issue of the magazine, is a prime example of psychological noir.

The story, like all psychological noir stories, is narrated in the first person. This particular first-person story is organized, like the celebrated modernisms of Conrad and James, around a frame narrative. The narrator, whose identity remains ambiguous until the very end of the narrative, recalls the life and violent escapades of "Bloody Dan," a worker in the Chicago stockyards. Bloody Dan, a.k.a. Dan Rouse, takes great pleasure in the dehumanizing work of slaughter: "The most blood thirsty being that ever donned a butcher's apron was Dan Rouse—a man with the form of a Greek god and the abortive brain of a devil from hell. He delighted in the terrified bleating of lambs in the slaughter pen. The agonized groans of the stricken ox and the shrill squeals of pigs when the blood smell assailed their nostrils were music to his ears" (119). His violence is described as being produced by an uncanny combination of the animalistic and the human: "Dan Rouse was a man who loved cruelty, brutality— ghastly brutality—the brutality of an animal. An animal he was—an animal dominated by human intelligence" (119). When he and his wife, Delia, have a child, named Danny, Delia hopes fatherhood will help to settle him down. Instead Bloody Dan becomes more violent than ever and begins to school his kid in the ways of violence. During "the panic" (one of the periodic depressions that punctuated the late nineteenth and early twentieth centuries), Dan loses his job in the stockyards and moves the family to North Dakota. There Delia meets and falls in love with the much gentler Henry. They spent a lot of time together but the story implies that they are otherwise chaste. Dan gets wind of them spending time and plans a brutal revenge in which he will place the most vicious dog he owns in a cave that can only be accessed and exited by a rope. He will then lure Henry inside the cave, allowing the dog to tear him to pieces. When he goes to set up this trap, though, his very young son follows him and "innocently" undoes the rope while his father is down in the cave with the dog. Dan meets the same fate that he had planned for Henry.

The son doesn't remember this except for a few hazy details. He has barely learned to speak at the time it happens. We discover in the last line that the narrator is the son and that he just discovered the truth by searching the cave:

> Yesterday I made an investigation. I wanted to find out what lay at the bottom of the little Danny Rouse's strange dreams of that babyhood day. I traveled two hundred miles to learn the truth.
>
> It was with considerable difficulty that I found the cave entrance. Fastening a rope to the projecting rock, electric torch in hand, I lowered myself through the opening.

On the sand in the bottom of the cave lay the skeletons of a man and a dog. The man's bones were broken and splintered—showing the marks of canine teeth.

I left them where they lay.

For, dear reader, *I am little Danny Rouse!* (123)

These concluding lines demonstrate the psychologizing of crime in the gothic-influenced first-person noir narrative. While it has social roots, the violence of this story is uncanny—a force either animalistic or dimly remembered, beyond the conscious control of the perpetrator.[31] This figuration of violence as uncanny pushes in two different directions: toward an understanding of the relationship between social violence and the formation of specific subjective and unconscious dispositions toward violence (little Danny's Freudian undoing of the rope is clearly marked as understandable and perhaps even desirable given the violence that Dan has perpetrated on and instilled in him and his mother); or toward an understanding of violence as outside rational or social explanation, as the inexplicably monstrous.

Bloody Dan is clearly the story's figure for the monster. He is described, like the monstrous murderers in Halttunen's analysis of nineteenth-century true-crime narratives, in language that locates his violence outside the purview of rational motive or explanation. Yet even in the case of Bloody Dan, the text also suggests the social origins of his violence: the description of his brain as "abortive" suggests that it has been halted in its development by the very dehumanizing conditions of his job. The same meaning is suggested by the description of him "donning" his butcher's apron, implying that his job becomes an identity he takes on, though this language can be contrasted to descriptions such as "blood-thirsty being" that imply that Dan's violence is somehow ontological. The mix of ontological and sociological explanations suggests the hybrid nature of the psychological noir story.

Unlike the gothic true-crime narratives that locate the violence they describe as beyond the purview of what can be comprehended within Enlightenment rationality, this psychological noir story seems to mix sociological and biological explanations, suggesting not only the ties of the psychological noir story to the type of socioeconomic conditions allegorized by the sociological noir story but also the ways in which the emerging discipline of psychology, including the radical branch of it called psychoanalysis, had as one of its initial motivations the attempt to understand subjective responses to socioeconomic phenomena. The psychological in this sense represents both a turning-away-from and an embodiment-in-microcosm of the social. The most radical aspects of the discourse attempt to understand, rather than elude, the relationship between the social and the subjective. It is this understanding of the social in miniature that is the most radical possibility embedded in the psychological noir narrative. Yet this form, like the gothic narratives that precede it, also tends to hypostatize subjectivity as either a biological or an inexplicable given.

This partial turning away from social explanations combined with a first-person narrative that, uncomfortably or otherwise, works to fuse reader consciousness with that of the story's protagonist, opens up these stories, and the hard-boiled fiction that follows them, to a more positive (and in this context ideological) set of phantasmatic meanings. Subjectivity and its relationship to violence tend to be hypostatized in these stories. Thus, even as the story gestures toward the social roots of Bloody Dan's violence and even more of little Danny's unconsciously violent act, it turns on an ontologizing representation of male subjectivity in which the link between masculinity and violence appears natural, even atavistic. This is especially true of the representation of Bloody Dan, whose violence is located in the discourse of not only the monstrous but the animalistic. The description of Dan's violence as animalistic connects it to the figuration of black masculinity as animalistic and violently misogynist that was central, as we saw earlier, to post-Reconstruction ideologies of white supremacy and to the representation of "blackness" in Poe's antebellum gothic and detective stories. Bloody Dan as "an animal dominated by human intelligence" becomes a version of the remarkably human-seeming orangutan in Poe's "Murders in the Rue Morgue," which, as a number of analyses have suggested, is clearly a displaced figuration of black masculinity, one that was a fictional parallel to the explicitly and implicitly racialized murderers of the gothic true-crime fiction. The masculinity embodied by Dan, a masculinity that is both ontologized and linked to his role as a slaughterhouse worker, demonstrates the way in which the discourse of animalism, like the discourse of criminality with which it mixed, conflated racial and class meanings.

Dan's animalism is linked to his masculine appeal: he is described as having the form of a Greek god, though one mixed with the abortive brain of a devil from hell. This description of the mixed, or miscegenous, character of Dan's masculinity, with its exteriorized emphasis on super-human appearance and strength, marks it as a specifically modern conception of male identity. Like the hard-boiled masculinity that would appear just a year later in the pages of *Black Mask*, Dan's masculinity is structured around an externalized conception of male identity and is modeled on, even as it defines itself partially against, a primitivized conception of black masculinity. Thus, in place of the opposition between detective and orangutan in "Murders in the Rue Morgue," Dan represents a miscegenous composite of both.

The linking of an ontologized conception of masculinity with violence and with racial borrowing is at the core of the phantasmatic meanings that structure the representation of male subjectivity in the psychological noir stories and that situate these stories as the immediate precursor to hard-boiled fiction. In order for this male subjectivity to emerge as unambiguously positive, however, the responsibility for the violence he perpetrates has to be shifted from the monstrousness of the male subject to the monstrousness of an other, specifically a female other. In effectuating this shift, the psychological noir stories again follow the lead of the gothic true-crime narratives, which, as Halttunen demonstrates, in the 1820s and 1830s underwent a shift in which the monstrousness of the criminal's actions was transferred to the sexuality of the female victim, who in her fallen state was constructed as the true root cause of violence.

This shift in the psychological noir stories is evident in Carroll John Daly's "Dolly," which appeared in the October 1922 issue of *Black Mask*, mere months before his first hard-boiled story. In this story, the first by Daly to appear in the pages of the magazine, a gothic plot straight out of Poe is seamlessly blended with a noir crime narrative centered on an elaborate grift. The story begins with the narrator's confession that he is in a madhouse. We also learn that his father, at the time the story he is about to narrate takes place, is a "doctor—a well known alienist" and his mother is dead (57). The story begins with his obsession with a woman named Dolly, whom he is dating during his final year in medical school. He is utterly infatuated with Dolly and his preoccupation especially attaches itself to her throat: "But it was her throat that held me spellbound; her throat and neck. Soft, velvet, pearl-like satin—not an alabaster white, nor a creamy white; perhaps more the whiteness of milk—a very thin and very clear milk. But it had the touch of silk and was warm and palpitating as I ran my fingers along its velvety surface" (57).

The narrator brings Dolly to a restaurant where his father often dines in hopes of gaining his approval, since the father "bore, in puritanical abhorrence, a deep animosity against the stage. And Dolly was of the chorus of a big musical revue" (58). Rather than approving of her, the father forbids the narrator to see her: "He did not ask me to decide. I do not think that he even considered that. He just laid down the law. I must give up Dolly" (58). The narrator then devises a plan with Dolly and her brother, who seems always to accompany her. He will pretend that he is on the edge of insanity in his obsession with Dolly and will write obsessively about her and especially her throat in his journal, which he and his father always look at and talk over in the evenings. He will say that he has to have her, and if he can't, he will strangle that beautiful throat so that nobody else may possess her. The narrator then refuses to let his father read his journal, hinting at the dirty secret within. This, of course, produces the desired effect: his father reads the journal.

The plan works perfectly. Worrying about his son's health, the father relents and allows him to marry Dolly. The marriage takes place and all of them, including Dolly's brother, live together under one roof. Things go on this way for some time, with Dolly and her brother taking frequent trips to the south to "visit her relatives." When Dolly makes a request for yet another trip south, the father gets angry and says that there is no more money for her trips. After that day, the father becomes increasingly ill. The son confesses his plot to him on his father's deathbed; the father then sits up and looks accusingly at Dolly with hate in his eyes, but speech fails him. Immediately after the father's death, the narrator's attitude toward Dolly changes—he sees how coldly she looked at the father during his death and how she is absolutely furious when the will leaves no provision for her. Over the next few days, things continue to deteriorate between Dolly and the narrator until one evening he discovers her in the arms of her brother exchanging passionate kisses and he realizes that he is not her brother at all—but her long-term lover and that he has been the object of an extremely elaborate grift. He then performs an autopsy on his father and finds that he has been poisoned.

At breakfast the next morning the narrator talks jovially and increasingly insanely with Dolly and her brother. The brother goes off to get a doctor, and while he is gone the narrator strangles Dolly to death. The narrator, as he calculated, is judged insane—because of his journal and the way he acted that morning and because Dolly and the brother were already having him secretly examined in the hopes of having him declared insane. It is unclear whether the narrator is sane or insane at the end of the story.

The gothic elements of this story are quite visible. The narrator with his fixation on Dolly's throat is a dead ringer for one of Poe's obsessive and haunted narrators. Moreover, the violent act he perpetrates on Dolly is straight out of horror narratives like "Bernice," "The Black Cat," or "The Fall of the House of Usher." Yet these gothic elements are mixed with a plot that ties this story to the sociological noir that precedes it and to much later noir narratives, such as Jim Thompson's *The Grifters*. The grift plot, which is actually a triple grift since the narrator starts by duping his father and at least claims to be fooling the authorities with his supposed performance of insanity at the end of the story, links what is in Poe a purposefully ahistorical and almost metaphysical narrative of violent obsession to the specific context of the instrumentalized economic and social relations produced by Taylorism and the growth of commodity culture in the early twentieth century. For the grift narrative, as with the crime narratives of noir more generally, seems to suggest that, like Taylorist reorganizations of the factory floor, social relationships are reducible to economic relationships. In contrast to the crime narratives of earlier centuries, which situated criminality and its punishment within the context of an essentially moral framework, the grift or crime noir narrative constructs the criminal act as an entirely economic transaction.

Here, however, the gothic framing of the grift narrative situates the affectively negative structure of the noir form, in which transactions and people seem to cancel each other out, within the context of the libidinally charged gothic narrative. Thus what this narrative produces is a phantasmatically more positive narrative than the purely negative transactions of the sociological noir form, in which the narrator is offered as a narratively stable, if psychically unstable, locus of readerly identification. And even the more unnerving aspects of the gothic crime narrative, in which the reader seems to be sealed into the consciousness of a monstrous protagonist, are alleviated by the grift plot. For like the criminals in the gothic true-crime narratives of the 1820s and 1830s, the guilt of the protagonist is mitigated and even cancelled out by the machinations of a sexually and economically manipulative woman.

This dynamic of projection in which the woman becomes the bearer of all the monstrousness that is excised from the subjectivity of the protagonist even affects the allegory of the (criminalized) subject's relationship to the law that, as I have argued, is part and parcel of the noir narrative. Here the subject's relationship to the embodiment of paternal law in the story, a figure who is initially marked as arbitrary and tyrannical, is displaced by his relationship to the scapegoated woman, Dolly. This deflects the negative energy of the noir narrative away from either a critique of the arbitrariness of the law and the economic system it underwrites or from a form of autocritique in which the violence of the protagonist is interrogated. Instead the negativity is displaced onto a scapegoated other, later to be named as the femme fatale of the hard-boiled narrative. In this way the gothic crime narrative is used to positivize the resolutely negative phantasmatic work done by the noir narrative, yet the violence associated with the gothic protagonist is eluded by recourse to the grift narrative, which enables the protagonist to project his violence onto the woman, whose grift betrays the benign paternal embodiment of law in the figure of the father and provides a pretext for the protagonist's violence.

Toward the Hard-Boiled

This playing of narratives off each other—the gothic and the grift narrative, the psychological and the sociological noir narrative—becomes one of the hallmarks of hard-boiled fiction. And indeed what follow from stories like "Dolly" and "The Passing of Bloody Dan" in *Black Mask* are stories by Daly and Hammett that are hard-boiled in all but name but that clearly indicate their debt to the noir fiction that preceded them. Hammett's story "It" appeared in the November 1923 issue of *Black Mask* and focused on an unnamed protagonist situated almost perfectly between crime and the law, the noir hero and the private detection of the Continental Op, Hammett's private eye who would be featured in almost every story he wrote for the remainder of the decade. Similarly, Daly's "The False Burton Combs" in the December 1922 issue of *Black Mask* featured a hero who "ain't a crook" and he ain't a cop or a private detective either (3). Instead he's a self-described "soldier of fortune" (5).

What is striking in this narrative of the genesis of hard-boiled fiction out of noir fiction, however, is the way in which the turn toward psychological noir, combined with the sociological noir that preceded it, laid the phantasmatic groundwork for the emergence of hard-boiled fiction. In this earlier noir fiction an ambiguous hero is born, one who is modeled on an iconography of black masculinity and on the transgressive identity of the class rebels common to the dime novel and the sociological noir fiction that followed in its footsteps, but one who can also manifest, through a structure of projection in which women and other racialized and sexualized figures become the bearers of the monstrousness the protagonist disavows, a relatively stable set of positive and culturally less disruptive meanings. Yet this new figure of the hard-boiled detective—a figure who would be born in the pages of *Black Mask* in June 1923—still bore within his representation the dark phantasmatic currents that we term noir.

As I have already suggested, the presence of these dark currents is indicated in part by the name of the first hard-boiled protagonist, Race Williams. The name both encodes and displaces the racial borrowing that is at the heart of the hard-boiled narrative and of the noir narrative that precedes it. The name "Race" suggests that Williams is a racially marked figure—for it is nonwhite forms of racial identity that are conventionally marked as such in U.S. culture. Yet the name also carries with it the suggestion that Williams is the hero of the (white) race, a notion that had much currency in the 1920s, a decade infamous for its nativism and for the popularity of the Ku Klux Klan; this popularity, as we have seen, was exploited by *Black Mask* in the very issue Williams first appeared. The name of the first hard-boiled hero thus symptomatically enacts the complex forms of disavowed racial borrowing that enable the construction of whiteness in the new genre. The hard-boiled story inherits, and fully exploits, a set of racial and gendered meanings from psychological noir that carry both misogyny and racism within their phantasmatic charge.

Hard-boiled fiction is thus inaugurated around duel disavowals, the disavowal of its relationship to the cultural negativity encoded in the noir crime story and the disavowal of the forms of racial and gendered negativity encoded in its inheritance from and positive reconfiguration of psychological noir. It is these twin forms of negativity, both contained within the apt condensation performed by the signifier *noir*, that return to haunt the hard-boiled form again and again, providing some of its most radical and radically negating moments. It is to the construction of hard-boiled masculinity out of these divergent materials and to the forms of noir negativity that continue to haunt its constitution that I now turn in my analysis of that most negative of hard-boiled novels, Dashiell Hammett's *Red Harvest*.

2

Going Blood-Simple
in Poisonville

> There is a certain gesture of virility, be it one's own or
> someone else's, that calls for suspicion.
> —*T. W. Adorno*, Minima Moralia

The Limits of a Critique

Red Harvest can best be described as hard-boiled fiction's first auto-critique. After developing and refining the technology of the hard-boiled narrative in the single-issue story format, Dashiell Hammett, near the end of 1927, turned to writing a longer episodic narrative. This extended narrative, published first as a serialized set of short stories in *Black Mask* in 1927 and 1928 and then as the novel *Red Harvest* in 1929, represented more than just an expansion of the techniques perfected in the shorter fiction. Instead, Hammett used the longer format to reflect on the economic and cultural changes that had helped to inaugurate the hard-boiled form as well as the political consequences of the conception of masculinity he pioneered. In doing so, Hammett tapped the negative phantasmatic construction of both the protagonist and the law that is central to noir fiction and that still persisted as a resource of critical negativity in the hard-boiled form.

Much of this critique is focused on Hammett's hard-boiled protagonist, the Continental Operative (or Op, for short). Unlike Hammett's earlier fiction, which generally presented the Op as a masterful and potent, if not always ideal, figure, *Red Harvest* narrates the limits of his control and potency. More importantly, the text reveals the cultural costs of his ethic of amoral detachment and instrumental rationality, linking this ethic to the increasing rationalization of economic and social life in the 1920s.[1] By adhering to his seemingly rational code of self-interest, the Op emerges as violently out of control: a "blood-simple" vigilante who produces more violence than he prevents. The novel thus replays within the context of the hard-boiled form what I described in the previous chapter as the negative fantasy central to sociological noir, in which neither the law nor criminality is presented as a stable or morally defensible site of identification.

However, as forceful as *Red Harvest*'s autocritique is, it remains incomplete. While the novel is able effectively to interrogate the relationship between the construction of hard-boiled masculinity and the transformation of everyday life in the early twentieth century, it seems unable to address critically the forms of affect and fantasy that invest this masculinity with social significance, forms that derive in part from the hard-boiled genre's inheritance from psychological noir. I want to suggest that this limitation is more than just an oversight; it stems from the novel's continuing formal investment in the very process of rationalization that it criticizes on the level of content. Thus the celebrated economy and detachment of hard-boiled prose can be read as a textual analog to the streamlined and rationalized factory spaces produced by Taylorism and incipient Fordism in this period.[2] This rationalized aesthetic is produced through the purging of affect from the text's first-person narrative, creating a form of split narration in which what are perceived by the male narrator to be "objective" social relations form the explicit text of the narrative while the narrative's phantasmatic and affective investments form its largely unspoken subtext. This split is the textual equivalent of the split that Lacan describes as characterizing subjectivity, with the materials purged from the space of representation forming a kind of textual unconscious.[3] This textual unconscious becomes a privileged site for exploring the workings of cultural fantasy, for a culture's fantasy investments are legible not only in the narratives it produces but even more in the gaps and fissures, condensations and displacements that suggest what such narratives can't fully articulate.[4] It is the materials of this textual unconscious that *Red Harvest* cannot critically engage and that everywhere overdetermine its political investments. The text can interrogate what it constructs as the abstract relationships of economics and interactions between men, but it cannot fully address relationships that it codes as affective: those organized by gender difference, sexuality, race, and nation.[5] The work of this chapter, then, will be to undo the ideological division between the objective and the phantasmatic in Hammett's text, a division that characterizes much of the writing in the hard-boiled tradition.

Recasting Manhood

First appearing in the pages of the detective pulp magazine *Black Mask* in the early part of the 1920s, the hard-boiled male represented a distinctly new figuration of American manhood, one formed through the modernization and conflation of a set of earlier masculine icons, from the social bandits and crime story protagonists discussed in the previous chapter, to the gentleman detective, to the frontier hero. Since I have already traced the emergence of hard-boiled masculinity from earlier representations of criminality in dime novels and true-crime narratives, I will here briefly chart his relationship to earlier figures of law and order: the gentleman detective and the frontier hero. Combining the rationality of the positivist with the chivalric code of nineteenth-century manhood, the gentleman detective grew up at the center of the detective story itself.[6] As popular male icons, gentlemen detectives such as C. Auguste Dupin, Sherlock Holmes, and Philo Vance embodied the basic principles of nineteenth-century manliness, which were predicated on an ideology of civilization emphasizing physical and psychical restraint and which opposed themselves to both the explicitly racialized figure of the black rapist and to the implicitly racialized figure of the underworld criminal.[7] This discourse of manliness also emphasized a largely interiorized conception of male identity, casting white, middle-class men as the intellectual and moral centers of the projects of evolution and civilization. A second genealogical precursor to the hard-boiled male was the mythic frontier hero who, as Richard Slotkin has demonstrated, was essential to earlier American fantasies of male autonomy and potency and who had a complex, usually opposed but sometimes intertwining relationship to the dime-novel figuration of social banditry.[8] Central to the lasting appeal of the frontier hero was his seemingly effortless embodiment of a contradictory set of American values: democratic egalitarianism and an imperializing sense of gender and racial privilege; artisanal self-sufficiency and a commitment to capitalist enterprise; a suspicion of luxury and an idealization of success; heterosexuality and a celebration of the community of men without women.[9]

The social and economic conditions under which the dual figures of the gentleman detective and the frontier hero first emerged had radically changed by the beginning of the twentieth century. The closure of the frontier combined with the radical transformation of society by urbanization, the growth of mass culture, and the shift in U.S. capitalism from a competitive and entrepreneurial stage to a corporate and managed stage all threatened the ability of these figures to embody convincingly the American fantasy of masculine individualism and thus mediate the social contradictions with which they were invested.

One solution to this challenge was to resurrect a composite of these two heroic figures within various forms of mass-market historical romances. The geography of the frontier could be literally revived, as in genre of the western, or its imperializing dynamics could be transposed to various overseas contexts, as in the revitalization of the adventure romance in the 1890s.[10] Ironically, it was the technology of the emergent mass culture that enabled the dissemination of these fantasies of return to a mythic era or space of masculine individualism and artisan autonomy. Although on one level this contradiction between content and form had the effect of suturing protest against modernization to the very forms of modernization itself, on another level, the mass dissemination of these popular fantasies provided a vital, if often deeply conservative, site of what T. J. Jackson Lears has described as antimodernist protest (4–58).

The figure of the hard-boiled male represented a different imaginary solution to the contradiction between the cultural fantasy of masculine autonomy and the emergence of mass and corporate culture. Rather than invoking mythic fantasies of a bygone era, he represented an adaptation of this cultural fantasy, through the figure of the lone detective or urbanite, to the rationalized, mass-cultural landscape of the modern city. This adaptation was achieved by jettisoning many of the romantic and sentimental trappings of the earlier figure of the gentleman detective and instead fashioning, as we saw in chapter 1, an image of the detective modeled on the criminals populating the prohibition-era crime fiction already filling the pages of *Black Mask* in the early twenties. This new masculinity seemed fully adapted to the rationalized and instrumentalized logic of life in the twenties. At the same time, the hard-boiled male had to resist the disposability and exchangeability of individual subjects implicit in the commodified logic of mass culture and the reification of labor in corporate capitalism.[11]

This double imperative produced the form of split narration that I have described as characteristic of the hard-boiled narrative. On one level, it seems fully adapted to a rationalized landscape. The first-person narration of the male protagonist consists largely of seemingly objective recounting of events ordered by an instrumentalized view of social relations. But on another level this narrative is overdetermined by the persistence in displaced form of the affect and sentiment that is seemingly purged from it. The hard-boiled narrator acts out the very phantasmatic and emotional investments that are excised from his narration. Thus the hard-boiled narrative seems to function as a discursive analog to the process of "exteriorization" that Michael Kimmel has described as characterizing twentieth-century conceptions of masculinity, which formed in opposition to the more interiorized nineteenth-century conception of manliness (191–221). Male identity became defined by a set of externally measurable quantities and actions with concepts of physicality and personality replacing Victorian notions of character. The hard-boiled protagonist's masculinity is embodied as both a physical quantity, one that can be measured in terms of active performance and embodied hardness, and a controlling, affectless personality that situates the detective, like the social scientist of the early twentieth century, as the detached observer and recorder of events.

Yet this masculinity is overdetermined by the persistence in displaced form of the affect and sentiment that are seemingly purged from it. The persistence of this sentiment in displaced form suggests that the hard-boiled text, for all its seeming modernity, is still intimately bound with the historical romance form and the more expressive forms of masculine subjectivity narrated within it. It is also bound up with the set of murderous racial and gender meanings that are associated with the psychological noir. As I argued in chapter 1, the psychological noir is a modernized descendent of the gothic, and the latter, in turn, as Karen Halttunen has pointed out, represents the violent inversion of the nineteenth-century discourse of romantic love central to the romance form (172–207). It is in part the disavowed persistence of the romance and the gothic within the hard-boiled text that enables it to link a seemingly outmoded discourse of masculine individualism to a representation of contemporary life in the era of mass and corporate culture.[12] Thus the purging of affect from the modernized surface of the hard-boiled narrative produces a historically specific form of textual unconscious. This unconscious overdetermines the autocritique advanced by *Red Harvest*.

Red Harvest *as Autocritique*

The novel begins with the Continental Op's arrival in the small and thoroughly corrupt mining city of Personville, which has been rechristened "Poisonville" by local residents. He has been hired to do some investigative work by Donald Willsson, the son of Elihu Willsson, Personville's leading capitalist and de facto patriarch. Donald is the publisher of Personville's one daily newspaper and the town's lone reformer. His murdered body is discovered before the Op has a chance to speak with him. The Op stays in town to find Donald's murderer and is soon hired by Elihu to empty the town of its "crooks and grafters," whom Elihu originally employed, along with the National Guard, to suppress a strike at his Personville Mining Corporation and who have temporarily wrestled control of the town away from him.[13] The Op begins the job by throwing in with the town's police force (so corrupt that it is indistinguishable from the town's other criminal organizations), but he is immediately double-crossed by the police chief, Noonan, and is almost killed. He then allies himself with Max "Whisper" Thaler, one of the local mob bosses. Meanwhile, he discovers and extracts a confession from Donald's murderer, ironically an otherwise innocent bank clerk named Albury with no connections to the city's crime syndicates. The next day, Elihu, who has mended fences with the leaders of the various criminal factions, attempts to call the Op off the job. The Op, however, refuses—partly because he dislikes Elihu, partly because he wants revenge on Noonan, and partly because he has begun to enjoy the violence his presence in town is creating. The Op continues the job of cleaning up the town by pitting its various illegal and nominally legal factions against each other, directly or indirectly producing at least nineteen murders. The most dramatic of these is that of Dinah Brand, Max Thaler's girlfriend and the text's femme fatale. Dinah makes her living through blackmail and playing the stock market and becomes one of the Op's allies in his mission to open the town up "from Adam's apple to ankles" (62). After a laudanum-fueled night at Dinah's house, the Op wakes to find his hand on an ice pick that has been plunged through her heart. While continuing violently to purge the town of its criminal elements, the Op spends much of the last third of the novel attempting to absolve himself of Dinah's murder, which he finally does by forcing a confession from a dying mob boss (Reno Starkey) in the closing pages of the novel. The novel ends with the cleaned-up town firmly under Elihu Willsson's control and "ready to go to the dogs again" (203).

The novel's critique of the political and economic conditions of everyday life in the early twentieth century is already apparent in this brief summary.[14] Driven by profit and a rationalized, objectifying conception of social relations, all actors in Personville are equally corrupt. The novel collapses distinctions between legal and illegal, wealthy and criminal, suggesting that such distinctions are meaningless in an environment ruled by force and economic exploitation. The collusion of public and private sectors in the novel (in which the police, the National Guard, and even the governor, as we later learn, function in tandem with Willsson's economic interests) suggests the new alliance between big business and

government in the teens and twenties. This newly complicitous relationship—evidenced by the expanded role of the commerce department, the
relaxation of antitrust laws, the passage of the Federal Reserve Act, the
formation of organizations like the National Foreign Trade Council,
and the rationalization of government-controlled industry during the
First World War—enabled the emergence of more managed and rationalized forms of capitalism. Hammett's novel, then, calls attention to
the violent suppression of organized labor, the instrumentalization of
social relations, and the growth of the "unofficial" or criminal economy
that forms the underside of this new economic regime. In this context,
Elihu Willsson's last name seems less than accidental given that President Woodrow Wilson was one of the main architects of the new economic order and used federal troops to suppress the 1919 strike by U.S.
Steel workers.[15]

The setting of the novel in the fictional Personville, an allegorical U.S.
anytown, further indicates the national dimensions of the novel's critique
of economic and social relationships. The name "Personville," clearly
echoing medieval "everyman" plays, announces the allegorical status of
Hammett's narrative[16] and suggests the U.S. ideal of a civic space defined
by democratic participation:[17]

> I first heard Personville called Poisonville by a red-haired mucker named
> Hickey Dewey in the Big Ship in Butte. He also called his shirt a shoit.
> I didn't think anything of what he had done to the city's name. Later I
> heard men who could manage their r's give it the same pronunciation.
> I still didn't see anything in it but the meaningless sort of humor that
> used to make richardsnary the thieves' word for dictionary. A few years
> later I went to Personville and learned better. (3)

The transformation of "Personville" into "Poisonville" in this opening
paragraph of the novel establishes the devolutionary movement of the
national allegory and foreshadows the poisoning of democratic ideals by
corporate and criminal interests that the Op will find in Personville.[18]
Significantly, this passage locates the sign for this transformation in the
popular speech and slang that constitute a defining feature of hard-
boiled prose. By doing so, the text suggests that the poisoning of democratic ideals is bound up with the transformation of economic and social
spheres that form the historical context for the emergence of the hard-
boiled aesthetic. The text thus alludes to its autocritical function in the
opening paragraph.

What is most striking about the passage, however, is not its obvious
allegorical resonances but the Op's blithe lack of awareness of them. The

Op's dismissal suggests that he is too embedded in this new world defined by thieves' language to realize the significance of the social and economic transformation that it signifies. The Op's blindness toward the significance of this transformation—literally his inability "to see anything in it"—foreshadows his later willful participation, as an ostensible representative of the law, in the vigilante code of Poisonville that forms what Slavoj Žižek describes as the official law's obscene underbelly (*Enjoy* 149–93). Furthermore, the ironic transformation of the "dick" in dictionary into the proper name "Richard," linking the new thieves' slang (as well as "hard-boiled dicks" like the Op) to the world of proper names, emphasizes the connection between the criminal classes and the Richards of this world.

As this opening paragraph suggests, the text's autocritique of hard-boiled masculinity emerges out of its larger critique of capitalist exploitation. The central figure of this critique is, of course, the Op himself. Hammett employs the structures of reader (especially male reader) identification that he has built up over the course of sixty-odd short stories to add force to *Red Harvest*'s critique, utilizing the Op's popularity as a protagonist in order to implicate his mass audience in the Op's increasingly unjustifiable acts of violence.[19] The critique builds slowly. The first fifty or so pages of the novel—what was roughly the first story, "The Cleansing of Poisonville," when it appeared serially in *Black Mask*—proceed much like any other Continental Op story, ending with the successful arrest of Albury. However, over the next hundred and fifty pages the Op begins the ominous cleansing promised by the first story's title, directly or indirectly producing the nineteen murders. While the Op directly participates in some of the murders, the text represents the instrumental rationality that informs his tactics of "stirring things up" as an equally significant source of violence, echoing the more abstracted and bureaucratic forms of violence that characterize life in the era of modernization.

The Op explains these tactics to Dinah Brand after both have witnessed the violent results of the Op's unfixing of a fixed boxing match:

> [The Op states:] "The closest I've got to an idea is to dig up any and all the dirty work I can that might implicate the others, and run it out. Maybe I'll advertise—*Crime Wanted—Male or Female*. If they're as crooked as I think they are I shouldn't have a lot of trouble finding a job or two that I can hang on them."
>
> "Is that what you were up to when you uncooked the fight?"
>
> "That was only an experiment—just to see what would happen."

GOING BLOOD-SIMPLE IN POISONVILLE | 65

"So that's the way you scientific detectives work. My God! for a fat, middle-aged, hard-boiled, pig-headed guy, you've got the vaguest way of doing things I've ever heard of."

"Plans are all right sometimes," I said. "And sometimes just stirring things up is all right—if you're tough enough to survive, and keep your eyes open so you'll see what you want when it comes to the top." (84–85)

Nowhere is the metacritical dimension of *Red Harvest* clearer than in this exchange between Dinah and the Op. The passage directly alludes to the conventions of both the hard-boiled narrative and the classical tradition that precedes it. Both traditions are mockingly critiqued: the hard-boiled for its "pig-headed" ethic of producing solutions through violence, and the classical for cloaking the same ethic in the garb of a scientific experiment. The passage highlights the instrumental rationality that informs the Op's tactics of stirring things up, in which he will resort to blackmail and the incitement of violence (as he has just done with the fight) in order to achieve his ends. Rather than justifying these actions on moral grounds as Holmes or Dupin might do, he invokes a rhetoric of toughness, replacing the moral rhetoric of Victorian manliness with the instrumentalized ethos of hard-boiled masculinity. The repression that accompanies this ethos of toughness is underscored by the last line of the passage. While the Op's statement that "you'll see what you want when it comes to the top" seems to argue for the efficacy of his tactics, it also suggests that he *only* sees what he wants to see. This representation of the detective as a selective viewer is part of Hammett's more general critique of the epistemology of the classical detective story and, as Steven Marcus has noted, runs throughout his fiction.[20]

The most dramatic representation of the amoral instrumentality of the Op's tactics is the "peace conference" he calls between the various warring factions in Personville (146). After the violence has escalated to the point that even hardened veterans of Personville, such as the police chief Noonan, declare that they are "sick of this butchering," the Op calls a meeting of the various warring factions with the stated goal of returning things to business as usual, with the casual but limited violence that this state of affairs implies (144). Instead, the Op orchestrates the outcome of the peace conference to ensure an escalation of the violence and the immediate murder of Noonan. An apparent allusion to the treaty of Versailles (with Willsson at its head) as well as a parody of a corporate board meeting, the "peace conference" effectively allegorizes the contradictory imperatives that define the role of the corporation and the nation-state in an increasingly corporatized world system: those of collusion and competition. Each of the conference's participants wants to secure alliances that will ensure his survival, if not prosperity, while each also views the other participants as competitors to be either exploited or eliminated. The result of this fully instrumentalized view of social and economic relations is the increased violence that follows from the conference.

While placing the Op at the center of the violence (and of the critique of this violence), the text resists making him its cause. Instead, his increasingly brutal tactics are presented as one more symptom of the town's (always already) "fallen" condition. The Op himself underscores the link between the town's ethic of profit-driven violence and his increasing vigilantism in a conversation with Dinah:

> "This damn burg's getting to me. If I don't get away soon, I'll be
> going blood-simple like the natives. There's been what? A dozen and a
> half murders since I've been here. . . . I've arranged a killing or two in
> my time, when they were necessary. But this is the first time I've ever
> got the fever. It's this damn burg. You can't go straight here. I got
> myself tangled at the beginning." (154)

In linking the Op's "blood-simple" vigilantism to the town's ethic of capitalist exploitation and violent self-interest, the text avoids the depoliticized or right-wing representation of the vigilante that divorces the violence from any larger social context. In making the Op's violence an effect of the town's corruption, however, the text also runs the risk of diluting its critique of instrumental rationality. If the town has caused the Op to go "blood-simple," then the violence of his behavior is limited to this one particular locale. Even the allegorical dimension of the text, which transforms Poisonville into an anytown of the 1920s, does not entirely alleviate the problems produced by the tropes of "going blood-simple" or "going native." The question then becomes whether the Op's violence can be read as the logical outcome of his hard-boiled code or as a break from its principles of amoral detachment.

Traversing the Form's Gender, Racial, and Sexual Unconscious

In order to address this contradiction, we need to account for what the text's autocritique does not or cannot fully articulate. Only by turning to the historical and phantasmatic investments that overdetermine the structure of the hard-boiled text can we begin to account for this aporia. From this theoretical vantage, the two terms of the contradiction—

going blood-simple versus amoral detachment—emerge as complementary and even constitutively dependent on each other rather than simply opposed.

It seems less than accidental that the Op uses the trope of "going native" in describing his adherence to the customs of Poisonville. The Op contrasts these "blood-simple" customs to the usual dictates of his hard-boiled code, but the trope of going native encodes in displaced form a phantasmatic racial borrowing that, as we saw in the previous chapter, structures the figuration of hard-boiled masculinity and lends a surreptitious set of racial meanings to the signifier "noir." While the natives of Poisonville are marked by criminality rather than racial otherness, the conflation of these two categories is a long-standing discursive tradition in both U.S racialist discourse and the discourse of criminality.

As a reworking and repudiation of the chivalric ideal of manhood associated with the historical romance and with the contemporaneous fictions of the Ku Klux Klan, the fantasy of hard-boiled masculinity initially appears to be a rejection of the forms of racism attaching to this chivalric ideal. Indeed, Sean McCann has theorized the hard-boiled story's emergence in opposition to the nativist rhetoric of the Klan.[21] However, McCann's reading of the hard-boiled story as representing a world where "ethnic distinctions become ultimately insubstantial" and "association is based not on inheritance but on shared criminal interests" misses the way in which the construction of race and masculine subjectivity in the hard-boiled text is structured around the conflation of race and criminality ("Constructing" 700–701). As we saw in chapter 1, this conflation has a long history in the popular fiction of the United States. Its presence in *Red Harvest* and other hard-boiled texts is also predicated on the emergence of more rationalized and social-scientific forms of racism that work precisely through this conflation as well as through the association of racial otherness with the category of the primitive as it emerges in the discourse of modern anthropology in the early twentieth century.[22]

The emergence of these more rationalized forms of racism produce their disavowed phantasmatic counterpart in white fantasies of going native as individualist transgression against the rationalized order of modern society itself. Thus hard-boiled masculinity can be read as one end point of what Gail Bederman has described as a discursive shift from a nineteenth-century conception of manliness that opposed itself to the ideological figure of the "primitive" black criminal—or rapist—to a valorized conception of primitivized white masculinity that is borrowed in a disavowed manner from the same ideological figure (1–44). As we saw in chapter 1, this disavowed borrowing can be read as symptomatically informing the naming of two of the genre's early protagonists, Race Williams and Sam Spade, as well as lending a racial resonance to the title of the magazine, *Black Mask*, in which hard-boiled fiction first appeared. The rationalization that characterizes the emergence of hard-boiled masculinity and modern forms of progressivist and social-scientific racism produces a phantasmatic doubling that is structured by a form of what Slavoj Žižek has termed "enjoyment theft": white hard-boiled masculinity gains its racialized identity through a disavowed borrowing from and envy of the perceived pleasures of black masculinity, fantasized as a less fully civilized and more enjoyably transgressive form of subjectivity (*Tarrying* 201).[23]

The opposition that the Op maintains between his code and the code of going native records this disavowal, revealing that his code is in fact predicated on a fantasy of emulating such imagined "native" customs as criminality and gendered violence. "Going blood-simple" similarly suggests this structure of disavowal, simultaneously invoking racialist fantasies of nonwhite "simple" (i.e., primitive) blood and disowning this phantasmatic miscegenation by asserting that the blood is "simple" (i.e., unmixed). Thus, on the level of the signifier, the text indicates that the opposition between the Op's code and his "going blood-simple" is spurious even as the rhetoric of the text remains conflicted on this point. This conflicted rhetoric also indicates the limits of the text's autocritique, marking the racial divide that the text phantasmatically traverses but must represent as intact.

Red Harvest's reworking of the phantasmatic investments that structure the representation of gender and sexuality in the hard-boiled text forms another important site of cultural dream work, one that also helps to explain the seeming contradiction between the text's critique of the Op's code and its rhetoric of going blood-simple. In the hard-boiled text, the textual representation of hard-boiled masculinity is structured around the purging of subjective affect from the first-person narrative, suggesting a form of consciousness that seems fully adapted to the rationalized and instrumentalized landscape of everyday life in the 1920s. The text replaces affective description and conventional representation of interiority with deflationary humor and affectless parataxis connoting hardness and objectivity. In *Red Harvest*, the textual repressions that structure the hard-boiled aesthetic begin to return and haunt the Op's narrative, revealing the affect that the discourse of hard-boiled masculinity works to disavow and that shapes its relationship to a rationalized social sphere.

The passage cited above provides one example of the return of the repressed in the Op's discourse. In his conversation with Dinah, the Op distinguishes between his usual disinterested attitude toward killing as a "necessary" part of the job and the homicidal "fever" that has infected him since entering Poisonville. The rhetoric of necessity suggests a similar structure of disavowal to that of race and criminality in the hard-boiled text, a rhetoric in which the "fever" of sadistic enjoyment in killing is masked by the instrumental logic of necessity. The appeal of this enjoyment surfaces more fully later in the Op's discussion with Dinah: "Play with murder enough and it gets you one of two ways. It makes you sick, or you get to like it. It got to Noonan the first way. He was green around the gills after Yard was knocked off, all the stomach gone out of him, willing to do anything to make the peace" (155). The Op obliquely admits his murderous enjoyment by contrasting it to Noonan's going green around the gills. The description of Noonan as "green" implies a standard of masculine toughness in relation to which Noonan is a mere rookie, one who can't stomach the job. The comparison undoes the opposition between the Op's code and the enjoyment of murder: in being tough enough to like murder, enjoyment becomes the logical conclusion of his ethic of hardness, rather than its antithesis. The phrase "play with murder enough" also undoes this opposition with its implication that murder has been a game that the Op "got to like" a long time ago. The passage, then, suggests that what is troubling the Op is not the enjoyment of murder itself but the fact that this enjoyment is becoming too apparent both to himself and to others. The masculine ethic of "doing one's job right or wrong" no longer fully enables him to disavow the affective pleasure of doing a "wrong" job.

It is significant that the Op confesses his going blood-simple to Dinah Brand, since the disavowal of sadism also structures the Op's relationship to Dinah, and more generally the hard-boiled male's relationship to the femme fatale in the larger organization of gender, sexuality, and sexual desire in the hard-boiled text. The figure of the femme fatale functions as an important nexus of displaced textual affect, revealing the phantasmatic economy of projection that structures most hard-boiled narratives. As a figure, she allegorizes all the forms of connection—economic, national, sexual, or racial—that the hard-boiled male disavows. Thus, as William Marling points out, Dinah is allegorically equated in *Red Harvest* with both capitalist and erotic speculation, two forms of connection that the Op disavows; she uses her connections with various boyfriends to further her dealings in both blackmail and the stock market (119).

The rejection of final union between the hard-boiled male and the femme fatale—implicit in the very adjective "fatale"—establishes the hard-boiled form's (equally allegorical) repudiation of the allegorical trajectory of the romance. Unlike the classical detective story—which, as Dennis Porter has noted, often reproduces the marriage plot of the conventional romance—the hard-boiled novel finds its roots in the gothic complications or refusal of this plot.[24] If, as theorists as diverse as Doris Sommer and Fredric Jameson have argued, the marriage that closes the romance allegorically represents a comedic resolution to the various conflicts (economic, national, sexual, racial) that organize the narrative,[25] then the hard-boiled text, as the immediate genealogical descendent of gothic fictional and true-crime texts, narrativizes a refusal of such resolution in its rejection of a final heterosexual union.[26] The femme fatale becomes the symbol of a rejected comedic resolution: a figure of repudiation on which the hard-boiled male can project and disavow his complicity with the economic and social system against which he defines himself. The ritual repudiation of the femme fatale in the hard-boiled text allows the male protagonist to maintain his fantasies of autonomy and individualist opposition to the dominant order.

Yet this repudiation forms only one affective pole of the hard-boiled male's relationship to the femme fatale, one that masks, while it also suggests, his continuing preoccupation with her. Both repudiation and investment are evident in the Op's initial description of Dinah, disrupting the seemingly smooth, objective surface of the prose:

> She was an inch or two taller than I, which made her about five feet eight. She had a broad-shouldered, full-breasted, round-hipped body and big muscular legs. The hand she gave me was soft, warm, strong. Her face was the face of a girl of twenty-five already showing signs of wear. Little lines crossed the corner of her big ripe mouth. Fainter lines were beginning to make nets around her thick-lashed eyes. They were large eyes, blue and a bit blood-shot. Her coarse hair—brown—needed trimming and was parted crookedly. One side of her upper lip had been rouged higher than the other. Her dress was of a particularly unbecoming wine color, and it gaped here and there down one side, where she had neglected to snap the fasteners or they had popped open. There was a run down the front of her left stocking. (32)

The length of this description is the first indication of the Op's affective investment. Personal descriptions in *Red Harvest* are almost never this detailed, being characterized instead by shorthand phrases such as "hog-jaw" that, as William Marling has pointed out, function by a logic of metonymy (117–18). His investment is also indicated by the explicitly connotative language that everywhere disrupts the illusion of denotation

that is central to the hard-boiled aesthetic. The eruption of the connotative into the detached parataxis of the hard-boiled prose indicates
the ambivalence that structures the hard-boiled male's representation of
the femme fatale. The prose of this passage vacillates between descriptions that suggest attraction ("broad-shouldered, full-breasted, round-
hipped body," "big muscular legs," "big ripe mouth," "soft, warm,
strong") and those that imply repudiation ("the face of a girl of twenty-
five already showing signs of wear," "coarse hair . . . parted crookedly,"
"faint lines . . . around her thick-lashed eyes"). This vacillation is present
even on the level of the individual sentence (her dress is both "unbe-
coming" and "gaping," her mouth is both "ripe" and crossed with lines,
and her eyes are both "blue" and "blood-shot"), suggesting the simul-
taneity of these feelings.

The ambivalence evident in the hard-boiled male's contradictory desires simultaneously to possess and repudiate the femme fatale suggests
that his preoccupation with her is structured by melancholia. Freud
defines melancholia as a form of mourning that is made interminable by
the subject's simultaneous phantasmatic incorporation of and ambivalence toward a love object that is perceived as lost.[27] The subject feels
aggression and resentment toward the object because of some imagined
or real act of abandonment or betrayal. This resentment conflicts with
the subject's idealized phantasmatic construction of the love object, a
construction that is now unconsciously simultaneously internalized and
figured as irrevocably lost in a nostalgic past, even when the object itself
is still present. Conventionally in melancholia, the internalization of
the object produces a form of self-loathing in which the aggression at
the love object now becomes directed inward as the object becomes in-
corporated into the subject's ego. However, in the melancholic cultural
fantasy that underpins *Red Harvest* and conventionally structures most
hard-boiled texts, the melancholic object and the aggression it provokes
become, like all other forms of affect, (re)externalized through projection. The femme fatale becomes the locus for this projection, allegorically becoming the gendered figure through which the hard-boiled male
narrates a larger sense of cultural loss and betrayal and toward which he
directs his displaced aggression and self-loathing.

Via this melancholic logic, the hard-boiled male constructs the femme
fatale in relationship to a specifically modernist figuration of the virgin/
whore opposition, one in which the "whore" becomes the representation
of femininity in the era of mass culture (repeating the ideological links
between the representation of femininity and that of mass culture described by Andreas Huyssen) while the virginal ideal of the nineteenth

century forms its melancholic subtext.[28] The aggression that the hard-boiled male demonstrates toward the "fallen" femme fatale can be read as an effect of this melancholic subtext, one that is directed at an internalized and always already lost ideal. This ideal is simultaneously sexual and, via the larger allegory of the national romance, national.

In order to fully understand the phantasmatic construction of gender and sexuality in the hard-boiled narrative, however, we need to read this melancholic rejection of the romance paradigm in relationship to a more constitutive melancholia that organizes what Sommer describes as the construction of "natural" desire in the romance plot (39). This more constitutive melancholia has been theorized by Judith Butler, who, expanding on Freud's definition, links melancholia to the always incomplete formation of normative sexual and gender identities. In Butler's account, the cultural prohibition on same-sex desire produces the subject's melancholic incorporation of the gender of the prohibited love object. Because of the prohibition, the subject identifies with this gender, while the other gender can be symbolized as an object of desire.[29] Reading this melancholic production of heterosexual desire in relationship to the ordering of the romance plot suggests why the hard-boiled narrative's rejection of this plot does not conventionally lead to the textual realization of radically alternative ways of organizing desire. The melancholic rejection of the femme fatale (precisely because it is melancholic and predicated on the phantasmatic persistence of the virginal ideal of the romance) does little to disturb the constitutive melancholia that orders the construction of heterosexual desire in the romance plot. Thus the rejection of heterosexual union in the hard-boiled text produces a homosocial space that is ordered by a homoeroticism that remains largely foreclosed.

The Hard-Boiled Form as National Dream Work

Appropriately enough, the only direct textual expression of the phantasmatic dynamics that overdetermine the representation of gender, sexuality, race, and nation in *Red Harvest* takes the form of what is either a dream or a laudanum-induced hallucination. A rebus containing, in coded form, not only the key dynamics that structure *Red Harvest* but also the hard-boiled form in general, the Op's dream/hallucination takes place during Dinah's murder. In the first part of the dream, the Op imagines himself sitting next to a woman whose face is covered by a veil: "I dreamed I was sitting on a bench, in Baltimore, facing the tumbling fountain in Harlem Park, beside a woman who wore a veil. I had come

there with her. She was somebody I knew well. But I had suddenly forgotten who she was. I couldn't see her face because of the long black
veil" (162). Initially the dream suggests a romantic connection between
the woman and the Op, who have arrived together to sit in the park like
lovers in a romance. These associations are furthered by first mention
of the veil, which is significantly not initially described as either black or
long, suggesting a wedding veil as easily as one worn for a funeral. It
therefore does not seem too much of a stretch to associate this couple
with the protagonists of a romance. However, the Op's selective amne-
sia (he can name the locale but can't remember the woman's name) and
the opaqueness of the veil suggest that the generic significance of this
figure must remain obscure for him.

And indeed, the second mention of the veil quickly refuses these
romantic connotations, unequivocally establishing it as a cloth of mourning. The significance of this funereal imagery becomes fully apparent
when the reader later learns that Dinah Brand is murdered during the
dream. The veiled woman of the dream, then, becomes metonymically
linked with the death of the text's femme fatale, encoding in displaced
form the often lethal repudiation of the femme fatale that forms one
pole of the hard-boiled male's ambivalent preoccupation with her. In
this larger generic context, we can read the woman's mourning as being
doubly significant: functioning as both a figuration of the femme fatale's
self-mourning that suggests the gendered social costs of the repressions
that structure hard-boiled masculinity and a projection of the hard-boiled
male's melancholic relationship to her. This melancholic relationship is
further suggested by the next part of the dream, in which the Op loses
sight of the woman and then runs after her, following her voice, but
finding "it was too late." The melancholia of the Op's search is figured
in its belatedness; his desire for the woman can only be articulated with
his loss of her. Thus the dream's movement from romantic union to representations of mourning and loss reproduces, in a displaced form, both
the hard-boiled novel's masculinist rejection of the marriage plot and the
aesthetics of melancholic ambivalence that replace it.

The Op's pursuit of the veiled woman is presented in explicitly
national terms:

> I walked streets hunting for her, half the streets in the United
> States . . .
> I walked more streets listening to her voice. She was calling a name,
> not mine, one strange to me, but no matter how fast I walked or in what
> direction, I could get no nearer her voice. It was the same distance from

me in the street that runs past the Federal Building in El Paso as in
Detroit's Grand Circus Park. (162–63)

This passage suggests a form of national allegory that is specific to the
hard-boiled text, one that replaces the allegory enacted by the resolution
of the romance marriage plot. In the passage, the nation is constituted
through the detective's melancholic desire for the femme fatale. In pursuit of her ever-vanishing image, the detective traverses the imaginary
space of the nation, here represented as an interconnected series of urban
streets. The nation, then, is phantasmatically constituted only through
the disappearance (or the melancholic repudiation) of the femme fatale
from its imaginary topography. Thus the virginal ideal of the romance
is replaced by a vanishing female figure, who can only be fully romanticized once she is dead, or at least safely "removed" from the imagined
community.

The specifically urban mapping of the nation in the passage should
also command our attention, suggesting a modernist reworking of the
nineteenth-century ideal of the nation as either agrarian utopia or expanding frontier. In this context we can read the virginal part of the
virgin/whore opposition that defines the femme fatale as a nostalgic
figuration that casts back as much to the tropes of "virginal landscape"
and nature as a mystical feminine force as to the virginal bride of the
romance.[30] These nostalgic constructions suggest the way in which the
text's economic critique is aligned, via the national allegory enacted by
the text, with the populist rhetoric that Michael Kazin and Richard
Hofstadter have argued forms a central facet of American political life.[31]
As Hofstadter notes, the "populists looked backward with longing to the
lost agrarian Eden, to the republican America of the early years of the
nineteenth century in which there were few millionaires and, as they saw
it, no beggars, when the laborer had excellent prospects and the farmer had
abundance, when statesmen still responded to the mood of the people
and there was no such thing as the money power" (62).[32] The fantasy of
the femme fatale as "whorish," then, clearly allegorizes the incursions
of such a money power, and, in rejecting her present embodiment for
an always already lost image of her as innocent, the hard-boiled male is
expressing a sentiment that is simultaneously anticorporate, nationalist,
and misogynist.

What emerges from the masculinized imaginary nation inaugurated by
the repudiation of the femme fatale is a homosocial space[33] that is characterized by either violent competition or a (usually implicit) homoerotic
longing.[34] In the second part of the dream sequence, these homosocial

dynamics take the form of the Op's pursuit, echoing the earlier pursuit of the femme fatale, of a criminalized male figure whom he is described as hating (163). Thus, in the dream sequence, as in *Red Harvest* in general, this homosocial space is primarily characterized by violence, underscoring the text's autocritique of the instrumental rationality that is central to the masculine imaginary of the hard-boiled male. Continuing its work of desublimation, the dream explicitly links this competitive violence to the racialized dimensions of the noir narrative, depicting the hunted man as a stereotypical Mexican or Chicano bandit figure: "He was a small brown man who wore an immense sombrero. He was standing on the steps of a tall building on the far side of a wide plaza, laughing at me" (163). While the disavowed racial borrowing that characterizes the discourse of white "primitive masculinity" is usually associated with the iconography of African American masculinity, the image of the Mexican can be read not only as a displacement but also as geopolitically specific, borrowing from the iconography of the Chicano "bandit" that is distinctive to the California landscape of much hard-boiled fiction. Thus the specific racial antagonisms that characterize the history of U.S. imperial aggression in California become one source for the racial borrowing that distinguishes the white male protagonists of both noir and hard-boiled fiction, a genealogy that here becomes explicit via the work of condensation that organizes the dream.[35] The contradictory desires that animate the hard-boiled male's relationship to this homosocial and racial other are dramatized near the dream's end: the Op embraces the man in an attempt to kill him, propelling the two of them off the roof of a building. This simultaneously erotic and homicidal embrace encapsulates the contradictory impulses that structure the homosocial national space.[36]

Unmasking a Constitutive Misogyny

The dream sequence, then, traverses in coded form the central phantasmatic investments structuring the hard-boiled aesthetic. The substitution of the phantasmatic landscape traversed by the dream for a direct representation of Dinah's murder also suggests its significance for the text's autocritique. In refusing to represent the murder directly, the text implicates the Op in the killing, while simultaneously withholding a full account of it. The reader and the Op wake from the dream, finding themselves holding the handle of an ice pick that has been plunged through Dinah Brand's heart. In this way, the text inverts a key aspect of the phantasmatic investment that structures the dynamic of suspense in the conventional detective novel. While suspense is still produced through what Roland Barthes has described as a form of hermeneutic delay, in which the answers to the questions proposed by the action or exposition of the narrative are withheld until the end of the novel, the readerly investment in the completion of the hermeneutic circuit is significantly altered.[37] Rather than eagerly anticipating the detective's masterly unmasking of the criminal, the reader is instead implicated in a narrativized form of self-revelation, in which the criminals for whom the Op and the reader are searching appear to be none other than themselves.

Since the opposition between criminal and detective has already been undone by the text's political and economic critique, this altered hermeneutic takes on a gendered specificity, one that echoes the phantasmatic landscape traversed by the dream sequence. Through the device of hermeneutic delay, Dinah's murder is distinguished from the other murders committed by the Op, the victims of which are male. Dinah's murder becomes the central narrative preoccupation of the final third of the novel while these other murders remain relatively incidental to its structural unfolding. The structural centrality of Dinah's murder, then, is ironically encoded through its elision from the representational space of the text. It is only because we do not witness her murder that the identity of its perpetrator can remain a hermeneutic preoccupation. This combination of structural centrality and representational elision reproduces the melancholic logic of the dream sequence, in which the competitive homosocial space of the hard-boiled narrative is inaugurated by the structural disappearance of the woman in the dream. Within the larger generic context mapped by the dream, then, the distinction between the representation of the other murders and Dinah's murder can be read as a larger division structuring the representation of violence in the hard-boiled narrative. Violence between men is figured as the result of public, visible, homosocial competition, whereas violence that crosses the divide of sexual difference, whichever direction the violence flows, is represented as necessarily private, a dark secret that the detective works simultaneously to expose and disavow. This double movement toward exposure and disavowal (or exposure as disavowal) is what is at stake in the Op's frantic search for another suspect in the murder of Dinah Brand. Until the closing pages of the novel, however, all signs point to the Op as Dinah's murderer, creating the textual possibility of exposure without disavowal, or, as I have already suggested, a dynamic of self-exposure, in which the detective reveals himself to have been the criminal all along.[38]

In developing this possibility, the narrative importantly links Dinah's murder to both the repression that characterizes the Op's ethic of detachment and to the rhetoric of going blood-simple that encodes his inability to fully disavow his sadism. In an ominous bit of foreshadowing, the Op contemplates murder by ice pick on the same evening of Dinah's murder. In response to Dinah's question, "Now what did you bring that ice pick in for?," the Op states:

> "To show you how my mind's running. A couple of days ago, if I
> thought about it at all, it was a good tool to pry off chunks of ice."
> I ran a finger down its half-foot of round steel blade to the needle point.
> "Not a bad thing to pin a man to his clothes with. That's the way I'm
> begging, on the level. I can't even see a mechanical cigar lighter without
> thinking of filling one with nitroglycerine for somebody you don't like.
> There's a piece of copper wire lying in the gutter in front of your
> house—thin, soft, and just long enough to go around a neck with two
> ends to hold on. I had one hell of a time to keep from picking it up and
> stuffing it into my pocket, just in case—"
> "You're crazy."
> "I know it. That's what I've been telling you. I'm going blood-
> simple." (157–58)

Here, the Op's "blood-simple" sadism takes form as fantasy. Initially, the psychoanalytically informed reader might read this scene as an important moment of libidinal recognition, one in which the Op symbolizes his desire for the first time in the narrative rather than projecting it onto Dinah or the town as a whole. Contrary to the literary logic of foreshadowing, such a reading might argue against the Op as Dinah's murderer, asserting that his ability to symbolize his murderous desire would preclude his acting it out in the form of a laudanum-induced hallucination. However, if we are to take this fantasy as a foreshadowing of the later murder, the gender of the victim is crucially displaced: "not a bad thing to pin a man to his clothes with." In this way, sexual difference remains crucially occluded in the Op's discourse, reproducing the fantasy of a purely homosocial space evident in the dream. The Op's disavowal of sexual difference, in turn, precludes any symbolization of his desire, murderous or otherwise, for Dinah. Thus, if we are to read the Op as potentially murderous in this passage, I would suggest it is because of this phantasmatic foreclosure of sexual difference, rather than because of the fantasy itself.

If the still partially disavowed sadism evident in the Op's fantasy is the flip side and necessary product of the Op's rationalized ethic of amoral instrumentality and affective detachment, then it is no surprise that, upon waking from his hallucination and possible murder of Dinah, the Op goes about assessing the murder in the same detached, affectless parataxis that characterizes the rest of his narrative:

> I was lying face down on the dining room floor, my head resting on my left forearm. My right arm was stretched straight out. My right hand held the round blue and white handle of Dinah Brand's ice pick. The pick's six inch needle-sharp blade was buried in Dinah Brand's left breast.
>
> She was lying on her back, dead. Her long muscular legs were stretched out toward the kitchen door. There was a run down the front of her stocking.
>
> Slowly, gently, as if afraid of waking her, I let go the ice pick, drew in my arm and got up . . .
>
> I examined the room. So far as I could tell, nothing had been changed in it. I went back to the kitchen and found no recognizable changes there. (164–65)

It is as if this murder is no different from any other the Op has been assigned to investigate; after describing the murder scene as he finds it, he proceeds with an examination of the room. However, this murder is not the same as one to which the Op has no connection and the narration's strained detachment and illusory objectivity, rather than connoting control, appears fully pathological. If, as I argued earlier, the affect purged from the narration is projected onto the figure of the femme fatale, then Dinah's murder becomes a way of further repudiating this affect. The return of the detached parataxis after the murder, then, takes on an all too lethal logic, indicating a complete repudiation of the partially disclosed affect encoded in the dream and the Op's murderous fantasy. Thus this passage suggests that central to the textual repressions that structure hard-boiled narration is a constitutive misogyny, one that is derived in part from the psychological noir and the forms of gothic narrative that preceded it. The femme fatale is figured as the bearer of all the forms of affect and social connection (via the allegorical structure mapped by the dream) that the detective must disavow in order to maintain his fantasies of objectivity and autonomy.

The disavowal and subsequent projection that structure this narration are underscored by a scene in which the Op confronts Helen Albury, a possible witness to Dinah's murder, who is willing to testify to the Op's guilt:

> She opened the door, made a choked, frightened sound in her throat, and backed away from me, holding both hands to her mouth.
>
> "Miss Helen Albury?" I asked.
>
> She shook her head violently from side to side. There was no truthfulness in it. Her eyes were crazy.
>
> I said:
>
> "I'd like to come in and talk to you a few minutes," going in as I spoke, closing the door behind me.
>
> She didn't say anything. She went up the steps in front of me, her head twisted around so she could watch me with her scary eyes.
>
> We went into a scantily furnished living room. Dinah's house could be seen from its windows.
>
> The girl stood in the center of the floor, her hands still to her mouth.
>
> I wasted time and words trying to convince her that I was harmless. It was no good. Everything I said seemed to increase her panic. It was a damned nuisance. I quit trying and got down to business. (184)

If we accept the Op as a reliable narrator, then this scene plays out as the hard-nosed, clear-headed detective confronted with a hysterical woman whom he needs to waste "time and words" talking sense into. However, all the details of the scene suggest that the Op is far from reliable in his assessment of the situation. In fact, all the qualities that he attributes to Helen seem to apply as easily to himself: a sense of "panic" (as is evidenced by the Op's increasingly frantic search for a suspect other than himself to pin Dinah's murder on), eyes that are both "scary" and "crazy" (the latter term is used by Dinah to describe the Op right before her murder and the applicability of the former term can be gauged by the fearful reactions of those who encounter the Op, including Helen in this scene), and a lack of truthfulness in his discourse (however we interpret Dinah's murder, the Op is far from "harmless"). In fact, nowhere in *Red Harvest* is the projective dynamic that characterizes the hard-boiled narrative more visible. It is notable that many of the visible traces of this projection are centered on the eyes, suggesting that the Op's ideology of detached observation masks a fundamental subjectivism in the field of visual perception. Much like the unreliable narrators of Henry James's *The Turn of the Screw* or Nella Larsen's *Passing*, the Op fundamentally misrecognizes his investments in the intersubjective dynamics that structure his relationship to the social field. This misrecognition stems not from an insufficiently objective viewpoint but from the desire for objectivity itself, explicitly manifested in the flat detachment of the Op's first-person narration. The purging of affect from the Op's discourse means that it can only appear in the space of the other, where this other is figured either as hysterical woman or monstrous criminal.[39] Both of these sites of projection begin to break down in the passage. Not only are the terms with which the Op characterizes Helen better applied to him but he becomes figured as monstrously criminal in this passage. This monstrous quality is most clearly evoked in the eyes of Helen, who reasonably sees him as a violent and dangerous man.

The reading of the criminal as a projection of the unacceptable or disavowed parts of the detective's personality is, of course, one of the central tenets of psychoanalytic accounts of the detective story, as well as one of its key inheritances from noir. And *Red Harvest* comes closer than most hard-boiled texts to desublimating the hidden identity of the two figures in relationship to violence against women. In the end, however, Hammett's text shies away from unequivocally presenting the Op as Dinah's murderer. In the closing pages of the novel, Reno Starky confesses to the murder ("Sure, I killed the bitch"), providing the reader and the Op with a seemingly stable site of disavowal (212).

Yet, as Steven Marcus has pointed out, because of the epistemological critique that is central to all of Hammett's fiction, all accounts of a crime—even confessions—have the status of fiction: "the 'reality' that anyone involved will swear to is in fact itself a construction, a fabrication, a fiction, a faked and alternate reality" (202). For the reader attuned to the ways in which the solution functions as a convenient fiction in Hammett's texts, the offhanded confession the Op extracts from a dying man becomes at the very least less than conclusive. Moreover, even if the reader accepts Reno's confession as truthful, the cultural work done by the novel as a whole suggests that actual or criminal guilt finally matters less than the Op's (and other male characters') participation in a larger set of material practices and phantasmatic disavowals that has as one of its results a lethal misogyny.[40] If the Op does not participate directly in Dinah's murder, his instrumentalist practice of "stirring things up" creates the context in which the murder is more than likely to take place. Similarly, if the Op didn't commit the murder, his actions and their relationship to his fantasy investments suggest that he is complicit with the forms of cultural misogyny (signaled here by Starky's use of the epithet "bitch") that contribute to violence against women. Thus, as with almost all attributions of individual guilt, Reno's confession functions as a locus of cultural disavowal; he becomes the scapegoat upon which the Op and the reader can project their own guilty complicity.

Red Harvest *as Cultural Dream Work*

Thus, while the novel retreats from a full desublimation of the hard-boiled detective's investment in a lethal misogyny, it exposes enough of the terms of this investment to make any readerly disavowal uncomfortable at best. However, the question remains as to why the text does not desublimate the hard-boiled genre's investments around gender, sexuality, race, and nation with the same sort of scrupulous rigor that it demystifies the economic and social ideology of the form. I would suggest that the answer lies with the division between what is constructed as phantasmatic and what is marked as objective that the novel not only records but in which it also participates. In maintaining this opposition, the text is not able to desublimate fully the way in which the seemingly objective structures of economic competition, rationalization of the social sphere, and instrumentalization of social relations produce a specific set of gendered, racialized, and national phantasmatic responses that become all the more determining for their exclusion from recognition in the field of the social. The objective of this chapter, then, has been to begin the work of undoing this ideological separation of the "real" from "the phantasmatic" in Hammett's text.

Nonetheless, it is the virtue of *Red Harvest* that it maps the relations among economics, politics, gender, and, to a lesser degree, race, nation, and sexuality—even though it does not fully present these categories as mutually constitutive. Thus, while there appear to be limits to its autocritical reflexivity, Hammett's text contains all the tools for extending this critique. In *The Interpretation of Dreams*, Freud emphasizes that the most important aspect of the dream is neither the contents of the dream nor the repressed "dream thoughts" but the work of transformation (or "dream work") that the dream undertakes between these two categories.[41] Similarly, while marking the limits of *Red Harvest*'s autocritique, I want to suggest that some of the most important work it does as a cultural text, whatever political commitments it may seem to manifest, is to reveal the traces of our cultural dream work, enabling us to begin to decode the phantasmatic investments that organize our fictions of the world, be they hard-boiled or otherwise.

3
The Hard-Boiled Male Travels Abroad

> It is not that Mr. Hemingway is, in the term which he uses in fine contempt for the big word, hard-boiled; it is that he is not hard-boiled enough . . .
> —*Allen Tate*

> It is awfully easy to be hard-boiled about everything in the daytime, but at night it is another thing.
> —*Jake Barnes*

Hard-Boiled Days and Sentimental Nights

Jake Barnes's meditation on the fluctuating ease of embodying hard-boiled masculinity appears early in Hemingway's chronicle of the lives and loves of Americans in Paris, framing much of the action that is to follow. The passage occurs after Jake, the novel's narrator, has the first of several frustrated encounters with the woman he loves, Lady Brett Ashley. After Brett leaves Jake's apartment to meet a potential lover, Jake, whose war wound makes conventional sex impossible, begins to feel "like hell" and then reflects on the difficulty of being hard-boiled at night.[1] It is striking that Jake thematizes his frustration in terms of a conception of male toughness associated with the contemporary pulp fiction of the period.

By 1926, the "hard-boiled" fiction of writers like Dashiell Hammett and Carroll John Daly had appeared in the pulp magazine *Black Mask* with ever increasing popularity for three years, and Jake's use of the term, whether or not a direct reference to the tough masculine hero popularized by this fiction, draws on the same set of cultural associations that made the term an apt moniker for this new hero.[2] If we are to see this as a direct reference, Jake's use of the term can be read as one of the numerous topical references to the departed American scene scattered throughout Hemingway's text.[3] However, while the novel's critics have regularly discussed the significance of the text's references to contemporary figures such as H. L. Mencken (who, perhaps uncoincidentally, was one of the original owners of *Black Mask*), and issues like prohibition and the Scopes "monkey trial," they have paid little attention to Jake's reference to popular detective fiction.[4] When the hard-boiled is invoked by Hemingway scholars, it usually is in the context of Hemingway's foundational influence on the genre, which is seen as beginning with *Red Harvest*, the first hard-boiled novel, in 1929.[5] However, as we saw in the previous chapter, *Red Harvest* was already a later novelistic elaboration and critique of a genre that originated in short-story form. The accounts of Hemingway critics, besides securing a genealogy of the popular form that locates its genesis in the pen of the modernist master, obscure the more complex and productive relationships among modernist and popular writers in this period: relationships that, among other things, were central to the construction, elaboration, and critique of the cultural fantasy of hard-boiled masculinity.[6] These relationships are evident in a number of different ways in *The Sun Also Rises*, from the novel's form to its narrative technique to its construction of gender and sexual relationships.

In addressing the representation of masculinity in *The Sun Also Rises*, I want to attend to the significance for the novel's mapping of social and sexual relations of these productive transactions or shared contexts across what Andreas Huyssen has described as "the great divide" between high and mass culture in the modernist period.[7] From this vantage, Jake's comment, with its opposition between day and night, hard-boiled masculinity and expressive manliness, becomes central to the text's ambivalent representation of the new gender and sexual roles associated with the "lost generation" of American expatriates in Paris, and more generally of the larger economic and social transformations that shaped cultural fantasies animating these roles. One gauge of this ambivalence is the divided critical response the novel has produced. As Rena Sanderson has concisely put it:

> A number of scholars recognize *The Sun Also Rises* as documenting
> the shift in gender constructions that followed World War I and the
> societal effects of that shift. . . . Though Brett and Jake are understood
> to embody new gender relations, there is no clear cut critical consensus
> on how we should interpret this couple or the clusters of bar-hopping
> men and women, adulterers, homosexuals and prostitutes that surround
> them. (177).[8]

Thus scholars such as Carlos Baker, Carole Gottlieb Vopat, and Allen Josephs read the novel as a moral rejection of what they consider the decadent and promiscuous lifestyle of the lost generation, while other scholars, such as Wendy Martin, James Nagel, and Scott Donaldson, read the novel as invested in the liberated, unsentimental mode of existence represented by the very same generation.

Rather than choose sides in this debate, I want to argue that the novel's ambivalence stems from its investment in both of these positions. This ambivalence shapes the text's conflicted representation of both masculine subjectivity and the larger social, sexual, and economic world in which this subjectivity is situated.[9] The opposition between the text as anti-modernist morality play versus a modernist celebration can be aligned with a number of other fantasy oppositions that the novel works to alternately construct and trouble. These multiple fantasy oppositions can be mapped in relationship to the opposition that Jake constructs between hard-boiled days and sentimental nights.

As J. Gerald Kennedy has pointed out, the novel in part turns on the opposition between Jake's daytime existence, associated with hard work, professionalism, and the Right Bank of Paris, and his nocturnal existence, which is associated with sexuality, leisure, and the Left Bank.[10] The novel's construction of a modern, hard-boiled masculinity can be squared relatively easily with Kennedy's mapping of the novel's representation of the Right Bank. The ethos of detached professionalism that Jake demonstrates in his role as reporter overlaps with the disinterested, professional demeanor of the hard-boiled detective. However, the sentimental manhood that Jake associates with his nocturnal existence fits less easily into the novel's representation of the Left Bank. While Jake, when his hard-boiled pose crumbles, intermittently attempts to pursue his sentimental desires on the Left Bank, the nightlife he finds does not provide a faithful mirror to the desires he consciously hopes to realize there—desires that seem in large part derived from the Victorian constructions of sexuality found in the popular romances of Hemingway's youth.[11]

Instead, the world of the Left Bank suggests a different series of modern desires, ones that seem to threaten both the professionalized ethos of the hard-boiled male and the romantic mythos of sentimental manliness that is its nocturnal flip side. What Jake finds on the Left Bank are desires associated with the emerging figures of the homosexual and the new woman as well as with a new world of mass cultural commodities.[12] Jake can neither pursue his sentiments nor consistently maintain the stoic stance of the hard-boiled male in this seductive world of modern nightlife. The desires that begin to emerge in the absence of these two reassuring poses motivate his flight to Spain, which is constructed as a fantasy of return to the space of the premodern. The contrast between

Paris and the Basque country of Spain forms the novel's other major fantasy opposition. If Paris is allied with commodification, modernization, amorality, and freedom from gender, sexual, and racial proscriptions, then the Basque country is aligned with an authentic folk culture, romance, a strict moral code, and a rigid racial, gender, and sexual hierarchy. Initially this fantasy landscape presents a reassuring contrast for Jake to the all-too-modern landscape of Paris. However, to paraphrase Theodor Adorno, this subjective dream of an escape from both the possibilities and limitations of modern life turns out to be objectively a nightmare, one that is very much the product of, rather than an escape from, the transformations of everyday life produced by high capitalism.[13] The nightmarish qualities of this fantasy of nostalgic return become increasingly evident over the course of the Spain section of the novel as the fantasy's commodified status and the violent implications of Jake's fetishization of hierarchy and purity become increasingly apparent. The full flowering of this nightmare provokes an ambivalent return to the cosmopolitan values of France, but the novel cannot finally effectively resolve the oppositions that it has put into motion.

The geographical organization of these oppositions is part of the novel's attempt to spatialize the transformations produced by modernization in this period, constructing a fantasy of a premodern and authentic Basque country in order to represent what has vanished, as well as suppress what has emerged, from the modernizing and commodified landscape of Paris. Like many modernist texts, then, *The Sun Also Rises* turns on the opposition between the exigencies and possibilities of modern life and a fantasized space of primitive certainty.

The missing term in this opposition is, of course, the United States, and it is important to read Hemingway's representation of both France and Spain in relationship to the departed American scene. It is equally important, however, not to reduce the novel's European context to a simple extension of the space of the United States, thereby reproducing an imperialist logic of appropriation that already functions too much in discussions of American literature of the period. Thus I want to read the novel's construction of masculinity both with and against the domestic code of hard-boiled masculinity as simultaneously an imperializing adaptation of this code to foreign soil and a critical meditation from the space of exile on its inadequacy for addressing the full range of possibilities and constrictions produced by the transformation of everyday life in the early twentieth century.[14]

In its opposition between hard-boiled masculinity and sentimental manhood, the novel recalls the split narration that I have described as characteristic of the hard-boiled text, in which the sentiment of the romance form (with its intimate generic links to both the sentimental and the gothic) is repressed from the text's seemingly objective narration, producing a textual unconscious that overdetermines the novel's construction of the social and sexual. However, in *The Sun Also Rises* the relationship between hard-boiled masculinity and sentimental manhood, as Jake's comment suggests, is directly thematized by the text, suggesting the possibility for a more critical and elaborated representation of this opposition.

This possibility is partially realized by the text, giving the lie to Allen Tate's assessment that the novel "isn't hard-boiled enough" (and suggesting the New Critic's own investment in a hard-boiled aesthetic) because "sentimentality appears for the very first time" in Hemingway's prose.[15] It is because Jake and Hemingway address the sentimentality masked by the hard-boiled code that the novel is able, to a certain degree, to examine critically the discursive construction of this code. However, in another sense, Tate is right, since at times the novel merely seems to revive rather than critically interrogate the sentimental materials it desublimates. Rather than working through this sentimental heritage in order to begin to engage both pleasurably and critically the emergent networks of desire represented by Parisian nightlife, the text can only locate its desire in a fantasy past.

Iceberg Aesthetics

The phantasmatic oppositions that organize the novel's content also inform its style. Since it is perhaps on the stylistic level that the parallels between Hemingway's novel and the hard-boiled narrative are most evident, I begin my analysis here. However, while it is important to address the stylistic convergences between the novel and hard-boiled prose, it is equally important to attend to their divergences. Hence I will analyze the way in which the shift from mass to high culture and from the mean streets of the American city to the bars and cafés of Paris shapes the textual representation of an emergent conception of masculinity.

Like *Red Harvest*, *The Sun Also Rises* is organized around the paratactic first-person narration of the text's male protagonist. Affect is largely absent from this narration. Instead, much of the narrative hinges on a flat and seemingly objective description of events and circumstances in which the larger moral or emotional import of the events is left for the reader to deduce. This is what Hemingway famously described as his "iceberg" prose style in which only a small fraction of the story's import is represented directly, the rest remaining under the surface. This description, with its suggestion of affective depths anchoring the surface of the prose, implies that the relationship between affect and its representation in Hemingway's narrative is at times somewhat different than the fantasy of the supercession of affect that animates Hammett's version of the hard-boiled aesthetic.

Certainly much of Hemingway's narrative functions in a manner similar to Hammett's prose: the flat, first-person narration both represses any direct representation of affective investment and suggests the narrator's mastery of the social situation. Take, for example, Jake's account of his actions just before leaving the *bal mussette* with Brett, a moment that, as we learn more fully later, is fraught with intense and contradictory emotional investments for him:

> We left the floor and I took my coat off a hanger on the wall and put it on. Brett stood by at the bar. Cohn was talking to her. I stopped at the bar and asked them for an envelope. The patronne found one. I took a fifty-franc note from my pocket, put it in the envelope, sealed it, and handed it to the patronne. (23)

The narration here seems composed entirely of objective description. Only through knowledge gained in other parts of the text do we have any indication of the affective investments that organize this scene. Jake is leaving with Brett for what they both know will be another frustrated encounter. This frustration has manifested itself in displaced form earlier in the evening when Jake expresses homophobic rage toward a group of gay men who have come to the *bal* with Brett. That this displacement is informed in part by a prior displacement of homoerotic desire, one that overdetermines Jake's ambivalent relationship to Brett, I will pursue at length below. For the moment it is only important to note the way in which Jake's internal state in the above passage, like the Op's in much of *Red Harvest*, can be derived only from his actions or by following a chain of affective displacements, and not by any direct narration of his feelings. The other actions in this scene are similarly loaded. Jake's casual notation of Robert Cohn's conversation with Brett masks the jealousy he feels about Robert's interest in her, a jealousy that mixes poorly with Robert's chivalry at lunch the next day when the two men almost come to blows. Meanwhile, Jake's leaving of the fifty-franc note for Georgette, the prostitute he has hired as an escort, may initially suggest his mastery of social codes, but paying Georgette merely to spend the evening out with him also suggests, as Arnold Davidson and Cathy Davidson have noted, that Jake is paying "to keep up appearances," an act that cannot be without its psychic resonances.[16] Thus a narrative sequence given entirely to action displaces any interiorized account of these affective investments.

At other moments, however, the laconic narrative style of *The Sun Also Rises* is used to indicate, rather than displace, affective investment. A description of Jake looking at his wound in a mirror presents a clear example of this second form of narration: "Undressing, I looked at myself in the mirror of the big armoire beside the bed. That was a typically French way to furnish a room. Practical, too, I suppose. Of all the ways to be wounded. I suppose it was funny. I put on my pajamas and got into bed" (31). This passage achieves its effect through the ironic opposition between the seemingly flat denotation of the narration and Jake's clearly distraught state. The submerged portions of the iceberg are indicated here not only by the simple declarative statement "of all the ways to be wounded," and the implied spectacle of Jake's wounded nakedness, but also in his attempt to distract himself by free-associating about the organization of the room. Ironically, this attempt only serves to emphasize the randomness of his wound, with the "way" of arranging objects in a room—one way among many—echoing the "way" in which he has been wounded—again one way among many. Thus the flatness and paratactic qualities of the prose can be used to suggest defensiveness and vulnerability as well as the toughness and mastery associated with the Op's narrative in *Red Harvest.*

These moments suggest the possibility of a radical reworking of the laconic prose style characteristic of both Hemingway and Hammett, a reworking in which the narration is able to indicate directly rather than displace the affective investments of the narrator. However, this possibility is only intermittently realized in *The Sun Also Rises*, owing to Jake's inability to engage critically his investments in a conception of sexuality and manhood derived largely from Victorian ideals of the popular romance. While at a number of key moments the narration is able to indicate the male protagonist's affective investments, allowing the sentimental attachments that are repressed from hard-boiled prose to return to the surface of the text, this return of the repressed generally produces only a repetition, rather than a working through, of the ideological significance of these attachments. Thus, while the text is able to desublimate a number of its phantasmatic investments, it only intermittently is able to critically engage, rather than simply embrace, these desublimated materials.

Central to the text's adaptation of a sentimental ideology to the conditions of modern existence is the representation of Jake's wound. It is no accident that the above example of one of the novel's expressive moments centers on the significance of that wound. On one level, it is important to read the wound in a relatively straightforward manner, as a representation of the violence produced by the First World War. On another level, the wound and its sexual implications clearly participate in the larger web of symbolism woven by the text; any number of critical discussions of the significance of the wound see it as symbolizing the impotence and/or woundedness of (take your pick) Jake, Hemingway, the lost generation, modern man, or all of the above.[17] Such symbolic readings generally present the wound as rendering Jake impotent, an interpretation that overlaps much of the time—though not always—with Jake's own conception of his wound. Not only are such readings contradicted by one of the famous elliptical moments in Hemingway's text when Jake and Brett appear to perform some sort of sex act (which is indicated by the passage of time and a question from Brett: "Then later: 'Do you feel any better darling?'") but they also reproduce the phallic cultural logic that conflates sexual and cultural value with a symbolic valorization of the male sex organ (55).[18] Rather than repeating the logic of such arguments (i.e., his wounded genitals must represent a lack of any functional sex life), I want to propose an alternate reading of the wound, one that interrogates the fantasy that equates phallic male sexuality with sexual potency and cultural authority. I want to read Jake's wound as symbolizing a blow to the cultural fantasy of what Freud has described as normative genital sexuality.

In *Three Essays on Sexuality*, Freud makes a distinction between a genital organization of sexuality that is "assumed to be normal" and the various forms of "perversion" that deviate from the aim or object of this sexuality (2).[19] In this relatively early and denaturalizing account of sexuality (one that can be read, in part, against his later more normativizing stage theory of sexuality), Freud opposes "the wide dissemination of tendencies to perversion" to the naturalizing beliefs of "popular opinion," which understand genital copulation between the sexes as sexuality *tout court* (1, 97). Jake's wound, then, can be read as an injury to this popular opinion—one that thematizes the threats to the ideology of phallic masculinity represented by various and contradictory forces of modernity. This reading of the wound would not reject the interpretation of the wound as symbolizing the violence of World War I so much as suggest that this violence itself and its effects on fantasies of heroic male mastery need to be understood within the larger historical context of the transformation of everyday life in the early part of the twentieth century. This transformation, in part, involves the rationalization and instrumentalization of daily life discussed in my reading of *Red Harvest* in the previous chapter and finds its negative apotheosis in the violence of the two world wars. However, *The Sun Also Rises* is at least equally engaged with two other emergent aspects of modern life: the growth of commodity culture and the emergence of new and contestatory sexual and gender identities in the early part of the twentieth century. Jake's wound and its sentimentalization as a signifier of a loss of male potency need to be understood in relationship to the decoding and recoding of desire represented by these transformations.[20]

Paris: The Contradictions of Modernity

Like the Op in *Red Harvest*, Jake prides himself on the work ethic and detached professionalism required by his job. As a reporter for the *New York Herald*, he demonstrates a commitment to work as its own justification, separate from any social or political role it performs, evident in his summary of a typical morning's work:

> Up-stairs in the office I read the French morning papers, smoked, and then sat at the typewriter and got off a good morning's work. At eleven o'clock I went over to the Quai' d'Orsay in a taxi and went in and sat with about a dozen correspondents, while the foreign office mouthpiece, a young Nouvelle Revue Française diplomat in horned-rimmed spectacles, talked and answered questions for half an hour. The President of the Council was in Lyon making a speech, or, rather he was on his way back. Several people asked questions to hear themselves talk and there were a couple of questions asked by news service men who wanted to know the answers. There was no news. (36)

Jake's work ethic is carefully noted in the first sentence of the passage: "and I got off a good morning's work." While this mention may seem casual, the experienced Hemingway reader will note that Jake attaches the definitive Hemingway adjective to this activity: "good." Within the minimalist parameters of the Hemingway prose style, "good" signifies all that is superlative or authentic—all that is too sacred to be translated into thick description. Such is the value of work for Jake. The vision of work presented by Jake, in fact, seems to elude the reification of the labor process produced by the rationalization that characterized the economic development of the United States and, in a slightly more incipient way, Western Europe in this period.[21] Instead, Jake's labor conjures a fantasy of the artisan. He seems to set his own hours and the pace of his work. Moreover, his use of the adjective "good" implies that he has an unalienated relationship to his labor.

The rest of the passage, however, demonstrates how detached from any larger social context this sense of work is, as the reification that Jake resists returns on another scene.[22] Jake's narration refers to a speech by the President of the Council, yet it reveals none of its content. Apparently the content is not important, as the last line of the passage ("There was no news") also suggests. In part, the passage seems to be suggesting the emptiness of the President's political discourse, reflecting the suspicion of career politicians shared by Hemingway and many of the post–World War I generation. This cynicism is, of course, a central characteristic of the hard-boiled protagonist and, in the passage above, it inspires some of Hemingway's most overtly hard-boiled writing. The description of the "foreign-office mouthpiece" and the people asking questions to "hear themselves talk" could come straight out of Hammett. However, as in the pulp narrative, this kind of deflationary humor cuts both ways, suggesting the limits of the narrator's instrumentalized worldview fully as much as the pretensions of the figures being mocked. Jake seems to dismiss both the askers and their questions because, unlike his fellow reporters, they are not asking questions that have simple factual answers but instead may be taking on larger political and social issues that cannot be reduced to a simple series of objective facts. Thus, while Jake maintains a commitment to a work ethic that seems to resist the rationalization of work produced by the emergent culture of corporate capitalism, the work to which he scrupulously adheres bears the traces of this rationalization in the reified code of the news reporter.[23]

Jake's commitment to work is paralleled by an insistence on paying his own way in the sphere of leisure. In contrast to the other characters associated with the lost generation, Jake is scrupulous about his debts and about paying his way up front. Like his commitment to work, these economic scruples seem at first to be pleasingly anachronistic, a marked contrast to the free-spending, debt-ridden ways of the rest of his companions, who embody the values of an emerging credit and consumer economy. Brett, Mike, and Robert all receive money from friends, relatives, or former spouses, and Mike, who is perhaps the novel's greatest negative exemplar of the new credit economy, is "an undischarged bankrupt" (79). However, while Jake's values around money and consumerism seem to contrast with those of his friends, these values are enmeshed in a commodified understanding of the world and its possibilities that is part and parcel of the new consumer economy.

Jake's investment in the ethic of "paying one's own way" and its relationship to commodification is most clearly articulated in one of his drunken nocturnal reveries during the fiesta at Pamplona:

I thought I had paid for everything. Not like the woman pays and pays
and pays. No idea of retribution or punishment. Just an exchange of
values. You gave up something and got something else. Or you worked
for something. You paid some way for everything that was any good.
I paid my way into enough things that I liked, so that I had a good time.
Either you paid by learning about them, or by experience, or by taking
chances, or by money. Enjoying living was learning to get your money's
worth and knowing when you had it. You could get your money's worth.
The world was a good place to buy in. (148)

This passage, beginning in a simple "exchange of values" and ending with
"the world was a good place to buy in" reads like a parody of the famous
first chapter of *Capital*, in which the world historical logic of commodity fetishism emerges from the initially simple equation ten yards of
linen=one coat.[24] Yet while it may be parodic, the passage, like many
others in *The Sun Also Rises*, cloaks pathos and serious intent in the guise
of parody and irony.[25] What emerges, then, from this curious mix of
humor and seriousness is the characteristically ambivalent tone of Jake's
narration. Jake is simultaneously elaborating his code and mocking it.
Yet, for all his mockery, he can construct no alternative and remains fully
invested in it. Similarly, while Marx may be parodied here, he is also
invoked in all seriousness, since commodification, as it transforms social
relations among people into relations among things, is the social dynamic
with which Jake is wrestling.

In the face of this transformation, Jake attempts to elaborate a code
organized around responsible and knowledgeable consumerism: "Enjoying living was learning to get your money's worth and knowing when
you had it." The dictates of this code structure Jake's behavior throughout the novel. He is endlessly concerned with being a smart consumer,
demonstrating that he knows how to get the best drinks, meals, and hotel
rooms, all at the right price. Yet the consumerist aspect of this pursuit is
mediated through a sense of ritual, in which the way in which something
is consumed is as important as what is consumed.[26] Take, for example,
Jake's insistence that he have an olive in his martini, when he and Brett
are drinking in Madrid: "I like an olive in a Martini" (244). What's striking in this demand is that Jake doesn't use a definite article (the martini,
this martini) but instead uses the indefinite article (a martini)—asserting
that this is the ritual by which he personalizes and consumes the generic
commodity, "martini." This consumerist code, with its focus on defining
oneself through external acquisitions and the rituals associated with them,
translates the exteriorization and instrumentalization characteristic of

hard-boiled masculinity to the world of leisure. When not working, Jake approaches the world of objects as being simultaneously instruments of commodified pleasure and metonymies of self-definition. Even the much vaunted cult of *afición*, while seemingly outside these modern commodity relations, can be read as an extension of this code to the realm of the bullfight, which is, after all, a spectator sport for Jake.

In fact, what emerges in this passage, with its description of the world as "a good place to buy in," is a vision of the ever more capitalized globe as an emporium for tourists. And while Jake tries to distance himself from the role of the tourist through his insider knowledge and *afición*, the passage suggests that this distancing is illusory. Jake may be more in the know, but his relationship to the commodity form and the privilege of the tourist is the same.

However, if on one level the passage suggests Jake's consumerist privilege, on another level it encodes the threat that commodification represents for him. Jake attempts to masculinize his code of proper consumption and spending by contrasting it to "the way the woman pays and pays and pays." However, the very exchange logic of the commodity form itself suggests the possibility of an uneasy equivalence between Jake and the abstract woman to whom he compares himself. In part, this contrast is one of Jake's more progressive moments, as he recognizes that the abstract equivalence implied by the emergent consumer economy does not necessarily translate into material equality for women but instead often produces its opposite. As Wendy Martin argues, Jake recognizes that "financial and social compensation for men and women is dramatically different" (73). Yet his insistence on the exorbitant payment that society demands of women also bespeaks a certain anxiety that this difference may vanish in the new economy ruled by the logic of abstract equivalence. Moreover, Jake's insistence that sacrifice is linked with femininity can be read as a displacement of his anxiety about his wound, which is described by an Italian officer as the ultimate sacrifice: "Then he made that wonderful speech: 'You, a foreigner, an Englishman' (any foreigner was an Englishman) 'have given more than your life'" (31). For Jake, this anxiety bespeaks impotence, suggesting that he sees commodification as producing a feminizing alienation from full and authentic existence. However, from my own rereading of the wound as an injury to the ideology of phallic sexuality, Jake's anxiety merely suggests his own phantasmatic fear of a loss of male supremacy. Given either interpretation, Jake's attempt at masculinizing this new landscape of abstract equivalence and transformed desire seems at best tenuous.

Finally, the passage presents a similar logic of equivalence and quantification functioning in relationship to all values and experience, such that everything functions by the same logic of exchange: "I paid my way into enough things that I liked that I had a good time. Either you paid by learning about them, or by experience, or by taking chances, or by money." Through the paratactic logic of exchange in these sentences, experience, learning, and taking chances are all equivalent to money. All are useful only insofar as they secure a "good time." Parataxis is, of course, one of the signature features of the Hemingway style. And while a number of critics have read the generation of this style as a reaction against the commodification of sentiment in more ornate and hypotactic Victorian prose styles, few have attended to the ways in which this parataxis itself accurately mirrors the metonymic logic of the newly emergent consumer culture, in which all objects exist separately, linked only by the quantified equivalence of exchange.

The relationship of this paratactic style to the emergent consumer culture represented in the novel by the Parisian nightlife is most memorably captured by the opening sentence of chapter 3:

> It was a warm spring night and I sat at a table on the terrace of the Napolitain after Robert had gone, watching it get dark and the electric signs come on, and the red and green stop-and-go traffic signal, and the crowd going by, and the horse-cabs clippety-clopping along at the edge of the solid taxi traffic, and the poules going by, singly and in pairs, looking for the evening meal. (14)

In many ways this can be read as a paradigmatic Hemingway sentence: a carefully rendered series of discrete objects, joined by simple conjunctions. The hierarchy of hypotaxis is seemingly absent, as are the relationships among the various objects. Instead, the metonymic juxtaposition of the objects implies their equivalence. In the passage, the logic of equivalence is explicitly bound up with commodification, indicated by the beckoning electric signs and the chaotic crowds of urban life. However, any conception of equality suggested by this equivalence is undermined by the realization that the "poules," or prostitutes, are also part of this commodified logic of abstract exchange. While we may want to read these sex workers as constructing a form of agency by consciously commodifying and acting on women's conventional status as objects of exchange between men in patriarchal societies, the very terms of this agency suggest the continuing gender and class inequalities that structure the seemingly abstract logic of capitalist exchange. The only person who seems to be at a (fantasized) remove from this logic of equivalence is Jake, the masculine spectator.

If my analysis so far suggests some of the possibilities and limits for the transformation of gender and sexual roles represented by commodification and modernization, Jake's experiences in the nightclubs of Paris suggest others. I have already touched on the scene at the *bal mussette* in my discussion of the novel's style. But this scene is rich with phantasmatic resonances and is worth examining further. Particularly rich for the novel's fantasy mapping of gender and sexuality is the scene in which Brett enters the *bal* with a group of gay men:

> Two taxis were coming down the steep street. They both stopped in front of the Bal. A crowd of young men, some in jerseys and some in their shirt-sleeves, got out. I could see their hands and newly washed wavy hair in the light from the door. The policeman standing by the door looked at me and smiled. They came in. As they went in, under the light I saw white hands, wavy hair, white faces, grimacing, gesturing, talking. With them was Brett. She looked lovely and she was very much with them. (20)

This passage is striking for a number of reasons. First, it explicitly allies Brett with the gay men ("she looked lovely and she was very much with them"), suggesting parallels between the emergent and newly named possibilities for both "the new woman" and "the homosexual." While, on one hand, the recoding implied by naming suggests the juridical regulation of these identities as well as their possible commodification, it also presents the power of named, collective identity and records the impact of a prior decoding of traditional ways of mapping gender, sexuality, and desire. The collective representation of Brett and the homosexuals, then, suggests the collective and not merely individual possibilities produced by this dynamic of decoding and recoding.[27]

The passage also records Jake's ambivalent relationship to these possibilities. As readers, we receive our introduction to Brett in this scene, and it is striking that we meet her amid a crowd of gay men. In fact, Jake's narration lingers on the men, fetishistically repeating the same description of the men's hands and faces and only turning to note Brett's presence at the end of the paragraph. This initial description suggests Jake's erotic preoccupation with the men, one he almost immediately disavows via homophobia: "I was very angry. Somehow, they always made me angry" (20). While Jake's homosocial visual exchange with the policeman indicates, on one level, their mutual interest in the homosexuals, it also serves to explicitly reaffirm their homophobia. Jake, then, represses his homoerotic interest in the men by visually aligning himself with the masculine and homophobic representative of repressive state authority.

Since this is the first time we meet Brett, the scene can also be read as a sort of textual reenactment of the scene of the initial attraction between Jake and her. In terms of the plot (if not necessarily the story), Jake's desire for Brett seems to emerge at least in part out of a metonymic displacement of his initial interest in the men. As a number of recent critics have noted, this erotic preoccupation with men is further suggested by Brett's "male" name and the "boyish" style with which she wears her hair. Brett may be a more socially acceptable object, allowing Jake to hang on to what's left of his wounded phallic sexuality, but his interest in the newly christened sexual identity of the homosexual and the subculture that is emerging around it suggests some of the polymorphous "perversities" that entice him to think about sex in a different way. But Jake does not pursue these possibilities and remains in his wounded state, neither able to restore himself to full phallic authority, a state one suspects only exists in the idealized pages of the adventure romance, nor able to abandon the phallic paradigm of conventional genital sexuality.

Other aspects of Jake's description of the men suggest the larger social context out of which these sexual possibilities emerge. The homosexuals' "newly washed" hands and permed hair link them to a middle-class, modern urban existence in which indoor plumbing is just becoming available and a high social premium is placed on grooming. Jake also repeatedly associates the men with "whiteness," noting their "white hands" and "white faces." Given Jake's ambivalent preoccupation with the men, his linking them with whiteness suggests a corollary set of ambivalent racial and class fantasies to accompany his sexual fantasies. We can read the homosexuals' whiteness through the lens of racial and colonial discourse as another sign of their modernity. As figures for an emerging counterculture in the modernizing metropole, the gay men are associated with an almost preternatural whiteness. The preternatural quality of this whiteness suggests Jake's ambivalence toward it and toward the larger forces of modernity he associates with it. Whiteness, as a racialized and class-based corollary to Jake's homoerotic desire, both attracts and repels him. This suggests that while he identifies with the racial and class privilege associated with what Gail Bederman has described as the discourse of civilization, he also shares the fear of his hard-boiled contemporaries of becoming "overly-civilized" and thus unmasculine: a fear that seems fully realized in the figure of the middle-class, urban homosexual. In the previous chapter, we examined the way in which hard-boiled masculinity adjusted to this perceived threat through a phantasmatic borrowing from the iconography of black manhood. *The Sun Also Rises* initiates a similar search for a primitive and implicitly racialized source of phallic virility. This search, however, involves a traversal of geographic as well as phantasmatic borders.[28]

Border Crossing: The Mirror of Touristic Fantasy

In book II, the action of the novel moves from the streets and cafés of Paris to the Basque country of Spain. In the fantasy mapping performed by the novel, this journey becomes not only a movement through geographical space but also a movement through time to a landscape and culture that are figured as largely premodern.[29] This phantasmatic journey to the space of the premodern can be read in part as a journey into the textual unconscious of the hard-boiled narrative; Jake, our intermittently hard-boiled hero, attempts literally to return to the heroic world of the nineteenth-century romance. This fantasy of return, however, is continuously disrupted by the intrusion of the commodified and touristic underpinnings of the fantasy.

The temporal fantasy that underpins the novel's geographical movement is suggested by Jake's description of the journey that he and his friends take into the Basque country after their crossing of the official border between France and Spain:

> We all got in the car and it started up the white dusty road into Spain. For a while the country was much as it had been; then, climbing all the time, we crossed the top of a Col, the road winding back and forth on itself, and then it really was Spain. There were long brown mountains and a few pines and far-off forests of beech-trees on some of the mountainsides. The road went along the summit of the Col and then dropped down, and the driver had to honk, and slow up, and turn out to avoid running into two donkeys that were sleeping in the road. . . Down below there were grassy plains and clear streams, and then we crossed a stream and went through a gloomy little village, and started to climb again. . . Then we crossed a wide plain, and there was a big river off on the right shining in the sun from between the line of trees, and away off you could see the plateau of Pamplona rising out of the plain, and the walls of the city and the great brown cathedral, and the broken skyline of the other churches. (93)

Initially, this description appears no different from any other in the novel. Jake carefully describes the changing geography of the Basque landscape much as he carefully notes each Parisian street down which he travels. However, other aspects of the passage suggest the dimension of fantasy that shapes Jake's perception of this landscape. His assertion that "then it really was Spain," which attempts to distinguish between abstract geopolitical borders and what could be described as geocultural borders, performs a kind of ontologizing of national and cultural difference, suggesting that he has entered not merely a different state but a different state of being. The detail of the donkeys sleeping in the road presents this ontologically distinct locale as organized around premodern forms of transit, through which the motorcar moves as a modernist anomaly. The status of the car as an anomalous talisman of modernity is further confirmed by the "crowd of kids" that watches the car as it pulls into Pamplona (94).[30] Similarly, the description of Pamplona as dominated by churches imagines a premodern world in which religious faith serves as the focal point of the community and can be profitably contrasted with the bars that punctuate the secularized landscape of Paris. This contrast between the church as a premodern site of belief and the bar as its modern corollary becomes almost explicit near the end of the novel when Jake and Brett discuss religion while being presided over by a bartender who mixes their ritual martinis for them (243–45).

While the above passage works to construct the Basque country as a site of the premodern, other aspects of it suggest the commodified, and hence modern, status of this fantasy for Jake. The description of the landscape is flat and denotative with none of the carefully rendered detail that characterizes the representation of landscape in a story like "Big Two-Hearted River." The flatness of this and other descriptions of the Basque landscape in the novel is formed through the emptying out of qualitative distinctions in the narration, so that the landscape can only be mapped as a series of abstractly equivalent objects, interesting for the novelty of their presence but not for any intrinsic or particular qualities they may possess. The description of the landscape is organized by the same paratactic logic that characterizes earlier descriptions of Paris, suggesting that the landscape is produced as a similarly commodified space through Jake's touristic gaze. In contrast to the modern enticements of Paris, however, the commodified fantasy projected onto the Basque landscape is that of the genuinely uncommodified and authentic.

The relationship of such touristic fantasies to the adventure romance is parodically underscored earlier in the novel when Jake discusses Robert's desire to go to South America after reading R. H. Hudson's *The Purple Land*:

"The Purple Land" is a very sinister book if read too late in life. It recounts splendid imaginary amorous adventures of a perfect English gentleman in an intensely romantic land, the scenery of which is very well described. For a man to take it at thirty-four as a guide book to what life holds is about as safe as it would be for a man of the same age to enter Wall Street direct from a French convent, equipped with a complete set of the more practical Alger books. (9)

Jake's narration clearly disparages the romantic fantasies entertained by Robert; like the title character of Conrad's *Lord Jim*, Robert can only perceive distant lands through the commodified lens of the adventure romance. However, as I have noted, much of the novel's humor turns on Jake's mockery of the very dynamics in which he is invested. As Richard Hovey has demonstrated, Robert serves as a double for Jake throughout the novel, embodying all the romantic investments that Jake disavows or toward which he remains ambivalent.[31] Thus, while Jake condemns Robert for his romanticism in this passage, we find similarly romantic sentiments organizing his own faith in the ritual of the bullfight and the cult of *afición*, suggesting that far from being merely naive, Robert's romantic and commodified visions of travel are equally central to Jake's own seemingly more-informed travel narrative. Robert here becomes a scapegoat onto which Jake can project his own investment in commodification, foreshadowing the increasingly virulent forms of anti-Semitism used to scapegoat Robert in the Pamplona section of the novel. Indeed, the logic of this anti-Semitism is already suggested in this passage with the Jewish Robert being phantasmatically associated with all that is inauthentic and impure in the commodified modern world within which he and Jake travel.

The Basque Country: Fantasies of Atavism

In examining the romantic fantasies that structure Jake's relationship to the space of Pamplona, it is important to see them as overdetermined by a parallel yoking together of seemingly disparate spaces (in this case not only Pamplona and Paris but Pamplona and the United States as well), a connection that the fantasies themselves work hard to disavow. If, on a symbolic level, we can read Jake's pilgrimage to Pamplona as a flight from the contradictions and disturbing possibilities offered by the nocturnal world of the Left Bank and a fantasized return to a space of cultural purity and phallic sexuality, then this fantasy is continuously disrupted by the encroaching reality of commodification and the modernity of the tourist industry in Pamplona. In order to accommodate these disruptions, Jake develops a form of fetishistic split belief in which he recognizes the modern and commodified aspects of contemporary Basque culture even as he insistently locates the culture's true essence in its premodern past. This fetishistic search for premodern purity is joined by a number of the lost-generation characters, and the conflict between this belief and the commodified reality upon which it is projected leads to the violence that concludes book II.

Both Jake's romantic fantasy of a return to a premodern past and its disruption by the forces of modernity are visible in his description of the religious procession that begins the fiesta in Pamplona:

> That afternoon was the big religious procession. San Fermin was
> translated from one church to another. In the procession were all the
> dignitaries, civil and religious. We could not see them because the
> crowd was too great. Ahead of the formal procession and behind it
> danced the *riau-riau* dancers. There was one mass of yellow shirts
> dancing up and down in the crowd. All we could see of the procession
> through the closely pressed people that crowded the side streets and
> curbs were the great giants, cigar-store Indians, thirty feet high, Moors,
> a King and Queen, whirling and waltzing solemnly to the *riau-riau* . . .
> Some dancers formed a circle around Brett and started to dance. They
> wore big wreaths of white garlics around their necks. They took Bill and
> me by the arms and put us in the circle. Bill started to dance, too. They
> were all chanting. Brett wanted to dance, but they did not want her to.
> They wanted her as an image to dance around. When the song ended
> with a sharp *riau-riau!* they rushed us to the wine shop. (155)

The passage imagines the festival as a religious bacchanal, part Catholic ceremony and part pagan ritual. The synchronized movements and matching costumes of the *riau-riau* dancers construct a fantasy image of the premodern collective; bound together in religious ecstasy, they are removed from the secularizing and atomizing forces of modernity. Unlike the explicit homoeroticism represented by the group of homosexuals at the *bal mussette*, this collectivity is imagined as safely homosocial and Jake and Bill quickly join in the fun. Any sexuality between the men is deflected onto Brett, as the group transforms her into an object of worship. In contrast to the movement and sexual autonomy that defined her arrival at the *bal*, Brett is prohibited from dancing and reduced to an "image to dance around." The novel's quintessential "new woman" is thus transformed into an icon of traditional femininity: part Virgin Mary and part sacrificial virgin from Stravinsky's *Sacre du*

Printemps. The fantasized return to the space of the premodern thus enables a reestablishment of a clearly homosocial and phallic sexual order.

As my reference to Stravinsky's modernist watershed suggests, the fantasy of the premodern that Hemingway's novel presents can be allied with other modernist attempts to locate a premodern site of mythic certainty and vitality. Unlike most other modernist texts, however, *The Sun Also Rises*, to its credit, underscores the final impossibility of this fantasy even as it represents its protagonist's investment in it. Thus, while Jake's description of the waltzing effigies of kings, queens, and Moors constructs the symbolic world of the medieval romance, the image of the "cigar-store Indian" disrupts this premodern reverie, reminding both him and the reader of the commodified and modern context that underpins this vision. This image disrupts Jake's reverie in two distinct ways: first, it underscores the fictiveness of his romantic associations with the Basque country by suggesting Jake's conflation of these associations with associations derived from the imperialist tradition of the American frontier romance; and second, it asserts the commodified nature of these associations, as the figure of the romantic Indian becomes just another way to sell cigars. Far from simply being a premodern collective ritual, the procession and the larger fiesta of which it is a part represent the adaptation of older premodern forms to the ends of the modern, capitalist nation-state, indicated by the "civil and religious" dignitaries, and to the burgeoning international tourist trade.

Jake and his friends are not the only tourists at the fiesta. Near the end of the week-long festival, tourists swarm the event as they arrive by the carload:

> The town was crowded. Every street was full. Big motor-cars from
> Biarritz and San Sebastian kept driving up and parking around the
> square. They brought people for the bull-fight. Sight-seeing cars came
> up, too. There was one with twenty-five Englishwomen in it. They sat
> in the big white car and looked through their glasses at the fiesta. (205)

As this passage suggests, Jake's narration advances an implicit critique of tourism. The sightseers gaze upon the Basques as cigar-store Indians who are there to advertise a good time, one in which they will soon partake. The scene emphasizes the specularity of this touristic dynamic, with the Englishwomen and other sightseers staring at the spectacle of the fiesta. The specularity of this scene echoes that of the earlier Paris street scene, as the commodification of the latter space becomes equally defining of the former. However, in order to develop this critique of tourism, Jake, as we have already seen, needs to locate the essence of

Basque culture in its premodern past. Thus the modernity of the culture's fraught relationship to the encroaching forces of capitalism can only be represented as inauthentic in Jake's schema. Instead, the Basque participants in the festival, to the extent that they are authentic, can only be represented as unwitting and helpless victims to the despoiling forces of international tourism.

The same fetishistic logic of split belief organizes Jake's investments in the cult of *afición* and in the bullfighter Pedro Romero. This investment is, of course, also shared by some of the Basque characters in the novel, most explicitly the hotel owner, Montoya, who demonstrates the appeal of this ideology for the local as well as the tourist. Like Jake, Montoya is a member of the cult of *afición*, one of a select group of true bullfighting fans who recognize that *afición* is what distinguishes the great bullfighters from the merely good or popular bullfighters. Jake and the other aficionados bemoan the current commercialization of the sport, asserting that most matadors do not practice the true art of bullfighting. They hold out hope for a bullfighter who can return the sport to its former glory, by performing in the old ways.

This fantasy takes shape in the figure of Pedro Romero. Romero, who occupies the symbolic center of the Pamplona section of the novel, is a young bullfighter who performs in the old ways. On a symbolic level, he embodies the heroic image of premodern manhood that Jake associates with the adventure romance. In the eyes of Jake and Montoya, Romero, as the heroic embodiment of the premodern style of bullfighting, needs to be protected from the corrupting forces of modernity. After Romero kills his first bull, Jake and Montoya discuss the importance of keeping him from a dinner with the American ambassador:

> I finished shaving and put my face down into the bowl and washed it with cold water. Montoya was standing there looking more embarrassed.
>
> "Look," he said. "I've just had a message from them at the Grand Hotel that they want Pedro Romero and Marcial Lalanda [another bullfighter] to come over for coffee to-night after dinner."
>
> "Well," I said, "it can't hurt Marcial any."
>
> "Marcial has been in San Sebastian all day. He drove over in a car this morning with Marquez. I don't think they'll be back to-night."
>
> Montoya stood embarrassed. He wanted me to say something.
>
> "Don't give Romero the message," I said.
>
> "You think so?"
>
> "Absolutely."
>
> Montoya was very pleased.

"I wanted to ask you because you were an American," he said.
"That's what I'd do."
"Look," said Montoya. "People take a boy like that. They don't
know what he's worth. They don't know what he means. Any foreigner
can flatter him. They start this Grand Hotel business, and in one year
they're through." (171–72)

The critique of tourism and imperialism advanced by the code of the
aficionado is again evident here. Both Jake and Montoya associate the
corrupting influences that threaten Pedro with foreigners and most
explicitly with Americans. Yet in order to construct this narrative of corruption, they must recast the adult Romero as an innocent "boy" who is
blissfully unaware of the seductions of modernity. Rather than advancing a critique of imperialism that would be able to recognize Romero's
ability to negotiate the commodification of the bullfight while still skill-
fully performing as a matador, they split off what he means from the
world in which he operates, maintaining the purity of the former and the
inauthenticity of the latter. Jake's and Montoya's insistence on this split
belief suggests that it has more to do with their own disavowals than any
real concern for Romero. Maintaining this fantasy allows both of them
to disavow their different complicities in the imperializing forces they
critique. Through the discourse of *afición*, Montoya can define himself
as a curator of premodern Basque culture and disavow his own complicity as a hotel owner with the commercialization of the bullfight and with
the economics of tourism. In this context, Montoya's remark about "this
Grand Hotel business" can be read as a projection of his own complicities. Similarly, Jake can disavow his role as a tourist and instead pursue
his fantasy of contact with a heroic avatar of premodern manhood.

The passage also suggests the homosocial pleasures associated with
the cult of *afición*. Montoya's embarrassment can be only partially attrib-
uted to the awkwardness of discussing American economic imperialism
with an American. There also seems to be an embarrassed yet shared
pleasure in their secret association as aficionados. The dynamics of this
interaction, in fact, seem to echo in inverse form Jake's interaction with
the policeman at the *bal mussette*. While both interactions are homosocial, Jake's interaction with the policeman is based on explicitly reaffirm-
ing homophobia, while his interaction with Montoya is organized around
a barely concealed homoerotic pleasure in their interaction and in their
mutual fascination with Romero.

The disguised erotics of this preoccupation with Romero become
nearly explicit in Jake's initial meeting with the matador:

The boy stood very straight and unsmiling in his full bull-fighting clothes. His jacket hung over the back of a chair. They were just finishing winding his sash. His black hair shone under the electric light. He wore a white linen shirt and the sword-handler finished his sash and stood up and stepped back. Pedro Romero nodded, seeming very far away and dignified when we shook hands. Montoya said something about what great aficionados we were, and that we wanted to wish him luck. Romero listened very seriously. Then he turned to me. He was the best-looking boy I have ever seen . . . We wished him "Mucha suerte," shook hands, and went out. He was standing, straight and handsome and altogether by himself, alone in the room with the hangers-on as we shut the door. (163)

The passage constructs an image of Romero as conquering hero. Attended to by underlings, he yet stands "altogether by himself." Romero thus seems to embody the manhood that Jake seeks—a manhood defined by phallic fullness and patriarchal privilege. As Jake's racialized fantasy of premodern manhood, Romero seems to represent the negation of the disturbing possibilities represented by the homosexuals in the *bal mussette*. However, Jake's climactic encounter with this masculine fantasy disturbingly reanimates the specter of homoeroticism from which he has fled. His description lingers lovingly over every detail of Romero's appearance, from the way his hair shines under the electric light to his facial expressions to his state of dress. The erotic charge produced by this encounter is further underscored by the way Jake explicitly emphasizes Romero's good looks. Thus, in fleeing from the possibilities of modern desire with its explicit naming of homosexuality, Jake turns to a romantic fantasy of premodern manhood, only to find his desire written there as well, albeit in a seemingly more secret script.

Viewed from the vantage of this desire and Jake's need to guard against its full recognition, the famous scene in which Jake "pimps" Brett to Romero reads very differently. The triangular relationship that develops among Jake, Brett, and Romero is, of course, attributable in part to Brett's desire for Romero. Her agency in this interaction complicates mainstream critical accounts of this scene, which, as the language of pimping suggests, tend to read the scene as a transaction made entirely between men. However, while it is important to account for Brett's agency in this interaction, Jake does play a pivotal role in facilitating Brett and Romero's liaison. It is thus equally important to address his investments in the interaction as well. In conventional readings of the novel, Jake's decision to assist Brett in getting Romero into bed is one of the more undermotivated events in the novel. The decision seems to transgress all of Jake's stated beliefs. In bringing Romero and Brett together, Jake breaks with his aficionado's commitment to protect Romero from foreign temptations, destroying his friendship with Montoya. It also goes against the jealous possessiveness that Jake had earlier demonstrated toward Brett.

In order to account for Jake's motives, we need to turn again to the complex set of fantasies that overdetermines his relationship to Brett, Romero, and the space of Pamplona. If Jake's journey to Pamplona represents his attempt to return to the premodern space of heroic manhood, then Romero, as the fantasized embodiment of this manhood, can serve in part as an idealized surrogate for Jake. Within this context, Romero is imagined as performing with the kind of phallic sexuality that Jake, in his ambivalent embodiment of modern masculinity, does not possess. However, while fulfilling Jake's fantasy, this surrogacy also negates it, underscoring the fact that Jake himself is barred from living this fantasy. Moreover, the surrogacy emphasizes the phantasmatic nature of this idealized manhood, suggesting that it can only be imagined as fully existing in the space of the other.[32] The ambivalence of this relationship of surrogacy indicates that Jake's investment in bringing Romero and Brett together has other sources as well. By underwriting this heterosexual encounter, Jake is also able to displace his homoerotic attraction to Romero. In this sense, the surrogacy works both ways: Jake not only identifies with Romero and desires Brett but he also identifies with Brett and desires Romero. Thus the possibilities of polymorphous "perversity" that Jake flees Paris to avoid return in slightly sublimated form in Pamplona. A final motivation for Jake's complicity in this triangle is suggested by the imperialist dimensions of the fantasies he attaches to Romero. His participation in what from the point of view of the aficionado is the willful destruction of a promising young bullfighter uncovers the thinly veiled aggression that underwrites his paternalistic investment in the ideology of *afición*.[33] A form of what Renato Resaldo has called "imperialist nostalgia," Jake's construction of Romero as a premodern naif already implies the bullfighter's destruction by the forces of modernity. Jake, then, merely attempts to speed this process along.

Romero, however, refuses to adhere to this script, marking the subjective limits of Jake's fantasy space. Far from destroying him, Romero's fling with Brett does not seem to affect his bullfighting at all. But Jake fetishistically hangs onto his fantasy construction of Romero, even as it is negated by Romero's ability to negotiate the world of modernity and the touristic economy of desire in which he is complexly if exploitatively positioned.

A number of the other lost-generation characters share both Jake's fetishistic preoccupation with phallic virility and his association of it with the Basque country, specifically with festival space of Pamplona. Brett, of course, becomes fascinated with Romero as an image of phallic prowess, commenting repeatedly on the tightness of his pants while watching him perform. Moreover, the other male characters become increasingly preoccupied with ideas of traditional manhood in the fantasy space of Pamplona. Throughout the novel, most of the leading male characters vie for Brett's amorous attentions. It is only in Pamplona, however, that the competition over these attentions becomes divisive, eventually leading to violence.

The relationship of these fantasies of phallic prowess to violence is metaphorically suggested by the group's conversation after they have just witnessed the goring of a steer (a castrated bull) by one of the bulls that will participate in the bullfight:

> "I say," Mike said, "they *were* fine bulls, weren't they? Did you see their horns?"
>
> "Did I not," said Brett. "I had no idea what they were like."
>
> "Did you see the one hit that steer?" Mike asked. "That was extraordinary."
>
> "It's no life being a steer," Robert Cohn said.
>
> "Don't you think so?" Mike said. "I would have thought you'd loved being a steer, Robert."
>
> "What do you mean, Mike?"
>
> "They lead such a quiet life. They never say anything and they're always hanging about so."
>
> We were embarrassed. Bill laughed. Robert Cohn was angry . . .
>
> "Come off it, Michael. You're drunk," Brett said.
>
> "I'm not drunk. I'm quite serious. *Is* Robert Cohn going to follow Brett around like a steer all the time?"
>
> "Shut up, Michael. Try and show a little breeding."
>
> "Breeding be damned. Who has any breeding anyway, except the bulls? Aren't the bulls lovely? Don't you like them, Bill? Why don't you say something, Robert? Don't sit there looking like a bloody funeral. What if Brett did sleep with you? She's slept with lots of better people than you." (141–42)

The group seems mesmerized by the bulls, commenting on their horns and noting the animals' "lovely" appearance. That the violent scene that they have just witnessed provokes fascination rather than disgust or pity suggests the characters' investment in the masculine ideal that the bulls metaphorically embody. Rather than being put off by the violence, they identify with the bulls' power—a power that is explicitly allied with masculine potency through the contrast with the castrated steers. In their dialogue the characters extend the metaphorics of this scene to their own interaction. Mike compares Robert to a steer, suggesting that Robert is less than fully masculine and implicitly threatening him with the violence they have just witnessed. As we learn in the last line of the passage, the vehemence of Mike's attack is motivated in part by sexual jealousy: he is furious with Robert for sleeping with Brett, his fiancée. This triangular battle between men over a woman, then, presents a locus classicus of competitive homosociality, recalling the image of the riau-riau dancers circling Brett and contrasting with the more "perverse" triangle formed by Romero, Jake, and Brett. Interestingly, though, this homosocial dynamic only acquires full force via the characters' projections onto the space of Pamplona. As Mike himself says, Brett's "slept with lots of better people" than Robert, but it is only here in Pamplona after witnessing the phallic spectacle of the bulls that Mike takes the issue up with Robert.

Mike's assertion that only the bulls have breeding complicates the passage further. In part, it betrays an anxiety as to distinguishing clearly between bull and steer among the lost-generation characters. While Mike insists that Robert is the steer, his comment also implies that the position of bull is unattainable by any of the characters. Mike's comment thus underscores the phantasmatic dimension of the group's perception of the bulls, suggesting that, like Romero, they represent an ideal of pure manhood attainable only in fantasy. Moreover, it is unclear whether Robert would be the steer if measured by this masculinist standard. If the homosocial competition between Mike and Robert is ostensibly over Brett, then it seems that Mike is more likely to be wearing cuckold's horns than bull's horns. Similarly, as many critics have pointed out, Jake, with his wound and his seemingly masochistic social interactions, is as likely a candidate for the steer as Robert.

However, Jake and the other lost-generation characters insist on treating Robert as a steer, making him the scapegoat for all that goes wrong in Pamplona. It is in this context that the eugenicist metaphorics of Mike's comment about "breeding" become significant. For part of Mike's objection to Robert is his Jewishness. He says later in the same scene: "Brett's gone off with men. But they weren't ever Jews and they didn't come hang about afterward" (143). Thus, while Mike mocks the idea of pure breeding in his comment, he is also very much invested in the idea, as his fury at Robert's and Brett's miscegenous fling suggests. As we have already seen, this anti-Semitism is not unique to Mike but is voiced at various points not only by Jake but by Bill and Brett as well. What is striking about these anti-Semitic comments, however, is that they occur with few exceptions only in book II, the part of the novel set in the Basque country. Moreover, while Jake's narration begins with a gratuitous joke about Robert's nose, Robert and Jake are reasonably good friends throughout most of book I.

The emergence of this anti-Semitism in the Basque country suggests that it has some relationship to the fantasies of cultural purity and phallic potency that the characters project onto this space. As the exchange between Mike and Robert indicates, the more the characters fetishize a phantasmatic state of premodern purity and potency, a state jointly symbolized by Romero and the bulls, the more anxious they become about their own ability to return to this state. One way of alleviating this anxiety is to construct a scapegoat on which to project their own sense of impurity and inadequacy. Robert, then, becomes this scapegoat.

It is only as the characters become transfixed by the fantasy of a return to a space of premodern and patriarchal purity, a fantasy that overlaps in notable ways with emergent fascist ideologies in this period, that they turn to anti-Semitism as a fetishistic means of disavowing their own anxieties about being adequate to this purity. The fetish of anti-Semitism works in an inverse way to the fetish of pure manhood represented by the bulls and Romero, yet the two function as complementary on an ideological level: in the fantasy of pure manhood the fetishistic logic of disavowal asserts, "I know very well that his masculinity is no more pure than mine, but nevertheless he represents pure manhood"; in the fantasy logic of anti-Semitism, on the other hand, the disavowal claims, "I know very well that I am as impure as he or she is, but nevertheless he or she embodies impurity." Moreover, the geographical fantasy mapping performed by the novel, with its border crossings and its construction of Basque country as a space of primitive otherness, suggests that this very fantasy of masculine purity already contains the trace of racial or ethnic alterity in its very construction, further underscoring the intimate connection between the two forms of fetishism.

The affect generated by these two forms of fetishism inevitably leads to violence as three of the major male characters get into fistfights with Robert. Moreover, the fiesta itself is metaphorically allied with warfare: rockets that signal the beginning of the fiesta leave a "shrapnel burst in the sky," the café becomes a "battleship stripped for action," fireworks explode on the ground, nearly killing some people, and a man is killed running from the bulls (153).[34] These images of warfare suggest the violent consequences of the nostalgic fantasy of returning to a premodern space of purity, one that is seemingly outside the commodified logic of capitalist exchange but which is actually produced by that very same logic.

Return: Reengaging Modernity

Fleeing from the violent consequences of his attempt to literalize fantasy, Jake returns to the French Riviera, which he allies with the modernized space of Paris. This return, however, can only be ambivalent, since it marks the death of his fantasy of masculine renewal. This ambivalence emerges most forcefully when Jake overtips a waiter to make up for sending back a liqueur made from the flowers of the Pyrenees that the waiter had recommended. After overtipping the waiter, Jake ironically meditates on the (phantasmatic) differences between France and Spain:

> The waiter seemed a little offended about the flowers of the Pyrenees, so I overtipped him. That made him happy. It felt comfortable to be in a country where it is so simple to make people happy. You can never tell whether a Spanish waiter will thank you. Everything is on such a clear financial basis in France. It is the simplest country to live in. No one makes things complicated by becoming your friend for any obscure reason. If you want people to like you, you have only to spend a little money. I spent a little money and the waiter liked me. He appreciated my valuable qualities. He would be glad to see me back. I would dine there again some time and he would be glad to see me, and would want me at his table. It would be a sincere liking because it would have a sound basis. I was back in France. (233)

By refusing the drink derived from the flowers of the Pyrenees, Jake signals his abandonment of the fantasies that he sought to fulfill in the Basque country of Spain. Instead, he orders a *vieux marc*, indicating his new allegiance to France. This signaling of national affiliation through the purchase of a commodity suggests a more modernized form of nationalism, one that contrasts with the more atavistic fantasy of cultural and racial purity projected onto the Basque country.

Jake's irony suggests his ambivalence about returning to this fantasy space of modern France. As in the passage when he describes his consumerist version of the hard-boiled code, here Jake mocks the values in which he is invested. Yet the passage indicates that he remains invested in them nonetheless. He ironically invokes the "clear financial basis" on which everything functions in France, whereby friendship becomes commodity and people's "valuable qualities" are transformed into abstract and exchangeable quantities. Yet he also seems genuinely relieved to have escaped to a space devoid of immediate affect in which "no one makes things complicated by becoming your friend for any obscure reason" and in which any violence or exploitation is safely mediated through the abstract logic of exchange (even as they form a necessary correlate to such forms of exchange).

The consequences of this return to the fantasy space of modernity for the novel's representation of masculinity and sexuality become apparent in its famous last scene. While the scene takes place in Madrid, the city is represented as merely another urban space filled with good restaurants, bars, and hotels. The Spanish capital can thus be phantasmatically allied with Jake's understanding of France as the generalized space of capitalism. Moreover, the history of colonial occupation of the Basque country by the expanding Spanish and French states (a history that, as we have seen, the novel replays in miniature form) also allies Madrid with France and against the Basque country.

It is while riding in a taxi through another urban, modernizing fantasy space, then, that Jake and Brett exchange their final words of the novel:

> I settled back. Brett moved close to me. We sat close against each other. I put my arm around her and she rested against me comfortably. It was very hot and bright, and the houses looked sharply white. We turned out onto the Gran Via.
>
> "Oh, Jake," Brett said, "we could have had such a damned good time together."
>
> Ahead was a mounted policeman in khaki directing traffic. He raised his baton. The car slowed suddenly pressing Brett against me.
>
> "Yes," I said. "Isn't it pretty to think so?" (247)

This final scene finds Jake (and Brett) in the same predicament as when the novel began. He wants to achieve an idealized heterosexual union with Brett, one predicated on fantasies of heroic manhood derived from the romance tradition, but is prohibited from doing so by his wound. Reading the wound, as I have done, as symbolizing an injury to the ideology of phallic manhood enables me to regard Jake's condition as allegorizing a certain set of challenges to traditional conceptions of manhood in the early twentieth century. Interestingly, Jake appears disenchanted with his nostalgic fantasy ("isn't it pretty to think so?") in this final scene. The impossibility of this fantasy has already been inscribed in his flight from the Basque country, but his verbal recognition of this impossibility is suggestive. While this disenchantment might suggest that Jake is now completely locked into the logic of capitalism and commodity culture, without even his nostalgic fantasies of escape remaining, this disenchantment also seems the first step in developing a different masculine subjectivity as well as imagining a more effectively critical relationship to the forces of capitalism.

The image of the policeman holding the phallic baton provides a perfect corollary to the possibilities of Jake's disenchantment, suggesting that perhaps Jake really is seeing the world differently. In contrast to Jake's homosocial identification with the policeman at the *bal musette* (and with Montoya), this passage presents an image of the policeman as negating. There is no understanding or kinship between Jake and the policeman. Instead he wields the baton of phallic authority that Jake lacks. But the prosthetic nature of this baton radically distinguishes this image of empowered masculinity from the previous images presented in the novel. Here manhood and patriarchal authority are not fantasized as inner essences that need to be reclaimed but are instead represented as entirely a function of social power—the social power of the modern capitalist state.

Beyond Nostalgia's Lure

The hard-boiled male travels to Europe in *The Sun Also Rises*. However, he does not make this journey untransformed. The representation of masculinity in Hemingway's novel contrasts in important ways with its representation in *Red Harvest*. While Jake and the Op generally share a code, a style of narration, and many of the same phantasmatic investments, the novels' differing representations of these commonalties present two very different views of this male figure. *Red Harvest* is much more rigorously negative in its representation of its hard-boiled narrator, demonstrating the Op's amoral complicity with corporate capitalism and the criminality it produces. In contrast, *The Sun Also Rises* is much more sympathetic toward its narrator. While Hemingway's novel represents the larger social dynamics of imperialism and capitalist exchange, it is much more ambivalent about Jake's complicity with these dynamics.

This sympathy seems to hinder *The Sun Also Rises'* critique of the socioeconomic underpinnings of hard-boiled masculinity. Yet it also enables the novel to investigate more thoroughly the phantasmatic investments and contradictions that structure hard-boiled masculinity and its relationship to this socioeconomic field. Because the text regularly, if quietly, registers Jake's affect and readily aligns itself with his phantasmatic investments, it is able to represent these investments in much greater detail. To take just one example, rather than having to read against the grain to uncover the romance narrative that overdetermines hard-boiled masculinity, the text stages an elaborate fantasy of return to the world of the romance. This narrative sympathy thus opens up the critical possibilities of working through as well as the dangers of repetition.[35]

Jake's trajectory in the novel implicitly suggests the importance of such a phantasmatic politics of working through for leftist praxis in general. Jake's fantasies of purity and immediate escape from the logic of capitalism find their unlikely echo in the asceticism and fantasies of purity that can limit certain strains of contemporary leftist discourse.[36] The Pamplona section of the novel suggests limitations and even dangers of such fantasies of purity. Instead, it is only at the end of the novel that Jake seems potentially able to develop a critical understanding of capitalism and his investments in it, one not structured around a logic of disavowal. The importance of this subjective dynamic of working through to achieving such a critical understanding suggests the irreducible importance of a politics of subjectivity and fantasy for rethinking contemporary leftist discourse. Such a politics would emphasize what Marx himself demonstrated long ago: that the only way to supersede capitalism is by working though and finally beyond the very logic of capitalism itself.[37]

4

Not Your Average Joe

Sometimes he would remember how he had once tricked
or teased white men into calling him a negro in order to
fight them, to beat them or be beaten; now he fought the
negro who called him white.
—*William Faulkner,* Light in August

Faulkner Reads Pulp

Soon after being introduced to Joe Christmas in William Faulkner's
Light in August, [1] the reader is presented with a scene of Joe reading: "He
ate his breakfast with his back against the tree, reading the magazine
while he ate. He had previously read but one story; he began now upon
the second one, reading the magazine straight through as though it were
a novel." [2] Described by Faulkner as being "of that type whose covers
bear either pictures of young women in underclothes or pictures of men
in the act of shooting one another with pistols," the magazine Joe reads
is clearly a pulp (110). In fact, it would only take a minor bit of historical conjecture to think that Faulkner, when writing this scene, had in
mind *Black Mask,* the pulp magazine that oversaw the birth and early
success of hard-boiled fiction. By the time *Light in August* was published
in 1932, *Black Mask* was the nation's leading publisher of hard-boiled
fiction and often featured covers that included either men with guns,
scantily clad women or, most often, both. [3] Faulkner, moreover, seems to
have had hard-boiled fiction very much on his mind in 1932, having just
published *Sanctuary,* which he described as his attempt to write in an
explicitly commercial style and which has been compared in terms of
both style and subject matter to Dashiell Hammett's fiction. [4]

The scene of reading occupies a prominent position in the novel.
Located at the beginning of Christmas's narrative, it occurs on the
morning of the day that Christmas kills Joanna Burden, framing both

the action that is to follow and Joe's life history, which is narrated in flash-back.[5] Like most fictional depictions of reading, the scene also suggests a metacritical or self-reflexive dimension: reading Faulkner writing about reading. Yet relatively little critical attention has been paid to this scene of popular reading and its relationship to the novel in which it is situated. This critical oversight is not incidental; it reflects the cultural divide that has historically informed Faulkner scholarship and, indeed, the project of modernist criticism as a whole.

It is a critical commonplace that Faulkner's writings can be divided into opposing cultural camps with relative ease.[6] On one hand, there are the stream of consciousness modernist masterworks such as *Absalom Absalom!* and *The Sound and the Fury*, which are sometimes cited by patriotic Americanists as proof positive that the modernist novel existed in the United States with all the formal and epistemological complexity that characterized European high modernism.[7] On the other hand, there are Faulkner's forays into mass or popular culture such as *Sanctuary*, *The Wild Palms*, *Pylon*, and his screenplay work. As these two categories are considered mutually exclusive in most Faulkner criticism, *Light in August* is usually classified as one of Faulkner's great modernist achievements (a recent critical text describing it as the "thoroughly modern novel") and any relationship it may bear to mass culture has generally been repressed.[8] Thus, while the relationship between hard-boiled fiction and *Sanctuary* has been intensively explored, there exists no fully developed analysis of a relationship between *Light in August* and hard-boiled and noir prose.[9]

The analysis to follow will posit that such a relationship exists and that it finds its most direct textual expression in the racialized figure of Joe Christmas. However, before turning to this relationship and in order to explore it more fully, it is necessary to rethink the relationship between Faulkner's work and the cultural divide that has shaped much of its critical reception.

This divide is, of course, not unique to Faulkner criticism but is a legacy of what were arguably the three most influential schools of modernist criticism: the New Critics, the New York Intellectuals, and the Frankfurt School. Despite political differences that ranged the spectrum from right-wing communitarianism through cold-war liberalism to leftist critique, these three schools shared many assumptions about the modernist work and its negative relationship to the world of mass culture. To broadly (and reductively) summarize, major practitioners of all three schools saw the modernist text as ideally removed from the everyday world, though for the New Critics this ideal remove functioned in the service of traditional values, while for many New York Intellectuals it confirmed the moral and aesthetic integrity of the work, and for the Frankfurt School it served as a negation of the inhumanity of the present capitalist order and a utopian index of the more humane order to come. Moreover, all three schools saw mass culture, or, as a number of the soon-to-be New Critics put it in their infamous Southern Agrarian manifesto of 1931, "industrial culture," as a pernicious and increasingly deterministic influence on contemporary society.[10] More recent writings by Andreas Huyssen and Fredric Jameson have challenged this view of mass culture, arguing for a more dialectical approach to the relationships between high and mass culture by asserting that the two forms are mutually constitutive and dialectically dependent on each other.[11] Jameson's and Huyssen's positions have, in turn, been refined and challenged by the most recent wave of modernist criticism, which has tended to deemphasize or entirely discard the high/low distinction in favor a nonhierarchical understanding of the entire range of modern writing practices.[12]

The possibilities opened up by this recent revisionist work promise to be particularly rich in the case of Faulkner, since, taken as a whole, his work has never fit comfortably on one side or the other of the cultural divide.[13] Indeed, the very visibility of this divide within Faulkner criticism and the subsequent need to denigrate so much of his written output as "inferior" suggests the enormity of the ideological effort undertaken to root him firmly in the camp of high modernism. What has been obscured by this effort is as visible in a work like *Light in August*, which became a celebrated part of the modernist canon, as it is in the many works that didn't.

In fact, *Light in August*, perhaps uniquely among Faulkner's output, can be read as advancing an implicit theory of the relationship between modernism and mass culture. Stylistically and thematically heterogeneous, the novel constructs a dynamic relationship between popular cultural forms such as the hard-boiled and noir narrative and the metanarrative techniques of the modernist novel.[14] Critics have long argued that Faulkner's novels are about storytelling, reading them as written metacommentaries on essentially oral forms of communication and community.[15] *Light in August* complicates this view by presenting the oral forms themselves as derived in part from the emergent world of mass culture. Thus the stories told by the town, the narrator, and the central characters in *Light in August* are not the simple, organic expression of folkways or the traditional community. Instead they are the product of the adaptation of this community and these folkways to the commodified narratives of mass culture, and vice versa.[16]

The novel's engagement with the effects of mass culture sheds light on the meaning of the allegory of reading with which we began. Joe reading the pulp becomes a reflection in miniature of the process of the novel as a whole. What we get in *Light in August* is Faulkner reading mass culture, simultaneously incorporating it into his narrative technique and developing a modernist metacommentary about its significance.[17] Yet this process does not just flow from high to low. Faulkner's modernist style is also transformed by this incorporation of popular cultural materials, rooting his modernist preoccupations with memory and perception in a relatively realistic and, at points, "pulpy" narrative structure.[18] The relationship between modernism and mass culture in *Light in August*, in fact, suggests a slightly different relationship between these terms than has been imagined by either Jameson and Huyssen or the most recent wave of modernist critics. The novel neither fully collapses high and mass culture into each other nor presents them as existing in a merely negative relationship but instead presents them as distinct yet deeply imbricated and overlapping spheres of cultural production that can positively, as well as negatively, interact with one another. Moreover, the novel's movement between the two spheres suggests that each has its formal and epistemological advantages and limitations. Thus Faulkner borrows modernism's complex engagement with questions of causality to complicate the more linear or mechanical understandings of causality that inform both cultural anxieties about mass culture and, often, the mass cultural text itself, while he draws on the mass culture's engagement with cultural fantasy to open out the often hermetic and purely subjective concerns of high modernism.[19]

To return more fully to the scene with which we began, a closer reading of the passage reveals the dynamics of this reciprocal relationship at work. Initially, Faulkner's language seems to echo that of traditional modernist critics. The description of Joe reading the pulp "straight through as if it were a novel" rather than jumping around from story to story seems to ironically underscore the distance between the two forms. Similarly, the vague description of the magazine's cover suggests the formulaic and disposable nature of the stories contained within. This disposability is confirmed when Christmas burns the magazine after reading it all the way through: "Then he struck a match to the magazine and prodded it patiently until it was consumed" (112).

However, Faulkner's description of the burning magazine as "consumed," suggesting a pun on the forms of commodity consumption integral to the reception of pulp magazines and the other types of mass culture rapidly transforming everyday life in the South of the thirties, hints that there might be a more complex engagement with popular materials in this passage than an initial reading would suggest. And, in fact, a more careful reading of the passage reveals that Joe's act of reading is anything but casual. The magazine is consumed by Joe's match only after he has lingered over and consumed much of its language, as words and passages from the pulp magazine intermingle with his perceptions of the day and his premonitions about killing Joanna Burden:

> Now and then he would look up from the page, chewing, into the
> sunshot leaves which arched the ditch. "Maybe I have already done it,"
> he thought. "Maybe it is no longer now waiting to be done." It seemed
> that he could see the yellow day opening peacefully on before him, like
> a corridor, an arras, into a still chiaroscuro without urgency. It seemed
> to him that as he sat there the yellow day contemplated him drowsily,
> like a prone and somnolent yellow cat. Then he read again. He turned
> the pages in steady progression, though now and then he would seem to
> linger upon one page, one line, perhaps one word. He would not look up
> then. He would not move, apparently arrested and held immobile by a
> single word which had perhaps not yet impacted, his whole being
> suspended by the single trivial combination of letters in a quiet and
> sunny space, so that hanging motionless and without physical weight
> he seemed to watch the slow flowing of time beneath him, thinking
> *All I wanted was peace* thinking, "She ought not to have started praying
> over me." (111–12, italics in original)

The process of consumption represented here is one of incorporation as much as simple popular cultural enjoyment, suggesting the power of mass culture to shape and organize subjectivity. As with the dietitian's toothpaste in his earliest childhood memory, Joe ingests the magazine's words and images with a kind of rapt attentiveness. Yet this process of incorporation is presented as neither mechanical nor unreflective. As the pulp's language mixes in Joe's consciousness with his perceptions of the day and his premonitions about killing Joanna, a complex representation of causality emerges, one in which mass cultural materials are neither ephemeral nor completely determining but rather part of a larger web of cultural meanings that impinge on Joe and help to organize his relationship to the surrounding world. Faulkner underscores this complex representation of causality by employing similes and words like "seem," "apparently," "perhaps" to emphasize the ambiguity or uncertainty of representation. Yet this modernist engagement with representation is brought to bear on a narrative that is straight out of a popular culture informed equally by the pulp stories found in *Black Mask* and the white-supremacist melodramas of Thomas Dixon: a violent and racially ambiguous drifter contemplates the murder of a white woman with whom he has been sexually involved.[20]

As part of these questions of causality, the passage also raises questions about Joe's agency in relationship to the mass cultural narratives he both reads and seems to embody. At one point, Joe imagines his fate as already determined ("'Maybe I have already done it,' he thought. 'Maybe it is no longer now waiting to be done'"), suggesting the power of mass cultural narratives and the larger social forces they symbolize to structure and even determine actions. Joe's understanding of his actions as fated is echoed at a number of other points in the narrative, forming, as Joseph Reed has pointed out, one of the dominant ways in which Joe organizes his relationship to the world.[21] Yet this determinism is contrasted with the agency that Joe demonstrates as a reader. Far from being merely a passive consumer, Joe is presented as an active participant in the process; his act of consumption is also an act of careful reading as he lingers on the pulp as one might a modernist novel, demonstrating that Faulkner's comparison between pulp magazine and novel is not entirely ironic. Thus, while the novel presents Joe as partly constrained on the level of action by the mass cultural fantasies that shape his subjectivity, the passage presents his power as a critical reader as an important corrective to this determinism, suggesting that as a reader he also has the ability to critically engage and perhaps work through these fantasies.

Indeed, this passage offers an exemplary model for critical reading, one that can be applied to *Light in August* itself: as a reader Joe both internalizes what he reads and transforms what he internalizes. Thus the process of reading also becomes a process of writing, a way of interpreting the meanings inscribed by the text to produce a different script. Similarly, in the pages that follow, I will present an analysis of *Light in August* that attempts to read both with and against the already quite dialectical and ambivalent logic of Faulkner's written text. In doing so, I hope thereby to script an understanding of the novel's representation of racialized masculinity and its relationship to the growth of mass culture and the transformation of everyday life in the South of the twenties and thirties that differs from the ones usually proffered by the novel's critics.

The placement of the scene of mass cultural reading near the beginning of Joe's narrative suggests that he himself can be read in part as a hard-boiled male. This possibility is further suggested by the way in which Joe's premonitions about killing Joanna mix with his reading of the pulp, suggesting the relationship between forms of cultural misogyny and the phantasmatic investments of hard-boiled masculinity. Following these leads, I will read Joe Christmas in relationship to the cultural fantasy of hard-boiled masculinity. However, this fantasy does not remain unchanged as it is adapted to the world of the modernizing, Jim Crow South. Just as the pulp story mixes with Joe's premonitions and his perceptions of the day, in *Light in August* the fantasy of hard-boiled masculinity mixes with cultural fantasies about black masculinity central to the maintenance of white supremacy in the segregated South of the 1930s. Yet this mixing does not so much add a new dimension to the hard-boiled male as make explicit the fantasy of racial borrowing that already formed an implicit part of his identity. The transplantation of the hard-boiled masculinity to the South merely makes explicit the ways in which white masculinity borrows from the racist cultural iconography of black masculinity for self-definition and to legitimate its embrace of gendered violence. The novel thus renders explicit the implicit dynamic of racial borrowing that structures noir and hard-boiled narratives, revealing the ways in which the negativity of noir is organized around a set of racialized meanings that usually remain buried but which everywhere shade its representation of masculinity and social antagonism. To read *Light in August* as bound up with popular forms such as the hard-boiled and noir narrative is to give the phantasmatic negativity associated with the latter term (and that is present in hard-boiled fiction as a genre informed and deformed by noir) an explicitly racial cast, one that makes explicit the dynamic of racial borrowing that remains implicit in the earlier texts I have examined. Such a reading of the novel also reveals that the racial borrowing central to noir and to the construction of hard-boiled masculinity can function in both directions: the white borrowing from the cultural iconography of black masculinity opens up a space for a reverse borrowing, one that can in part be used against conventional cultural constructions of black masculinity.[22]

Reading and Writing Racialized Masculinity

The novel's representation of the intersections and oppositions between differently racialized masculinities is predicated on the dynamics of cultural fantasy. These dynamics are linked in turn to those of mass cultural reading and writing. The text's representation of the relationship between technologies of writing and those of reading also extends beyond the novel's ambivalent engagement with mass culture to encompass a broader understanding of social power, shaping its representation of the relationship between individual forms of racialized and gendered subjectivity and larger forms of political-economic and cultural determination. The novel presents racialized and gendered subjectivity as the product of various forms of writing, from the writings of mass cultural texts to the subjective and cultural scripts produced by the workings of the political economy. Yet, as in the scene with Joe reading the pulp, this process of inscription is mediated by a countervailing one of readerly interpretation, one in which the subject negotiates and reconfigures the cultural meanings inscribed on him or her through these forms of cultural "writing."

It is this complex understanding of cultural power that shapes the novel's representation of racialized masculinity, one that is a product of a specific historical and socioeconomic context. As we have already seen in our analysis of Joe reading the pulp, the thematics of reading and writing are linked, in part, to the novel's representation of emergent forms of mass culture. This linkage is far from incidental. The exponential growth of mass culture represents one aspect of a larger set of cultural and economic transformations: the various processes of modernization that were reshaping life in both the American South and the nation as a whole in the twenties and early thirties. In the South, these transformations were part of the long and slow shift from largely agricultural forms of capitalist production to more industrial forms of capitalism.[23]

The growth of forms of mass culture such as film, recorded music, and the pulps represented one of the most visible, because cultural, manifestations of these transformations and, as such, provided one of the key sites of cultural contestation around the implication of these changes. Mass culture's growth was often thematized as the encroachment of various technologies of writing that produced deterministic cultural scripts. In these accounts, the individual subject became akin to the feckless protagonist of a naturalist novel whose fate and consciousness are entirely determined by the environmental conditioning of mass culture. It is into this cultural context, then, that Faulkner introduces his thematics of reading and writing, complicating the naturalist logic of these critical readings of modernization and the growth of mass culture by adding to them a theory of subjectivity and subjective fantasy that opens up a space of potential agency.

It is also in this context that the novel's representation of racialized masculinity is situated. The different fantasies of racialized masculinity that Joe embodies have their genesis in the opposition between modernist and antimodernist ideologies that shaped cultural life in both the South and the nation as a whole in the early thirties.[24] I have already examined, in chapter 2, the complex combination of modernist and antimodernist investments that shaped the representation of hard-boiled masculinity. In *Light in August*, these investments mix with an analogous set of investments specific to the American South. The South in the twenties and early thirties was ideologically split between advocates of a "New South" that would embrace processes of modernization, put aside sectional differences, and merge fully (if subordinately) with the economy of the nation as a whole, and antimodernist advocates, such as the Ku Klux Klan and members of various evangelical Protestant sects, who argued for a return to an agricultural economy and to what they defined as the traditional values of temperance, fundamentalist piety, and racial and sexual purity.[25]

The contest between these attitudes toward modernization shaped the material and phantasmatic organization of race and gender relations in the South in the twenties and thirties. Attitudes toward women's suffrage tended to divide along this axis. Similarly, while a majority of the region supported the Jim Crow laws, the reasons for this support alternated between a modernist rhetoric of racial harmony and sectional peace and an antimodernist rhetoric of embattled racial and sexual purity. Central to both constructions, but especially to the latter, was the cluster of cultural fantasies that are organized around what Angela Davis has termed the "myth of the black rapist."[26] Initially emerging, as we saw in chapter 1, as part of an elaborate post-Reconstruction rationale for the reinvigoration of white supremacy, the figure of the black rapist was revived as phantasmatic threat by the antimodernists' neo-Victorian rhetoric of sexual and racial purity. The ideological work done by this fantasy figure was central to the maintenance of the Jim Crow regime of racial terror, which was structured, Robyn Wiegman has argued, around the disciplinary practice of corporeal and carcerial violence in the forms of lynching and of panoptic surveillance produced by the ever-present threat of lynching. Central to this fantasy was the disavowal of its status as fantasy, constructing as real a scenario in which chivalric white men needed to protect pure white womanhood from a bestial black male sexuality. The fantasy thus enabled a transformation of political-economic questions of labor and citizenship into libidinal-economic ones of purity and transgression.[27]

Faulkner's reworking of the myth of the black rapist in his representation of Joe Christmas forms one key site of engagement with cultural fantasy. Christmas's trajectory in *Light in August* can be read in part as a fantasia on the cultural fantasy of the black rapist, one that both repeats its ideological coordinates and, crucially, opens up a space for their interrogation. For Joe's actions both conform to those of the mythical black rapist (he is reported to have black blood, he fits the stereotype of the threatening mulatto, and he eventually has a sadomasochistic sexual relationship with and kills a white woman in which questions of consent are at best confused) and significantly differ from it (it is unclear whether he really has any African American heritage, he kills Joanna Burden possibly in self-defense right before she was planning to commit a murder-suicide, and the sexual play in Joe's and Joanna's relationship underscore the myth's status as fantasy). Thus, as Eric Sundquist has argued, Faulkner's novel, in its ambivalence, provides us with both the myth of the black rapist and the tools for its undoing.[28]

However, while many recent readings have focused on Joe Christmas as a figuration of black masculinity or as a figure of racial indeterminacy, relatively little critical attention has been paid to his relationship to cultural constructions of white masculinity. Indeed, it is as if even in the most attentive of recent criticism the suggestion of Christmas's black blood is enough to establish his identity as generally "black" or, at least, "mulatto," thereby unconsciously replaying one of the central tenets of U.S. racial ideology. If we are seriously to attend to Joe's racial indeterminacy, then, it seems important to address the ways in which it is shaped by the production of fantasies about white as well as black masculinity. As already suggested, some of the central fantasies about white masculinity that the representation of Joe engages are those attaching to the figure of the hard-boiled male. What distinguishes *Light in August* from the other texts examined so far is that in Faulkner's novel the process of becoming hard-boiled is bound up explicitly with the process of becoming racialized and both are linked to the forms of gendered violence that I explored in chapters 1 and 2. If, as I have argued throughout, white hard-boiled masculinity was formed in part through its inheritance from the racialized dimensions of noir, including a disavowed borrowing from the figure of the black rapist, then the figure of Joe Christmas can be read as being poised equally between these two fantasies of violent masculinity.

Joe Christmas as Cultural Fantasy

As the novel's figure for miscegenation, Joe literally embodies the mixing of cultural oppositions that both shape and are shaped by the novel's production: oppositions between black and white, masculine and feminine, agrarian and urban, and high and mass culture. Traditional accounts of the novel have read Christmas's miscegenation as the novel's central problem, one that needs to find tragic resolution for order and traditional community to be restored.[29] If, however, the novel's focus on racial miscegenation is intimately connected with its interest in other forms of cultural and formal mixing, a very different *Light in August* emerges from the one canonized by the first wave of modernist critics. In this other *Light in August*, fantasies about racial mixture do not just function within the well-established coordinates of white supremacist ideology in the postemancipation South. They also become part of a more general set of fantasies about the cultural mixings produced by the process of modernization. Rather than defending an idea of traditional community against the encroachment of modernity, the novel can instead be read as interested in the possibilities as well as problems opened up by such cultural mixing. This interest is reflected not only in Faulkner's stylistic and thematic engagement with the new mass market genre of the pulp magazine and the forms of masculinity found within it but also in the way in which he challenges the potential stability of these emergent cultural forms by willfully mixing them with other cultural narratives, both high and low.

The links among hard-boiled masculinity, modernization, and miscegenation are suggested by the first full description we are given of Joe. Narrated from the vantage of Byron Bunch (who knows as little about Joe as the reader), this description is crucially alienated, based on a series of inferences and outward impressions. Indeed, Byron, like the rest of the town, plays the role of the classical detective, trying to glean Joe's essential character from a series of reified clues, such as the color of Joe's face and the quality of his clothes. Yet the semiotic confusion that Joe produces, like the mystery in a hard-boiled novel, refuses to resolve itself into a simple, convincing solution:

> Byron Bunch knows this: It was one Friday morning three years ago. And the group of men at work in the planer shed looked up, and saw the stranger standing there, watching them. They did not know how long he had been there. He looked like a tramp, yet not like a tramp either. His shoes were dusty and his trousers soiled too. But they were of decent serge, sharply creased, and his shirt was soiled but it was a white shirt, and he wore a tie and a stiffbrim straw hat that was quite new, cocked at an angle arrogant and baleful above his still face. He did not look like a professional hobo in his professional rags, but there was something definitely rootless about him, as though no town nor city was his, no street, no walls, no square of earth his home. And that he carried this knowledge with him always as though it were a banner, with a quality ruthless, lonely, and almost proud. . . And Byron watched him standing there and looking at the men in sweatstained overalls, with a cigarette in one side of his mouth and his face darkly and contemptuously still,

drawn down a little on one side because of the smoke. After a while he spat the cigarette without touching his hand to it and turned and went on to the mill office while the men in faded and worksoiled overalls looked at his back with a sort of baffled outrage. (31–32)

Joe here appears as a figure both familiar and opaque. The mystery his appearance creates owes not to the paucity of clues so much as their proliferation. In part his appearance seems to align him with knowable entities such as the hobo or the tramp, yet other aspects of his appearance (namely, his white shirt, tie, straw hat, and general demeanor) resist this coding, suggesting instead specifically urban connotations. Indeed, part of what remains illegible to the workers in the Jefferson planing mill are the signs that code Christmas as a hard-boiled male. From his straw hat, which is "cocked at an angle arrogant and baleful," to his much-worn urban clothes, to the contemptuous, efficient way in which he disposes of his cigarette, Joe seems to have leapt off the cover of a pulp magazine. Significantly, the hard-boiled connotations of Joe's dress and actions are echoed by the more intangible associations that his appearance suggests. Like Race Williams and the Continental Op, Joe is presented, via Byron's narration, as defining himself through his ruthless self-sufficiency and individualistic opposition to the larger social order; the passage describes him as wearing his rootlessness "as though it were a banner, with a quality ruthless, lonely and almost proud." Indeed, the adjective "lonely" is applied to Joe throughout the novel, presenting him as a figure of almost ontological isolation. If on one level this loneliness connotes social dispossession, on another it suggests a willful refusal of the ties of community and domesticity. In other words, Joe can be read as a "drifter" as much as a "tramp" or a "hobo." As a symbol of social disaffection and economic decay, the drifter was an ideologically charged figuration of masculinity in the Depression era—one that was both romanticized as a social rebel and criticized as a dangerous menace. As the noir aesthetic adapted to the differing socioeconomic and phantasmatic contexts of the Great Depression, stories with drifters as protagonists became increasingly common, James M. Cain's *The Postman Always Rings Twice* being the most famous. Joe Christmas as drifter thus stands near the beginning of this generic mutation, a hard-boiled male who is not a detective and who signifies as both urban and agrarian, rebel and menace. He thus returns the hard-boiled male to his noir roots, recalling the protagonists of the noir crime fiction discussed in chapter 1, who defined themselves against any association with collectivity and law and order, even the tenuous one manifested by the private detective.

Other aspects of Joe's identity remain opaque to the millworkers. His last name, Christmas, provokes anxious speculation that seems metonymically bound up with the semiotic confusion produced by his "parchment colored" face, which is repeatedly described as "dark" (34). The millworkers decide that he must be a foreigner, since nobody has "ever heard of a white man named Christmas," leading Byron to speculate on the potential significance of a name:

> And that was the first time Byron remembered that he had ever thought how a man's name, which is supposed to be just the sound for who he is, can be somehow an augur of what he will do, if other men can only read the meaning in time. It seemed to him that none of them had looked especially at the stranger until they heard his name. But as soon as they heard it, it was as though there was something in the sound of it that was trying to tell them what to expect; that he carried with him his own inescapable warning, like a flower its scent or a rattlesnake its rattle. Only none of them had sense enough to recognize it. They just thought that he was a foreigner, and as they watched him for the rest of that Friday, working in that tie and straw hat and the creased trousers, they said among themselves that that was the way men in his country worked. (33–34).

Here the town's perception of Joe (as narrated by Byron) dances around the possible "truth" that fetishistically lies at the heart of most, if not all, Southern fiction in this period: the "truth" of racial difference. The town tries to narrate Joe's possible difference (the "it" that they refuse to recognize) as an ethnic or national difference, since to admit to the possibility of Joe's identity as black would be to admit to the possibility of an autonomous black identity, one not already subjugated to the town's ethic of white supremacy. Joe's actions connote masculine autonomy rather than subservience, freedom of movement rather than constraint. But even beyond the possibility of Joe's blackness, what is most striking in this passage is how the millworkers create the "truth" that they disavow.

The construction of this disavowed "truth," as well as other potential "truths" about Joe, is thematized in Byron's meditations on Joe's name. The name retrospectively constitutes his appearance and identity as noteworthy.[30] As in the psychoanalytic account of deferred action (*nachtraglichkeit*), it is only after the later signifier fixes the meaning of what has come before that this previous material takes on significance, one that appears traumatic, or at least disturbing in its implications for the town.[31] John T. Irwin has noted the centrality of *nachtraglichkeit* to the epistemological structure of Faulkner's fiction, and this is clearly the case in *Light in August*.[32] This scene turns on the relationship between first impressions and their retrospective construction. Thus it is significant that Byron underscores the retrospectively constituted nature of his account of Joe's first appearance in the town, because it emphasizes that his narrative has been projected back onto an initial experience of indifference or meaninglessness ("it seemed to him that none of them had looked especially at the stranger until they heard his name"). It similarly indicates the irreducibly phantasmatic nature of the meanings that the millworkers project onto the multiplicity of possible significations that Joe's appearance could suggest. These meanings seem to become more fixed as Byron's account continues. Initially functioning as an arbitrary signifier that triggers a retrospective series of fantasy projections, Christmas's name becomes transformed into an index of his identity, one that can be read as an augur of his future actions, as the passage moves from radical underdetermination to strict determinism.

What lies between the two poles of underdetermination and strict determinism is Joe's figuration as uncanny. Once Joe's identity begins to accrue meaning, it is the very uncanniness of his appearance—he is both familiar and strange—that seems to disturb his viewers the most. As Freud posits in his celebrated essay on the subject, it is this very trace of the familiar in the unfamiliar that gives the uncanny its power to disturb, indicating that the unfamiliar is so in part because it connected with knowledge that has been repressed.[33] The initial description we get of Joe adds an important twist to this formulation, suggesting that what is repressed in the uncanny scenario is as much a construction as that which is perceived. Joe thus functions as a sort of mobile screen on which the town can project any of a number of differing and even conflicting fantasies. In addition to the "truth" of racial difference that the town projects onto Joe (and that he internalizes at certain points and rejects at others), he represents a kind of synecdoche for the forces of modernization itself. As a drifter, he conjures images of both city and town yet "no square of earth [is] his home." In this way, he becomes a disturbing mirror for the millworkers, who have presumably left jobs on the land to become part of the emerging industrial economy in the South. Similarly, his very inscrutability echoes the way in which the town disavows transformations produced by modernity. The urban associations his identity conjures, including those of hard-boiled masculinity, remain scrupulously unrecognized by the town, only showing up as incongruities that do not allow them to assimilate him fully to their world (or, more precisely, to their fantasy of their world). Yet these incongruities disturbingly mix with more rural associations. Even the racial "truth" that the town attempts to disavow about him becomes a mixed disavowal: one that functions as a disavowal of urban white masculinity fully as much as of the possibility of an autonomous urban or rural black masculinity. Thus Joe is uninterpretable precisely because he seems to come from both everywhere and nowhere, paralleling the way in which modernization in the South cannot entirely be located in an encroaching urban North but also must be understood as an internal process, one that must be disavowed and treated as "foreign" if the fiction of traditional community is to be maintained.

As befitting an uncanny figure, Joe's story begins in the South, moves to the North, and then returns to haunt his initial home. This geographical trajectory is charted in condensed form in chapter 10. The sentence that opens the chapter reproduces in microcosm the heterogeneous stylistic tendencies that inform the novel as a whole: "Knowing not grieving remembers a thousand savage and lonely streets" (220). The first part of the sentence, with its complex interweaving of different modes of psychological perception (knowing, grieving, remembering) seems to be firmly rooted in the psychological and temporal preoccupations of modernism, recalling the more famous opening sentences of chapter 6: "Memory believes before knowing remembers. Believes longer than recollects, longer than knowing even wonders" (119). However, the hyperbolic yet terse invocation of "a thousand savage and lonely streets" in the sentence's second half recalls the paratactic prose of the mass market pulp. This stylistic hybridity is mirrored on the level of content. The sentence's yoking together of "savage" and "lonely" suggests the conjunction of cultural fantasies of black and white masculinity, the adjective "savage" invoking the primitivized image of the black rapist while the word "lonely" conjures the solitary figure of the hard-boiled male.[34]

The conjunction of these two fantasies and their relationship to the novel's representation of modernization is suggested throughout the rest of the chapter. Like the dream sequence in *Red Harvest*, the chapter performs a form of fantasy mapping, charting Christmas's movements between North and South, city and country, black and white, suggesting the range of divergent cultural materials that inform his identity. And while the passage does not take shape explicitly as a dream, the work of condensation it undertakes suggests that it functions in a manner akin to the Freudian logic of the dream work.[35] The chapter, coming near the middle of the novel, compresses fifteen years of Joe's life into a few pages. This temporal condensation is mirrored by a similar spatial one: the chapter maps Christmas's travels during this time, noting his movement from the rural and urban South to the urban North and back again.

Faulkner metaphorizes these spatial and temporal condensations through the image of an endless street, this image itself a condensation of the thousand savage and lonely streets that open the chapter:

> From that night the thousand streets ran as one street, with imperceptible corners and changes of scene, broken by intervals of begged and stolen rides, on trains and trucks, and on country wagons with he at twenty and twentyfive and thirty sitting on the seat with his still hard face and the clothes (even when soiled and worn) of a city man and the driver of the wagon not knowing who or what the passenger was and not daring to ask. The street ran into Oklahoma and Missouri and as far south as Mexico and then back north to Chicago and Detroit and then back south again and at last to Mississippi. It was fifteen years long. (223–24)

Although brief, the spatial mapping performed in this passage is significant, allegorically suggesting that the formation of Christmas's identity can only be fully understood within a national and international as well as regional frame. The juxtaposition of different modes of transportation suggests the interlinking of urban and rural spaces. Christmas's identity can thus be read as a composite of rural and urban influences, yet the very metaphor of the continuous street encodes the transformation of the former by the forces of modernization embodied in the latter. The image also suggests the way in which this process of modernization is also a process of nationalization, as the construction of roads to coincide with the advent of the automobile furthered both processes in the twenties and thirties.

The passage allies Joe with the street and with various forms of transportation, suggesting that he can be read in part as an allegory for modernization itself. The passage represents his movement and illegibility as both threat and possibility, echoing what David Harvey has described as modernization's ambivalent promise of destructive creativity and creative destruction.[36] His racial indeterminacy and the various racialized and gendered fantasies that the text constructs around this indeterminacy are, in turn, linked to this allegorization. An ambiguous figure in a changing landscape, Joe is presented as both uncoded ("the driver of the wagon not knowing who or what the passenger was") and recoded as the passage constructs him in terms of the emergent, racialized identities of the hard-boiled male (he is described as "having the still hard face and clothes . . . of a city man") and the autonomous black migrant who, in part because of the nationalization of industry created by the First World War, is able to move from job to job and is no longer strictly tied to a semiautonomous Southern regional economy: "he was in turn laborer, miner, prospector, gambling tout; he enlisted in the army, served four months and deserted and was never caught" (224). It is these contradictory forms of racialized masculinity that Joe uncannily embodies for many of the residents of Jefferson and which they attempt to disavow in their encounters with him.

The town's double disavowal of an autonomous black masculinity and an urban white masculinity suggests a phantasmatic linkage between the construction and representation of the two, a linkage that the novel as a whole bears out. The novel's engagement with the cluster of racialized fantasies that circulate around the figure of the hard-boiled male forms the central locus of this linkage, shaping its portrayal of the different forms of racialized masculinity embodied by Joe and the different relationships to processes of modernization that these suggest.

Joe's identification with the iconography of hard-boiled masculinity is initially established in a passage in which Joe's Calvinist stepfather, McEachern, discovering that his business in town will necessitate eating lunch there, reluctantly takes the young Joe to a house of prostitution in order to purchase the cheapest lunch in town. At the house, which doubles as a diner, Joe sees a group of men who look like none he has ever encountered before: "The men were not in overalls and they all wore hats, and their faces were all alike: not young and not old; not farmers and not townsmen either. They looked like people who had just got off a train and who would be gone tomorrow and who did not have any address" (174). This passage echoes the first description we are given of Joe, suggesting that the older Joe has internalized the masculinity that these men embody. Like the adult Joe, these men appear to be drifters with no known address. Defined by the narrator in terms of what they are not, the men appear alien and indecipherable to the young Joe, much as he will appear in later years to the workers in the Jefferson mill. Yet, while the men are defined negatively, there are hints in the passage as to what has shaped their identity. Since their appearance conforms neither to the codes of dress and behavior associated with the town nor to those associated with the countryside, it points to the one space that lies outside both of these localities: the modern city. This urban association is reinforced by their hats, their lack of overalls, and the stereotyped sameness of their faces—a sameness that carries connotations of the homogenizing effects of mass culture. In sum, the passage presents these men as embodying the fantasy of hard-boiled masculinity.[37]

Within the terms of the town's fantasy, the coding of these men in relationship to a form of masculinity associated with pulp magazines functions negatively to associate them with the amoral encroachment of modernity into the traditional space of the town. However, if we read this passage against the fantasy of the town, the men also represent the phantasmatic power of mass culture to shape and transform everyday life. For the stereotyped quality of the men suggests the way in which they have conformed to an image repertoire derived from mass culture itself. Like Joe reading the pulp, the men have been transformed into the very images that they consume. This transformative power is presented as liberating as well as constraining, for while the men may appear stereo-typed, the conformity implied by this sameness represents a transforma-tion of the constraints and conformities of the town and countryside, symbolized here by the contrasting uniform of overalls.

It is important to underscore that the description of these men is constructed through the lens of fantasy—a fantasy that not only shapes Joe's memory of his youth but also organizes a larger set of cultural and regional investments. For, as we have seen, the workers of Jefferson pro-ject many of the same phantasmatic associations onto the adult Joe. The insistence in both passages on the foreignness and indecipherability of hard-boiled masculinity suggests that the fantasy is organized around a logic of disavowal. While the men may have traveled to the town by train from various locations, urban and otherwise, they are a defining and permanent feature of the town. Yet in order for the town to maintain its fantasy of existing as a self-contained, traditional community, this house of prostitution and the forms of masculinity found within it must be constructed as an alien incursion, one alternately and somewhat contra-dictorily associated with a dangerously itinerate class and an emergent form of urban masculinity. A disavowed and censured subjectivity, the masculinity represented by these men becomes an attractive site for trans-gressive identification for all those who wish to rebel against the antmod-ernist ethos of the town. Joe is no exception; the form of masculinity represented by the men becomes the perfect locus of identification for the young Joe. It allows him to enact an individualist rebellion against the antimodernist morality embodied by the town's leading male citizens while maintaining a masculine site of identification.

Joe's identification with the fantasy of hard-boiled masculinity em-bodied by these men is confirmed a few pages later as his first percep-tions of the establishment's proprietor mix with an account of how Joe later will adopt the same mannerisms:

> He was not a big man, not much bigger than Joe himself, with a
> cigarette burning in one corner of his mouth as though to be out of the
> way of talking. From that face squinted and still behind curling smoke

from the cigarette which was not touched once with hand until it
burned down and was spat out and ground beneath a heel, Joe was to
acquire one of his own mannerisms. But not yet. That was to come later,
when life had begun to go so fast that accepting would take the place of
knowing and believing. (178)

Corresponding to Joe's essential build and possessing the mannerisms
that Joe will soon adopt, the proprietor functions, in part, as Joe's double. Yet this doubling is displaced through time. Rather than mirroring
what Joe already is, the proprietor appears to reflect what Joe will
become. He is, if I may be permitted the pun, the ghost of Christmas
future. His function as an augur of Christmas's future is reinforced by
the narrative's mixing of temporal registers, so that retrospective descriptions of Joe's remembered experience blend seamlessly with accounts of
his future, a future that corresponds to the novel's temporal present. A
modernist break with the illusion of sequential time that characterizes
most realist and pulp narratives, this mixing of temporal registers initially
seems to present the future as predetermined. Yet it also can be read as
employing the irruption of the fictional past and future into the fictional
present to complicate the ontological status of each and to call attention
to the way in which the realist or pulp narrative is organized around a
similar logic of predetermination, in which the illusion of open-ended
sequential time central to the realist novel is belied by the inevitability
of its ending. The passage's engagement with issues of temporality recalls
the engagement with similar questions in the scene of Joe reading the
pulp. Indeed, this scene echoes the earlier scene in a number of ways.
Joe reads the proprietor just as if he were a character in a pulp magazine—seeing in him an ideal type, worthy of imitation. But just as in the
earlier scene, this process of inscription and internalization (with its
suggestion of a predetermined outcome) is mediated by the process of
reading and the possibilities for critical agency that this suggests. The
proprietor represents Joe's future only to the degree that their readings
of the fantasy overlap. Conversely, the way in which they will work
through or against the fantasy will differ to the degree that their readings differ. Thus the scene presents both the power of mass cultural fantasy to produce identification and the power of subjective interpretation
(what I have been calling "reading") to critically shape and engage this
identification.

The dialectical relationship between phantasmatic identification and
its critical elaboration is central to the way in which the racial fantasies
attaching to Joe intermix with the fantasy of hard-boiled masculinity. As

we have already begun to see, Joe's racial identity fluctuates ambiguously over the course of the novel, the signifiers white, black, and mulatto attaching to him in unstable and never fully convincing ways. While Joe is partly constrained by others' fantasies of his racial identity (a constraint that grows as the novel progresses, culminating in the scene of his castration and death, which can be read as a final violent attempt to "fix" the meaning of his identity once and for all), he also provides conflicting and contradictory self-definitions at various points in the novel.

Contradictory in terms of racial coding, these moments of self-definition are consistent in defining Joe in opposition to those around him. Joe employs racial discourse not as a means of blending in with those around him but as a means to stand out. He thus effectuates a form of what I want to term "anti-passing," calling attention to what he constructs or what is constructed by others as his racial difference. After sleeping with white prostitutes, he defines himself as black in order get out of paying for their services, even when this means he will be beaten up and run out of town as a result (224–25). Similarly, through the novel's intermittent use of free indirect discourse, he defines himself (or is defined) as the first white person to cross the threshold of Joanna Burden's house in over twenty-five years, in implicit contrast to the Negroes who cross it daily (259). These moments of anti-passing depend, in turn, on a previous instance of passing. It is only because the prostitutes assume he is white that he can in turn disrupt the transaction by asserting his blackness. Similarly, it is only because he functions as ambiguously distinct from the white community of the town (a distinctness that is constructed as foreign but is always implicitly racialized as well) that he would venture out to the Burden household, which has been shunned by all white members of the community for years. These moments of anti-passing thus emerge as a kind of insistence on the difference that is threatened by the incorporative logic of passing. They perform a radical refusal of community or commonalty, and as such call attention not only to the constructedness of race but also to the fantasy of the homogeneous community itself. For it is only by a process of collective erasure of differences that a fantasy of homogeneity is produced in the first place, just as the fantasy of difference is produced in part by the erasure of commonalities. This erasure of differences is produced not only through a constant policing of the phantasmatic and geographic borders of the community but also through a process of willed ignorance (what in psychoanalytic terms would be described as a disavowal), in which difference is insistently rendered nonvisible or incoherent. We have already seen this process at work in Byron's account of the town's initial perceptions of Joe—the aspects of Joe's identity that potentially do not match the millworkers' fantasy of their homogenous collective identity appear as opaque or are grouped under the unspecific and less threatening signifier, "foreign." Joe's insistence on his difference through the dynamic of anti-passing thus disrupts their willed ignorance, calling attention to the forms of difference that the town has attempted to disavow.

However, it is not merely difference, but antagonistic difference, that is inscribed by these moments of anti-passing. "Sometimes [Joe] would remember how he had once tricked or teased white men into calling him a negro in order to fight them, to beat them or be beaten; now he fought the negro who called him white" (225). Joe's reaction is equally aggressive toward those who define him as different as it is toward those who define him as similar, suggesting that it is the power of self-definition (or perhaps more precisely the fantasy of self-definition) that he is attempting to preserve.

The dynamic of anti-passing, with its challenge to definitions of community and its relationship to ideas of self-definition, can thus be read as enacting a complicated series of fantasies in relation to processes of modernization. As discussed above, Joe, as an emblem for various forms of cultural mixing, allegorizes the threat modernization poses to the antimodernist morality of many of Jefferson's residents. As a sexually promiscuous bootlegger of indeterminate racial status, Joe functions as an almost hyperbolic embodiment of the various ways of life and threats to purity censured by Southern antimodernists in the twenties and thirties. Joe's embodiment of all of the town's worst fears can be read in itself as a form of anti-passing. By methodically embracing all that the town rejects, Joe defines himself against the ethos of the community, refusing homogenization. The racialized identity that is both imposed on Joe and embraced by him at the end of the novel merely literalizes the conceptual anti-passing that he has already been enacting. This anti-passing, with its refusal of antimodernist definitions of morality and community, enacts a phantasmatic embrace of the modern. Yet this embrace of the modern remains ambiguous. For the dynamic of anti-passing, in its refusal of homogeneity and its individualist opposition to the dominant order, also can be read as enacting a corollary series of antimodernist fantasies, in which the individual is defined in opposition to the standardization and massification of everyday life.

The phantasmatic dimensions of these moments of anti-passing, with their contradictory relationship to modernization, overlap with the cultural fantasies that shape hard-boiled masculinity. Like Jake and the Op, Joe attempts to distinguish himself from both the community and the

larger society of which he is a part and, like the Op, he does this in explicitly antagonistic terms. In this way, Joe uses his ambiguous positioning within racial discourse to effectuate the individualist rebellion against
the social order that is one of the defining features of hard-boiled masculinity. His use of race to effectuate this individualist rebellion makes
explicit the racial borrowing that informs the construction of hard-boiled
masculinity and that structures the negativity of the noir narrative. For
it is the ideological figure of the black rapist, so central both to the racial
unconscious of the hard-boiled and noir narrative and to the maintenance
of white supremacy in the South of this period, that the fantasy of hard-
boiled masculinity draws on in constructing its antisocial investments.

There were a number of reasons why this figure was an appealing
site of ambivalent identification within the fantasy of hard-boiled masculinity. For one, it represented a break from the Victorian discourse of
middle-class manliness, with its commitment to the twin moral ideals of
civilization and progress. The transformations produced by the growth
of corporate capitalism, urbanization, and mass culture and by various
social shifts in the definitions of femininity and sexuality caused older
discourses of manhood to appear outmoded. The cultural fantasy of hard-
boiled masculinity emerged as one response to this perceived obsoles-
cence. On one hand, hard-boiled masculinity represented a modernization
of older forms of manhood, one that produced a phantasmatic reconcil-
iation between discourse of masculinity and an increasingly modernized
and instrumentalized world. On the other hand, the fantasy represented
a protest against these very processes of modernization and instrumentalization. Thus the fantasy was not only one of adaptation, in which the
hard-boiled male would become as instrumentalized, streamlined, and
amoral as the modernizing world that surrounds him, but also one of
rebellion against this world and the moral discourses of progress and civilization that continued to justify it.

The figure of the black rapist, then, represented both an amoral form
of masculinity on which the (white) hard-boiled male could model himself in his efforts to adapt to a modernizing world and one that in its
signification as both amoral and primitive opened up a space for protest against that very same world. As we saw in chapter 1, the negativity
of noir, a negativity that takes much of its force from its investment in a
metaphorical and implicitly racialized blackness, emerged in response
to the advent of corporate capitalism and the Taylorist transformation of
work. In its ambivalent rejection of white manhood and the discourse of
civilization that underpins it, the racial borrowing that characterizes the
construction of white hard-boiled masculinity draws on the negative set

of meanings embedded in the noir narrative. Yet this racial borrowing does little to disturb the workings of white supremacy. For while one form of privileged white male subjectivity is being abandoned through cross-racial identification, another one is being forged. The production of this new conception of white masculinity is secured through the disavowal of the very borrowing that enables its emergence.

It is this structure of disavowal that Joe disrupts by explicitly (if ambiguously) embodying the racial borrowing that only remains implicit in most noir and hard-boiled texts. For to the degree that we read Joe as white, his taking on of a Negro identity throughout much of the text literalizes the borrowing that remains implicit and disavowed in other noir narratives. Rather than just borrowing from the racist iconography of black masculinity while insisting on his whiteness, Joe defines himself as black in those moments of borrowing, revealing the dependence of this emergent form of white masculinity on an image of black masculinity to which it is ostensibly opposed.

Similarly by embodying certain fantasies of black masculinity while laying claim to whiteness, Joe performs a form of resistant reverse borrowing. This reverse borrowing refuses the association of black male identity with femininity produced by certain discourses of white supremacy. It instead challenges the dictates of white privilege by simultaneously embodying the opposite white supremacist fantasy of black masculinity as hypermasculine and laying claim to the full manhood that was constructed in the twenties and early thirties as the exclusive province of white men. As historians and theorists of the post-Reconstruction era have argued, the logic of white hegemony maintained contradictory associations of black masculinity with both femininity and hypermasculinity. This contradictory logic fetishistically manifested itself in the fantasies of the feminized "good darky" who knows his place and the hypermasculine black or mulatto beast with an inexhaustible appetite for the rape of white women.[38] Essentially a way of enforcing hierarchy and proscribing behavior, this fetishistic split was organized around the symbolic axis of masculinity. To the degree that black men acquiesced to the economic, political, and social disenfranchisements of the Jim Crow regime, they were relegated to the subordinate but relatively safe role of the good darky. Key to the performance of this proscribed role was the renunciation of any claim to the rights and privileges of manhood, including citizenship, access to the public sphere, and sexual privilege across racial lines. However, if a black man was perceived (or fantasized) as refusing to renounce his claim on manhood or on any of the economic, political, or social privileges accorded to it, the image of the good darky would be replaced by the hypermasculinized image of the black rapist; the disciplinary violence of either the lynch mob or the state judicial system would be called on to forcefully ensure his emasculation.

It is in the context of this constellation of racist and sexist cultural fantasies that Joe's reverse borrowing performs its disruptions. For by simultaneously embodying hypermasculine forms of both black and white masculinity, Joe both draws on the contestatory power encoded in the image of the black rapist while simultaneously refusing its dehumanizing implications by asserting his claim to the privileges of white manhood. However, while this dynamic of reverse borrowing opens up a space to challenge the cultural fantasies that underwrite white supremacy, it is organized by a repudiation of femininity and a phantasmatic logic that replays the masculinism and misogyny of the larger culture.

This repudiation of femininity, and the violent misogyny it underwrites, are evident at a number of points throughout the novel, from Joe's beating of Bobbie to punish her for menstruating to his final killing of Joanna. However, the scene that fundamentally dramatizes the relationship between Joe's violent repudiation of femininity and the larger forms of cultural fantasy about race and gender I have been examining is the scene in which the young Joe assaults a black woman whom he and some other white or white-appearing boys have paid to have sex with:

> His turn came. He entered the shed. It was dark. At once he was overcome by a terrible haste. There was something in him trying to get out, like when he had used to think of toothpaste. But he could not move at once, standing there, smelling the woman smelling the negro all at once; enclosed by the womanshenegro and the haste, driven, having to wait until she spoke: a guiding sound that was no particular word and completely unaware. Then it seemed to him that he could see her— something prone, abject; her eyes perhaps. Leaning, he seemed to look down into a black well and at the bottom he saw two glints like reflections of dead stars. He was moving, because his foot touched her. Then it touched her again because he kicked her. He kicked her hard, kicking into and through a choked wail of surprise and fear. She began to scream, he jerking her up, clutching her by the arm, hitting her with wide, wild blows, striking at the voice perhaps, feeling her flesh anyway, enclosed by the womanshenegro and the haste. (156–57)

On one level this scene must be read straightforwardly as one in which Joe violently asserts the twin privileges of whiteness and masculinity through the violent assault of a black woman. Yet the language of the scene is too phobic for this violence to be merely about privilege. Instead the scene reveals the phobic logic that has historically intertwined with and complicated cultural fantasies of racial and gender privilege in the United States. For the violence of Joe's repudiation of both femininity and blackness is partly motivated by a fear of being defined by them, of being "enclosed" by what he terms "the womanshenegro." This language of enclosure and engulfment is continued in the description of the "black well" Joe sees in her eyes. These images of engulfment and the confla-tion of gynophobia and negrophobia that they perform are repeated at key moments throughout the novel, most notably in a scene in which Joe walks through Freedman Town, the Negro section of Jefferson. He imagines himself "at the bottom of a thick black pit" in which "he and all other manshaped life about him had been returned to the lightless hot wet primogenitive Female" (114–15).

Central to this phobic language of engulfment is the confusion of the boundary between the internal and the external that both passages enact. On his journey through Freedman Town Joe imagines hearing "on all sides, *even within him*, the bodiless fecundmellow voices of negro women" (114, emphasis mine). Similarly, it is unclear whether the "choked wail of surprise and fear" that Joe is "kicking into and through" is the woman's or his own. This blurring of the distinction between internal and external suggests that the femininity and blackness that Joe is repu-diating must finally be located within himself. Indeed, these repudiated materials are described as "something in him trying to get out" and are compared to the toothpaste associated with a female dietitian at the orphanage where Joe is first raised.

At the orphanage, the young Joe initially enjoys ingesting the tooth-paste, its soft pinkness and its association with the dietitian becoming his first symbol of femininity; initially, then, Joe is not defined in oppo-sition to femininity. However, during a scene in which Joe overhears the dietitian being raped, he, in a panic, ingests too much of the toothpaste and then violently throws it up (120–22). While this act initially suggests a continuing empathetic identification with the dietitian, the expelled toothpaste becomes a foundational moment of excorporation, marking the end of his identification with femininity and the beginning of his repudiation of it, since it has now indelibly been associated in his mind with victimhood (a victimhood he could—and in fact does—all too eas-ily share). This association of femininity with victimhood continues throughout the novel, reinforced by, even as it functions as a condensa-tion of, the cultural fantasies that link acquiescent black male identity with femininity and those that define hard-boiled masculinity in oppo-sition to a dangerous and threatening femininity. The culture of white male violence then becomes phantasmatically displaced onto femininity, which is contradictorily constructed as both the locus of victimhood and as a ubiquitous threat.

It is this entire complex of associations that is invoked in the reference to the pink toothpaste in the passage above. Joe's phobic construction in the passage of blackness and femininity as an external threat must, then, be read as a displacement, in which he projects onto the space of the other precisely those characteristics that he has repressed in himself. The description of the black woman as "abject" reinforces this reading, suggesting that Joe's repudiation of blackness and femininity is organized by a phantasmatic logic of abjection, one that is at once subjective and cultural.[39]

The woman thus functions as a return of the repressed for Joe (just as he functions as one for Jefferson), representing precisely the forms of subjectivity that Joe has rejected: femininity and blackness to the degree that is associated with femininity. She also symbolizes the limits of the form of subjective agency that Joe enacts. For, since Joe contests the terms of the definition of manhood in the white supremacist South only from within the masculinist logic of that conception of manhood itself, his agency is premised on a foundational misogyny. Moreover, Joe's murder at the hands of a racist mob, a death made possible in part by his insistence on anti-passing, suggests some of the material limits of the forms of agency he embodies.

Joe's Agency (and Its Limits)

Joe's investment in this masculinist logic, with some notable if only fleeting exceptions, shapes his trajectory throughout the novel, demarcating the horizon of his political and cultural mobility. The relative fixity of Joe's gender identifications stands in contrast to the plasticity of his racial identification. Yet, as I have just demonstrated, the two poles of identification are linked in their very opposition. Joe embodies fantasies of black and white masculinity that share a common phantasmatic core, one organized around a repudiation of femininity and a corollary investment in antagonistic individualism. It is this common core, produced, in part, by the logic of white supremacy itself, that enables Joe to reveal the interdependence of fantasies of masculinity that were imagined in the culture of the interwar South as entirely distinct. Yet Joe does not merely reveal the interdependence of fantasies of white and black masculinity but also underscores the ways in which this interdependence reveals contradictions within the two forms of masculinity themselves.

In thus employing the work of cultural fantasy against itself, Joe's movements open up a space for a critical engagement with the culture that formed him. What I have termed various acts of subjective reading rescript the writing produced by the larger culture and political economy in which he is situated. And while Joe does not critically engage his gender identifications in the same manner that he engages his racial identifications, the novel suggests that such an engagement is possible. As I suggested above, Joe's identification with masculinity seems to be predicated on an initial identification with femininity, an identification that is recounted in Joe's earliest memories ("he was too young yet to escape from the world of women," 121). The malleability of Joe's gender investments is further suggested by consensual sexual role playing in which gender roles are sometimes exchanged ("it was like she was the man and I was the woman") that informs one pole of his relationship to Joanna Burden, a pole that can be read in opposition to the misogynist violence that finally concludes their involvement (261).

Thus the novel points toward the possibilities of transformation as well as reiteration enabled by the workings of cultural fantasy. This productive relationship to fantasy emerges in part through the novel's positive, as well as negative, engagement with mass cultural forms such as the pulp story, suggesting a very different understanding of the relationship between modernism and mass culture from the one shared by the most influential schools of modernist criticism. *Light in August* represents the power of mass cultural fantasies to mobilize identifications that can work against and not only with forms of cultural hegemony, thus opening up spaces for resistance as well as repetition, transformation as well as reiteration.

In order to achieve this complex representation of hegemony, Faulkner's novel draws equally on the metatextual and epistemological concerns of high modernism and the materialism and engagement with forms of cultural fantasy that characterize the pulp novel. It is only by mixing these generic and cultural forms that Faulkner's novel is able to provide a nuanced representation of both the possibilities and limits of individual agency in a world defined by the massive economic and cultural transformations produced by modernization and the growth of mass culture. In the next chapter I will turn to a novel that marks more fully the limits of the type of individual agency I have traced here, Chester Himes's *If He Hollers Let Him Go*. Without a larger transformation in the structures of collective fantasy, Himes suggests, individual forms of phantasmatic working through remain largely powerless to affect the workings of cultural power.

5
Freudian Knot or Gordian Knot?

> But it's a Freudian knot, not a Gordian knot, son.
> —*Chester Himes,* The End of a Primitive

Himes's Transgressive Aesthetic

The novels of Chester Himes resist easy categorization. Occupying a contradictory yet overlapping series of borderzones between high and popular culture, noir and hard-boiled fiction, the political and the psychological, modernism and postmodernism, social protest literature and expatriate modernism, African American and Anglo-American literary traditions, Himes's novels seem designed to disturb received notions of both canonicity and literary propriety. Officially, his writings can be split between the detective fiction written for the famous French detective imprint *Série Noire* and his more properly "literary" endeavors. Yet as soon as one begins to look closely at the novels themselves this generic distinction begins to collapse. Filled with the stuff of pulp and popular fiction—lurid crimes, illicit sexuality, populist anti-intellectualism, and the narrativization of popular fantasy—Himes's "literary" works transgress the boundaries of the literary itself. Similarly, Himes's detective fictions are often read as elaborate postmodern allegories or cosmic jokes of the type commonly associated with putatively high-cultural writers such as Thomas Pynchon and Don DeLillo. The contradictions of Himes's fiction do not end at the level of its generic transgressions. Rather these disruptions, and the formal contradictions they enact, form part of a more general will to transgress that shapes the themes and content of Himes's fiction fully as much as its form. Himes's novels are designed to shock or disturb, producing narratives that not only resist categorization but also

143

flaunt conventional morality and eschew easy recuperation by any single ethical or political position.

Interestingly, unlike those of many of his transgressive contemporaries (and here I am thinking of Jim Thompson and Patricia Highsmith as much as William Burroughs or Thomas Pynchon), Himes's novels have lost none of their ability to shock. They remain thoroughly disturbing reads.[1] This ability of Himes's fiction to elude the limited shelf life of most forms of literary transgression speaks to the continuing volatility of the subject at the center of many of his most transgressive texts: black/white sexual relations, specifically that most taboo of heterosexual, miscegenous relationships, sex between a white woman and a black man. Yet the transgression does not end with the mere representation of this relationship, for in Himes's fiction this relationship—whether consensual or nonconsensual—is conceived as violent. The explicit subject of Himes's fiction is thus the fantasy that lies buried in the heart of noir and hard-boiled fiction: the fantasy of violent, racialized sexual and political transgression.

On one level the representation of this violent fantasy may seem less genuinely transgressive, merely repeating the racist and sexist fantasies that formed the meat and potatoes of the postwar cultural imaginary. On another level, however, Himes' insistence on the violence of these encounters foregrounds, on the most intimate of intersubjective terrains, the simultaneously sexual and political libidinal aggressivity that is the inevitable product of this cultural imaginary. In this way, texts like *The End of a Primitive* and the text that will form the central subject of this chapter, *If He Hollers Let Him Go*, hold up a funhouse mirror to the racial and sexual imaginary of postwar American culture, reflecting back, in distorted and often parodic ways, the already fantastic sexual fantasies of a white-supremacist American culture. Himes is thus holding up his own funhouse mirror to another funhouse mirror—that of the racist and sexist cultural fantasies that shaped everyday American life in the forties and fifties. The distortions produced by this process seem at certain points corrective and at other points conducive to further, hyperbolic distortions.

This mix of the hyperbolic and corrective, the fantastic and the realistic, yet another site of stylistic transgression in Himes's fiction, contributes to the wildly divergent critical assessments of his work as well as to his exclusion, until recently, from the canons of both African American and American fiction. For to the degree that Himes is read as a writer of realist or social protest fiction, a mode of reading that as Henry Louis Gates Jr. points out has formed a litmus test for the canonical value of texts written by African Americans, his disturbing and almost gleefully nonredemptive representations of the violent intersectionality of race, gender, and sexuality have, until recently, made his novels nearly impervious to critical recuperation for the African American canon.[2] On the other hand, the realist elements in Himes's fiction, elements that indeed link him ambiguously to a tradition of social protest literature, bar its easy inclusion in what was at the time the emergent practice of transgressive postmodern writing. Thus Himes's novels haunt the uneasy borderlands between the realist and the experimental, the mimetic and the fantastic, the explicitly political and the seemingly absurd, and so they remain largely outside both the conventional American and African American canons.[3]

There is evidence, however, that this state of affairs is changing. After a long period in which very few of his texts were available, in the past fifteen years almost all of Himes's texts have returned to print. An analogous revival of critical interest has emerged, evidenced by, for example, the rapidly expanding number of articles appearing on Himes in the Modern Language Association database; a panel dedicated to his work at a meeting of the American Studies Association; the publication of two new biographies; and the inclusion of his *The Real Cool Killers* in the recent Library of America volume, *Crime Novels: American Noir of the 1950s*.[4]

The reemergence of Chester Himes as a writer of cultural interest has paralleled, perhaps not coincidentally, the rise of theories of intersectionality in the contemporary academy. The concept of intersectionality emerged out of the epistemological challenges produced by attempting to think simultaneously through multiple forms of difference, oppression, and subjectivity. Theories of intersectionality have attempted to provide a language for theorizing the intersections of race, class, gender, sexuality, and economics in the formation of individual and collective subjects. This theoretical innovation appeared initially within the fields of critical race theory and critical legal studies as a way of conceptualizing the multiple structural and discursive marginalizations experienced by women of color. As Kimberlé Williams Crenshaw puts it in her foundational article on the subject, "Mapping the Margins: Intersectionality, Identity Politics, and Violence against Women of Color," the concept of intersectionality enables the exploration of the "various ways in which race and gender intersect in shaping structural, political and representational aspects of violence against women of color" (358).[5] It is significant to note that Crenshaw's initial formulation of the term emerged in the context of theorizing forms of violence. For as the term has gained a wide academic currency in the last ten years as a means of theorizing multiply situated subjectivities and their relationship to cultural power,

Crenshaw's initial focus on the relationship between violence and intersectionality has been somewhat obscured.

Rethinking intersectionality through the lens of Himes's writings importantly restores Crenshaw's initial focus on the relationship between intersectionality and violence: in Himes's fiction intersectionality is almost always represented as violent or, at the very least, as a potential site of violence. Yet the representation of intersectionality that emerges from Himes's fiction also differs in important ways from even Crenshaw's initial formulation. It is, if anything, cast in even more negative terms. Himes represents sites of intersection as locations of negation in American culture, forming the fissures and uncanny contiguities through which the violence central to the maintenance of an unequal and exploitative culture plays itself out in ways intimate and social, individual and collective. These forms of intersectionality are experienced as an intrasubjective dynamic of psychic negation or division as much as an intersubjective one, modeled on the experience of subjective negation that Frantz Fanon describes as central to the experience of racism. Fanon describes the black subject's experience of racism in a white world as a negation of subjectivity that seals him or her into "crushing objecthood."[6] Himes's fiction suggests that objectification and negation are the experience of the marginalized at sites of intersection in American culture, whether these sites are out in the world or internalized within the psyche. In its emphasis on negativity, a work like *If He Hollers Let Him Go* draws on the forms of phantasmatic negativity encoded in noir and in noir-inflected forms such as the hard-boiled narrative. Himes's fiction makes explicit not only the racialized dimensions of noir but also the ways in which these racialized dimensions are saturated with phantasmatic negativity, a negativity that is available, as we will see, for a range of political meanings.

It is the representation of intersectionality as negation that forms the core of Himes's engagement with the noir aesthetic and, I would suggest, ensures the continuing capacity of his fiction to disturb. In tracing Himes's representation of negative intersectionality in *If He Hollers Let Him Go*, I want to argue that it has much to teach us about what is missing from most current theorizations of the intersections of race, gender, class, and sexuality in American culture. In advancing this argument, I will be brushing against the grain of most of the recent scholarship on Himes, which tends to deemphasize or minimize the violent and disturbing aspects of his fiction. I want to suggest that it is when his fiction is at its most disturbing that it has the most to teach us about thinking through and working through the polarities that organize the American cultural landscape.

The lessons that Himes's negativity has to offer are twofold: the first negative and the second, paradoxically, positive. First, his representation of violent intersectionality challenges the emphasis on positive representation found in much contemporary progressive scholarship. As Wahneema Lubiano has pointed out, to the degree that radical and progressive political change is conceived of as solely a question of transforming representation, such a politics is easily and readily appropriable by the liberal state.[7] We instead need to theorize, I would argue, the dynamic relationships between representations and material forms of culture, subjective forms of fantasy, and the larger political economy in which they are embedded. Indeed, forms of negative representation, such as Himes's, to the degree they are less appropriable and inscribe in the aesthetic realm cultural conflicts that we in our deeply and violently idealist society attempt to purge from the space of representation, represent in many ways a greater challenge to business as usual in the United States than an entire syllabus of positive and reassuringly contained representations of cultural diversity. In this way, Himes's fiction demonstrates the value of both theorizing and tarrying with the negative in analyzing the violent contradictions that organize American society.[8]

Second, Himes's representation of violent intersectionality suggests the importance of recognizing and working through the negative in attempting to construct a positive political program. It is only after we recognize and work through the negative as it shapes the relationship of individual and collective subjectivities to forms of economic, political, and cultural power that we can begin to think about an effective coalitional and liberatory politics. The negativity of Himes's fiction thus underscores the representational and political limits of a purely discursive understanding of cultural power, suggesting instead the need to understand the violent intersectionalities of American life as produced by both phantasmatic and material contradictions, or, as he puts it in the epigraph to this chapter, by both Freudian and Gordian Knots.

The Black Hard-Boiled Male

It is this dialectic between the negative and positive dimensions of negative representation that shapes the construction of hard-boiled masculinity in *If He Hollers Let Him Go*. In order to understand fully the positive potential embedded in Himes's embrace of negative representation, we must return to the broader discussion that animates *Hard-Boiled Masculinities* as a whole. It is only by considering the forms of masculine subjectivity narrated in the hard-boiled genre and the ways these intersect with the workings of cultural fantasy that, for the reader, Himes's negative representation takes on a set of culturally specific meanings.[9]

Himes was a regular reader of pulp fiction. He subscribed to *Black Mask* while serving a prison sentence for armed robbery in the thirties, the years of publication of his first short stories. When Himes turned to writing detective fiction in the fifties, he reread Hammett, Chandler, and Faulkner's *Sanctuary* and *Light in August* for inspiration. This sustained engagement with hard-boiled and hard-boiled-influenced fiction is evident everywhere throughout his writings. Almost all of Himes's fiction contains hard-boiled elements, including a terse, laconic prose style and a representation of masculine subjectivity that corresponds in its essential features to what I have been calling hard-boiled masculinity.[10] Moreover, certain texts, including *If He Hollers Let Him Go* and all the Harlem detective novels, are written explicitly in the style of the noir or hard-boiled novel.[11]

The positive work enabled by Himes's embrace of negative representation emerges most clearly in relationship to hard-boiled fiction and the forms of masculinity narrated by the genre. For his fiction can be read, in part, as a desublimation of the cultural fantasies that animate the hard-boiled narrative and the broader fictions of American culture from which this form gains much of its vitality and appeal.[12] Himes's fiction literalizes the racial borrowing at the heart of the noir aesthetic in a manner similar to Faulkner's desublimation of the same dynamic in *Light in August*. However, as I demonstrate in chapter 4, Faulkner foregrounds the interdependence of fantasies of black and white masculinity by making Joe Christmas's racial identity finally unknowable. Himes, in contrast, literalizes the borrowing by making his hard-boiled protagonists unambiguously black. By changing the subject-position of the protagonist, he not only underscores the dependence of the two fantasies of masculinity on each other but also transforms the ideological and narrative coordinates of the pulp forms with which he works. For the African American hard-boiled male cannot function in the same largely unmarked manner as his white counterpart. This inability to occupy an unmarked position transforms the mode of narration characteristic of much hard-boiled fiction. This transformation is especially notable in *If He Hollers Let Him Go*, which is written in the classic first-person style of most hard-boiled fiction, in contrast to the Harlem detective novels, which are written in the third person. Functioning as a racially marked subject in a white supremacist culture, Himes's protagonist, Bob Jones, can no longer maintain his fantasy of detached objectivity and dispassionate observation. He is clearly not only the subject of the gaze but also its object, and as such he becomes objectified as well as formed subjectively through the lens of various forms of cultural fantasy. [13]

The racialized protagonist's double role as both subject and object of the gaze transforms the cultural fantasy of hard-boiled masculinity.[14] The representation of masculinity in hard-boiled fiction enacts a phantasmatic resolution between American discourses of masculine individualism, on the one hand, and a newly corporatized, collectivized, and rationalized socioeconomic world, on the other. The narrative subjectivity constructed by the hard-boiled text's first-person narration is key to achieving this resolution: through the detached, affectless narration the hard-boiled male is imagined as embodying a subjectivity as rationalized and instrumentalized as the Taylorized world in which he operates. Yet even as the hard-boiled male's subjectivity reflects this new world, he is crucially imagined as its subject rather than its object. His consciousness and gaze are presented as rational and controlling, shaping both the terms of the narrative and much of the story's action, in contrast to the objectified others with whom he interacts and who become the fantasized bearers of all the affect that the protagonist has purged from his narrative consciousness.

This narrative dynamic and the fantasy of masculine subjectivity it underwrites become disrupted in Himes's narratives. For the double role of the African American hard-boiled protagonist as both subject and object of the gaze renders impossible to sustain the fantasy of detached and dispassionate subjectivity. Rather than allowing it to become a formal limitation, Himes employs this narrative impossibility as a means to further desublimate the fantasy investments that organize the hard-boiled and noir forms. In place of the cool detached narration of the Continental Op or Race Williams, we are presented with Bob Jones's passionate, affect-laden narration. The affect purged from the narrative consciousness and projected onto others in the conventional hard-boiled narrative is thus returned to the consciousness of the narrator, who symbolizes many of the aggressive and fearful impulses that are merely acted out in other hard-boiled texts.[15]

This symbolization of affect forms a key aspect of Himes's embrace of the forms of negative representation associated with noir, for it is through representing the unacceptable wishes, desires, and fears of his protagonists that his transgressive aesthetic is formed. Paradoxically, this form of negative representation and the forms of fantasy work it enables allow the narrative to suggest the positive possibility of constructing an ethical masculine subjectivity that contrasts in important ways with the dominant representation of hard-boiled masculinity.[16] This possibility is enabled by the work of desublimation undertaken by the novel, a work that is in turn enabled by Himes's initial act of desublimation: writing a noir narrative with a hard-boiled African American protagonist.

Much of Himes's fiction undertakes the work of desublimation, representing the narrative impulses and affective investments that remain unacknowledged or disavowed in most cultural narratives, literary or otherwise. In an interview with John Williams, Himes articulated the desire to write in a style that would allow the unconscious of a given character to be transferred directly to the page without mediation or censorship.[17] This impulse toward desublimation and disclosure informs the political stakes of Himes's transgressive aesthetic and his embrace of negative representation. By representing many of the unacceptable wishes and unacknowledged traumas that shape cultural fantasies about the intersections of race, gender, class, sexuality, and economics in the United States, the text enables the reader to engage in a kind of fantasy work, recognizing or disavowing his or her relationship to these wishes and traumas.

This cultural practice is modeled in *If He Hollers Let Him Go*, which presents a disjunction between the protagonist's fantasies and his actions. This disjunction is represented as opening up a space for subjective working through, in which the symbolization of fantasies and affect can enable individual subjects to move beyond the compulsion to repeat cultural fantasies on the level of action. But the novel also marks the material limits of this practice of subjective working through, at least when it is undertaken as a form of individual, rather than collective, practice. In representing the forces that constrain his protagonist, Himes thus constructs a model of power that takes into account both the phantasmatic and the material. As I have already suggested, the knots of contradiction and power in Himes's text are both Freudian and Gordian, requiring a praxis of both working through and cutting through.

This elaboration of the relationship between fantasy and action, the phantasmatic and the material, the psychological and the sociological, while present to some degree in all of Himes's texts, is particularly rich in *If He Hollers Let Him Go*. One reason for that richness is the text's reworking of the first-person narration of the hard-boiled and psychological noir forms in relationship to a racially marked protagonist.

Historicizing Himes's novel in relationship to the broad cultural and political shifts that occurred between the radical thirties and the cold-war fifties suggests another. Published in 1945, Himes's novel appears at a midway point in the transition from the radical cultural practices that Michael Denning terms "the cultural front" to the conservative constraints of cold-war culture that Alan Nadel names "containment culture."[18] While Denning's and Nadel's revisionist histories both overlap and contradict each other to a certain extent, the former providing a bottom-up, Gramscian account of cultural resistance and contestation, the latter constructing a top-down model of cultural constraint and complicity, the two accounts can also be read as complementing each other. Denning's long thirties and Nadel's long fifties not only represent different cultural moments but also warring tendencies within the same cultural moment.

As my own contribution to these differing revisionist histories, I want to suggest that we can see a broad shift in cultural narratives from the sociological to the psychological in the transition from the thirties to the fifties, with both here conceived as ideologico-cultural formations as much as distinct historical periods. In broad terms this shift can be read in terms of the common-sense narrative of the move from radical to conservative cultural politics. But such an understanding remains persuasive only if we leave intact the divide between the sociological and the psychological, the dismantling of which is the central theoretical project of *Hard-Boiled Masculinities*. Read through the psycho-Marxist paradigm that organizes my argument, the shift becomes a more ambivalent one, opening up the possibility of certain forms of political and cultural work, even as it has the potential to close down other ones. Thus, as I argue in chapter 2, the disavowal of the psychological and affective dimensions of culture in *Red Harvest* and other classic hard-boiled texts (dimensions they inherited from what I term the "psychological noir") limits the political efficacy of their seemingly radical sociological representations.[19] In contrast, noir and hard-boiled narratives of the fifties by the likes of Jim Thompson, Patricia Highsmith, and Himes himself present the affective and psychological dimensions of culture with much greater complexity, critically reanimating the forms of psychological negativity central to the psychological noir. The same divide can be seen to function when we situate Himes's novel in relationship to the two canonical pillars of midcentury African American fiction, Richard Wright's *Native Son*, published in 1940, and Ralph Ellison's *Invisible Man*, published in 1951. The broad political and social agenda and truncated character development of Wright's social-realist narrative is replaced by Ellison's stream-of-consciousness and surrealist account of his protagonist's resolutely individualist negotiation of the absurdity of race in the United States. As Nadel suggests, we can read the psychologized narratives of the fifties (especially when read in conjunction with early postmodernist fiction) as pointing toward postmodern forms of identity and subjectivity politics.

What becomes attenuated in these narratives, however, is the broad social and economic mapping that characterizes the writings of Hammett and his contemporaries. *If He Hollers Let Him Go* appears at a privileged ligature in this shift, in which the sociological critique had not yet been suppressed and the psychological, or to use my term of preference, the phantasmatic, critique was just emerging. What we get in Himes's novel, then, is a historically privileged working through of the relationship between these two modes of mapping the cultural and the political-economic.

An Affective Hard-Boiled Aesthetic

Himes's willful mixing of registers, between the seemingly objective and the affective, the material and the phantasmatic, the private and the public—in sum between Gordian knots and Freudian knots—manifests itself most immediately on the level of style. In contrast to the detached first-person narration conventional to the hard-boiled narrative, Himes writes in a style at once hard-boiled and affect-laden. In this way, his narrative technique constructs a representation of masculinity that differs in important ways from the forms of masculinity imagined in the fiction of Hammett, Daly, and other hard-boiled writers. In my analysis of *Red Harvest* in chapter 2, I argue that the hard-boiled story is organized around a form of paratactic, first-person narration that strives for an objective and detached description of events. This narration produces as its inevitable uncanny double a libidinally charged textual economy in which the affect purged from the text's first-person narration either becomes acted out— rather than symbolized—by the protagonist or becomes projected onto various racialized and sexualized others. In Himes's narrative this process is partly undone. While Bob Jones' narration retains the cynicism and the parataxis characteristic of the hard-boiled form, as well as many of the subjective investments that conventionally accompany this narration, including misogyny, individualism, and a homosociality that is alternately violently competitive and affectionately fraternal, it also becomes a vehicle for symbolizing Bob's affective investments in a manner that breaks in significant ways from conventional hard-boiled narration.

Himes's simultaneous adherence to and break from hard-boiled form are evident in a passage in which Bob Jones wakes from a series of disturbing dreams:

> Suddenly I came awake. For a time I lay there without thought, suspended in a vacancy. There was no meaning to anything; I didn't even remember having dreamed.

The alarm went off again; I knew then that it had been the alarm that had awakened me. I groped for it blindly, shut it off; I kept my eyes shut tight. But I began feeling scared in spite of hiding from the day. It came along with consciousness. It came into my head first, somewhere back of my closed eyes, moved slowly underneath my skull to the base of my brain, cold and hollow. It seeped down my spine, into my arms, spread through my groin with an almost sexual torture, settled in my stomach like butterfly wings. For a moment I felt torn all loose inside, shriveled, paralyzed, as if after a while I'd have to get up and die.[20]

Himes' investment in the hard-boiled aesthetic and his transformation of it are both evident in this passage. The opening half of the passage reads very much like any other hard-boiled narrative. Bob recounts his waking moments in a terse parataxis that catalogues actions and immediate perceptions rather than feelings or reflections. Similarly, the themes of the first half of the passage are those conventional to the hard-boiled narrative. In contrast to the epistemological certainty embodied by the hero of the classical detective story, Bob, as the hard-boiled protagonist, wakes up, devoid of knowledge, to grope blindly in a world in which "there was no meaning to anything." Immediately, then, the narrative establishes the themes of epistemological and existential uncertainty that are a hallmark of hard-boiled and noir fiction.

Yet this representation of epistemological uncertainty and existential absurdity is quickly replaced by the potentially lethal certainty of fear for a black person in a white-supremacist society. While the world around Bob Jones remains absurd, he cannot simply occupy a privileged position of uncertainty, for he is affectively certain of one thing: that the world in which he lives is organized around negating or subordinating his very existence. The absurdity of this world is specific. It is no longer just the generalized absurdity produced by the dissolution of nineteenth-century forms of scientific certainty; it is also the specific forms of absurdity that Himes, citing Camus, attributes to racism in the opening sentence of the second volume of his autobiography, *My Life of Absurdity*:

Albert Camus once said that racism is absurd. Racism introduces absurdity into the human condition. Not only does racism express the absurdity of the racists, but it generates absurdity in the victims. And the absurdity of the victims intensifies the absurdity of the racists ad infinitum. If one lives in a country where racism is held valid and practiced in all ways of life, eventually, no matter whether one is a racist or a victim, one comes to feel the absurdity of life.[21]

Bob Jones awakens to this absurd condition. His position as a victim of this condition produces a form of abject fear. For Bob is not only a detached subject attempting to make sense of this absurd world; as a victim of this absurdity, he is also objectified by it. As Frantz Fanon puts it in *Black Skin, White Masks*, a text that makes explicit reference to *If He Hollers Let Him Go*, racism renders its victim an "object among objects" (109). Bob fears this objectification and struggles against it for much of the rest of the novel.

Himes's representation of the fear produced by this threat of objectification transforms the conventions of the hard-boiled narrative. Although the passage starts out in conventional hard-boiled form, the introduction of the theme of fear radically transforms both the content and the form of Bob's narration. In contrast to the short, clipped sentences that characterize the opening part of the passage, the sentences in which Bob describes his experience of fear are longer and more drawn out, slowing down the rhythm of the passage to highlight the impact of fear on Bob's consciousness. Similarly, in place of the detached, affectless narration of the conventional hard-boiled narrator, Bob's narration is almost overloaded with affect. He cannot ward off this affect by projecting it onto the outside world; it instead invades his consciousness, threatening to overwhelm him.

Significantly, this threat is presented in explicitly sexualized terms. The fear is described as moving down his body and spreading through his groin with "an almost sexual torture," leaving him "torn loose" and "shriveled" inside. The sexualization of this fear suggests the explicitly sexualized and gendered terms through which white supremacy was perpetuated and maintained in the mid-twentieth-century United States. As Robyn Wiegman has argued, white supremacy in the post-Reconstruction period was organized around a sexualization of political and economic questions and a concomitant rhetoric of manhood (81–133). Manhood and the forms of political citizenship and economic power that it entailed were constructed as the sole province of white men, who were also charged with the duty of protecting white womanhood from a rapacious black male sexuality. The effectiveness of this ideology in organizing political, economic, racial, gender, and sexual relationships in the United States, an effectiveness that was ensured through the constant threat of corporeal violence in the form of lynching and various forms of sanctioned public violence, meant that most challenges to this system were constructed within the very terms of the system itself. Thus Bob Jones challenges the exclusion of black masculinity from white-supremacist definitions of manhood, but in doing so he leaves intact the masculinist logic on which this construction of manhood is founded. Within the masculinist and sexualized logic of white supremacy, the exclusion of black men from definitions of manhood was figured as a form of castration or emasculation, a symbolic construction that was sometimes violently literalized in the practice of lynching. In the context of this overdetermined network of meanings, we must read the representation of Bob as shriveled and torn apart by his fear as an image of castration—one that challenges his claim to manhood. In contrast to the detached and emotionless narration of the white hard-boiled protagonist, Bob's affect-laden narration situates him differently and more precariously in relationship to discourses of manhood. Bob's actions throughout much of the rest of the novel can be partly read as an attempt to ensure his right to lay claim to hard-boiled masculinity and the forms of whiteness and political and economic enfranchisement that it guarantees.

Bob's attempts to successfully negotiate both the forms of cultural fantasy that enmesh him and the relationship of these fantasies to his material actions in the world in which he lives and works become the central dialectic driving the narrative. The narrative presents fantasy and action, the subjective and the material, as deeply intermeshed and importantly distinct. Bob lives in a world in which racist cultural fantasy shapes the terms of his material existence. To take only the most obvious example, one I will return to below, the myth, or fantasy, of the black rapist dictates not only the segregated and unequal terms of Bob's employment but his very existence. In this way, Himes's novel represents the central role that fantasy and affect play in shaping not only intersubjective interactions but the very terms of material existence. The novel can thus be read as a kind of anti-hard-boiled narrative: rather than disavowing the relationship of subjective fantasy to the social, it instantiates its primacy. But this primacy is experienced as a nightmare by Bob, for the larger conflations of fantasy and materiality that shape the terms of his existence also threaten to negate it. In order to survive in this world and to find a viable and even ethical relationship to it, it becomes essential for him to recognize the crucial disjunction between fantasy and action. In order to do this, he must not only recognize the determining role that fantasy plays in the world in which he lives but also symbolize his own investments in these fantasies. Thus rather than conflating fantasy with reality by treating the former as the latter, as does the culture that surrounds him, Bob must recognize the formative nature of fantasy in relation to the material world he inhabits and the crucial disjunction between the two.

American Nightmare

The novel scrupulously maps larger phantasmatic and material coordinates of the landscape through which Bob moves. The former are detailed through a series of dreams that plague Bob before he wakes each morning throughout the five-day period chronicled by the novel. The latter are indicated via Himes's nuanced depiction of wartime Los Angeles, which becomes a synecdoche for the political-economic and cultural conditions of the United States as a whole in the mid-twentieth century. In the next few pages, I will first trace the socioeconomic mapping undertaken by the novel's representation of Los Angeles and then turn to the phantasmatic logic unveiled in Bob's dreams. However, the novel presents the material and the phantasmatic as interpenetrating, rather than as discrete. The relationship of the dream sequences to the rest of the narrative underscores this interpenetration, for Bob's dreams and his waking existence are nearly indistinguishable. If anything, the former represent merely a more succinct distillation, or condensation, of the fantasy logic that governs the latter. The dreams thus serve as both foil and explanation for the world he inhabits.

The novel is set in a wartime Los Angeles that is a contradictory emblem of both racial progress and xenophobic racism.[22] As such, Himes's L.A. becomes a symbol for the larger shift "from a modern racial regime to a postmodern one" that Michael Denning describes as largely taking place during World War II (33). Characterized by the dissolution of most systems of forced labor, the expansion of global labor migration, the rise of American extracontinental imperialism, and the implementation of "modern racial systems with their legal codes of segregation, exclusion, reservations, and anti-miscegenation," the modern racial regime extended from the end of Reconstruction roughly through the beginning of World War II (33). In contrast, the postmodern racial regime, which replaced it and which extends into our own time, is characterized by a "'postmodern rewriting of the color line that derived from new relations to Asia and Latin America," the emergence of powerful new forms of antiracist struggle (including the civil rights movement, movements for racial and economic justice, and various nationalist movements), the eventual institutionalization of forms of legal equality that were usually accompanied by continuing material inequality, and the concomitant shift from overt to covert forms of institutionalized racism (33–34).

As a worker in one of the newly, if only partly, integrated wartime industries, a naval shipyard, Bob exists at ground zero of this transformation. One of the first black leadermen in the Atlas shipyards, Bob is the beneficiary of the hard-won antiracist and prolabor struggles of the CIO and other "cultural front" organizations in the thirties and forties, which, as Nikhil Pal Singh has argued, served as an important, and in many ways more radical, precursor to the civil rights movement of the fifties (473–87).[23] He is also the beneficiary of the wartime need for African American labor in heavy industry and A. Philip Randolph's March on Washington Movement, which forced the Roosevelt administration to end officially sanctioned discrimination in the defense industries. This position enables the formerly working-class Bob to make a tenuous purchase on the middle class, symbolized in the novel most directly by his car: "I had a '42 Buick Roadmaster I'd bought four months ago, right after I'd gotten to be leaderman, and every time I got behind the wheel and looked down the broad, flat, mile-long hood I thought about how the rich white folks out in Beverly couldn't even buy a new car now and got a certain satisfaction" (13). The car is at once a symbol of class ascendancy and a claim staked in the name of racial parity. Bob derives satisfaction from the fact that he can purchase something not currently attainable to some rich whites; for him this is a sign that at least some part of FDR liberalism works according to its newly minted rhetoric of color-blind merit, rather than its ongoing practice of racial inequality. On one level, then, Bob's life reflects the new possibilities opened up by the larger shift from a modern to a postmodern racial regime and by the forms of collective struggle that precipitated this shift.

Yet, on another level, the individualist terms of these possibilities and their tenuousness also mark the ways in which the shift from a modern to a postmodern racial regime in the United States represented a transformation in the terms and organization of white supremacy, rather than its supercession. The retrenchment of racism within the ostensibly more egalitarian war effort is driven home by Himes's narrative. Based in part on Himes's own experiences working in the L.A. shipyards as part of the war effort, *If He Hollers Let Him Go* stands as an important corrective to Denning's and especially Singh's occasionally overly affirmative (though otherwise quite valuable) theorizations of the challenge to white supremacy and capitalist exploitation represented by the multiracial war effort. In contrast to Singh's description of the racial realignments of the forties as (borrowing a phrase from C. Vann Woodward) a "second Reconstruction," Himes presents wartime L.A. as a site of violent racial strife and antagonism—as much a retrenchment of white supremacy as a challenge to it. Moreover, this antagonism is not limited to the Zoot Suit riots and internment of Japanese-Americans but also characterizes working conditions in the newly integrated shipyards and interactions between civilians on the sidewalks and streets of L.A.: "It beat me. I began to feel conspicuous, ill at ease, out of place. It was the white folks' world and they resented me just standing in it" (75).

It is in these public and semipublic spaces that the negative intersectionality foregrounded by Himes's narrative becomes manifest. The parallel situation of black workers and white female workers as newly included and still quite marginalized members of the labor force produces no sense of alliance. Instead, the relationship between the two groups of workers is cast in negative terms: Bob loses his job when he responds to a white female worker, Madge, who has called him a "nigger" by calling her, in turn, a "cracker bitch" (29). When Bob goes to talk to Herbie, the Jewish union steward, about getting his job reinstated, their possible alliance becomes disrupted by warring racisms and conflicting alliances: Bob's anti-Semitism makes Herbie less than willing to go to bat for him, and Herbie's implicitly racist conflation of the workers' interests with those of the white workers negates any feeling of pro-union solidarity that Bob might feel (105–8).[24]

The novel's mapping of the social and economic conditions that characterized wartime Los Angeles and, by extension, the wartime United States is complemented by its mapping of the forms of fantasy and affect that shape intersubjective relationships within the domain of the social. This fantasy mapping is performed in part through Bob's nightmares, which in their indistinguishability from Bob's waking existence ironically underscore the intertwining of fantasy and materiality in his world. The novel's sociopolitical and socioeconomic mapping of the intersection of white supremacy with the wartime economy is mirrored, in condensed form, in Bob's second dream. The dream also records the forms of affect that the contradictions produced by this intersection generate in Bob. Bob dreams that he is being brutally beaten with a rubber hose by "two poor peckerwoods" in front of the Los Angeles Federal Building (67). The latter begin to take pity on him and question the morality and necessity of the beating but when they try to stop, they are ordered to continue by "the president of the shipyard corporation dressed in the uniform of an army general" who is flanked by policemen (67). The beating is interrupted by "two old colored couples in working clothes" who look at the "peckerwoods with dull hatred" (68). The shipyard president smiles at the black couples and says, "'There should be something done about this. . . . All of us responsible white people are trying to keep these things from taking place but you boys must help us'" (68). The dream ends with Bob unable to speak and the black couples looking at the shipyard president "as if he were a good, kind god" (68).

This dream sequence narrates in condensed form the power relationships that organize the novel as a whole. Indeed, in many ways the dream constructs a clearer picture of these relationships than Bob's waking narrative. In contrast to the immediacy of affect and antagonism in his waking narration, Bob's dream mediates these immediate forms of antagonism by marking them as ideological instances within a broader account of political and economic power. While in his waking narrative Bob's relationship to white workers is constructed along the lines of pure antagonism, in the dream the antagonism between him and the white working-class men (or "peckerwoods") is figured as ideologically reproducing the interests of the state (represented in the dream by the policemen) and the emerging military-industrial complex (invoked, in a particularly apt condensation, by the shipyard owner dressed in the uniform of a general). In this way, Bob's dream articulates the possibility of working through the immediate forms of affect produced by negative intersectionality as the first step toward producing more politically productive alliances and forms of affect.

The relationship between class and race mapped by the dream corresponds in its essential components to Nikhil Pal Singh's account of the relationship between racial formation and class formation in U.S. history. The historical divisions and confluences between working-class whites and working-class blacks are central to Singh's account, providing the logic by which hegemony is challenged or reproduced in a culture that is at once capitalist and white supremacist. The alliances of the thirties and forties represent the reemergence of a coalitional politics that had its first articulation in the union organizing of the Knights of Labor and the early Populist alliances of the latter half of the nineteenth century. The intervening suppression of this coalitional possibility was achieved through the disarticulation of race and class. Class politics were constructed as the sole domain of white workers, a tendency that was reinforced by the racial exclusions practiced by the AFL and other craft-based unions, and racial politics were seen as the sole concern of African Americans. Bob's dream, like his waking narrative, indicates this disarticulation of race and class. The white working-class men are represented as violent antagonists, rather than allies. Yet the dream also indicates that this antagonism functions as a displacement of the real source of antagonism: the hegemonic interests represented by the state and the military-industrial complex. By indicating the ideological nature of this antagonism, Himes implicitly suggests the possibility of the same sort of pro-labor, antiracist coalition that Singh valorizes. The difference between their two positions is that Himes foregrounds the importance of negative affect in setting initial limits on the possibility of developing an effective coalition while Singh gives an entirely positive account of this coalition as an embodiment of already achieved multiracial radicalism. Indeed, if we read Himes's representation of this negative affect through the lens of contemporary debates about the meaning and political character of cultural conflict in the United States, it stands as an important challenge to overly redemptive or positive forms of historiography. Himes's narrative suggests the way that even the most radical versions of the latter run the risk of reproducing the appropriative logic of American liberalism to the degree that they articulate a merely positive account of intersectionality in which all negativity, especially that experienced by the most marginal members of a coalition, is foreclosed from representation.

This negative intersectionality and the forms of negative affect it generates are foregrounded by Himes's narrative. Yet, *If He Hollers* does not merely valorize this negative affect without also suggesting the possibility of working though it, a possibility that can be generative of more effective forms of negativity, directed at more productive targets.

Bob's first dream, with which the novel opens, narrativizes the forms of cultural fantasy that organize his existence. The content of this initial dream and the phantasmatic logic it instantiates frame much of the action that follows. After an initial section of the dream in which Bob imagines a police search for a black murder suspect (a search that foreshadows his own encounter with racist law enforcement at the end of the novel), Bob turns over in bed and dreams the following scenario:

> I was asking two white men for a job. They looked as if they didn't want to give me the job but didn't want to say so outright. Instead they asked me if I had my tools. I said I didn't have any tools but I could do the job. They began laughing at me, scornfully and derisively. One said, "He ain't got no tools," and they laughed like hell.
>
> I didn't mind their not giving me the job, but their laughing at me hurt. I felt small and humiliated and desperate, looking at the two big white men laughing at me. (6)

This dream sequence emphasizes the persistence of white supremacy on unofficial and phantasmatic levels in the now ostensibly egalitarian space of the job. In doing so, it presages the on-the-job racism Bob encounters throughout the rest of the novel which, by costing him his position as leaderman and his military deferment, effectively bars him from realizing the egalitarian promises of the newly expanded terms of American liberalism in the Roosevelt era. This exclusion is cast in homosocial terms and explicitly sexualized, underscoring the libidinal dynamics that organize the workings of white supremacy in the United States. The synchronized responses and laughter of the two white men construct the privileges of whiteness in fraternal terms, bonding them together and pitting them against Bob. This homosocial bonding is achieved through their sexualized joke about Bob's lack of tools. Their pun on the word "tool" casts the opposition between the men and Bob in terms of a rhetoric of manhood. Lacking tools, Bob is castrated and excluded from the privileges of manhood, which is constructed as the sole province of white men.

The dream's condensation of the sexual and the vocational, a condensation that is crystallized by the two meanings of the word "tool," highlights the way in which the phantasmatic and the material are thoroughly intertwined in Himes's text. This intertwining is centered on cultural definitions of masculinity, yet as the image of castration, especially with its symbolic link to the practice of lynching, implies, the intertwining of this fantasy logic with Bob's material existence is threatening on a bodily level. In order to negotiate his way through this threatening and potentially lethal landscape, Bob must begin to separate fantasy from action. He can only do this, though, by working through the forms of fantasy that both construct his racialized masculinity and threaten to negate his very existence, fantasies that have their genesis in the overlap between hard-boiled masculinity and cultural constructions of African American masculinity.

Lethal Fantasies

The novel's intertwining of cultural fantasies about hard-boiled and African American masculinity transforms not only the form but also the ideological coordinates of the hard-boiled narrative. In this transformation, the novel demonstrates the intersectionality of race, gender, and sexuality in twentieth-century American culture. The novel reveals the way in which transforming the racial identity of the hard-boiled protagonist produces concomitant changes in the gendered and sexual fantasies that organize the narrative. These changes, in turn, point beyond the confines of the genre, indicating the forms of cultural fantasy that shaped and delimited the construction of black masculinity in the mid-twentieth-century United States.

Transforming the race of the protagonist transforms the homosocial economy that organizes the hard-boiled narrative. Like the Continental Op and Jake Barnes, Bob Jones exists in a world defined largely in homosocial terms. However, unlike these unambiguously white precursors and like Joe Christmas, Bob must confront the racialized nature of this homosocial world. These racialized terms are equally constitutive of white hard-boiled masculinity. However, because whiteness remains the unmarked term in the black/white binary opposition that forms the dominant paradigm for American race relations, the white hard-boiled male has the privilege of disavowing his racialization. As a visibly racialized subject, Bob Jones lacks this privilege.

He must instead confront the cultural meanings and the forms of negation encoded in what Fanon terms "the fact of blackness" (116). Fanon employs this phrase to describe the way in which the black subject is "overdetermined from without" via a conflation of appearance, race, and value. Race is thus epidermalized and produced as a visible "fact." This fact is in turn experienced as negating: "In the white world the man of color encounters difficulties in the development of the bodily schema. Consciousness of the body is solely a negating activity. It is a third-person consciousness" (110). This third-person consciousness produces the fraught and affect-laden character of Bob's narration, for in trying to narrate his own first-person story, Bob must resist the forms of third-person objectification produced by the "fact of blackness." Since it is only experienced in the white world, this "fact" should not be taken as objective or prediscursive; it is instead produced as one of the elementary ideological effects of white supremacy. Judith Butler describes the production of such seemingly material "facts" as a process of "materialization" that "stabilizes over time to produce the effect of boundary, fixity and surface we call matter. That matter is always materialized has, I think, to be thought of in relation to the productive and, indeed, materializing effects of regulatory power in the Foucaultian sense" (*Bodies* 9–10). To Butler's Foucauldian reading of the materializing effects of regulatory power, I would add my own account of the materializing effects of cultural fantasy. For the "fact" of blackness experienced by Bob is one produced by a materialization of fantasy and charged with libidinal meaning.

It is this fact of blackness, and the cultural meanings encoded in it, that overdetermine the homosocial economy in which Bob, as a hard-boiled male, operates. Like the Continental Op, Bob finds himself in libidinally charged relationships with other men that are organized either around competition or collusion. For the Op, these relationships take on a seemingly objective character, appearing to operate by abstract laws that echo those of the market; their libidinal character remains hidden. For Bob, in contrast, these homosocial relationships are libidinally charged in immediate ways. He recognizes the ways in which they are organized around a logic of white supremacy, a logic that materializes his blackness in terms at once libidinal and objectifying.

Earlier I discussed how white supremacy in the first half of the twentieth century was formulated in terms of access to manhood and the privileges accorded to it. In the context of this conflation of whiteness and manhood, the homosocial logic that structures white supremacy and that organizes Bob's actions becomes fully legible. For this culturally sanctioned form of manhood is opposed to the culturally abjected forms of blackness that Fanon describes. This abjection is produced in part through the dual sexualizing myths of the black rapist and the promiscuous black woman. Thus black bodies become bearers of the affect and sexuality purged from the homosocial relations between white men.

Like Joe Christmas, Bob attempts to challenge this abjection by asserting his right to the same cultural privileges that are accorded to white masculinity. In doing so, the competitive logic that structures homosociality takes on a specifically racialized character, one that both challenges the racial exclusions produced by white supremacy and reinforces the masculinism of its logic. This competitive homosocial logic structures Bob's attempts at class ascendancy. We have already seen how Bob's car becomes infused with competitive significance. A similar logic structures his sexual encounters and dating life. The organization of Bob's sexuality affirms Eve Sedgwick's assertion that homosocial relations between men are produced through the construction of women as objects either of exchange or competition.[25] This logic is evident in Bob's relationship to white women, with whom he sleeps as a kind of challenge to white men. However, this is equally true of his relationship to black women. Throughout most of the narrative Bob dates Alice Harrison, the light-skinned daughter of one of the wealthiest black families in Los Angeles. This relationship is explicitly linked to Bob's ambitions to become part of the middle class: when the two imagine their future together, Bob thinks of saving up his money in order to go to law school, a move that would ensure his entry into the black bourgeoisie. This claim on middle-class status is simultaneously a claim on manhood, one that challenges the conflation of manhood and whiteness. For in staking his claim on a form of middle-class masculinity, a form of masculinity that carries with it privileges such as property ownership and the ability to dictate the work of others, Bob is implicitly challenging the conflation of whiteness and manhood.

The phantasmatic homosocial competition that underpins this challenge infuses Bob's relationship to Alice. While it is important not to efface the novel's suggestion of Alice's agency (Bob is "proud of what she demanded from white people," 10), in his eyes she represents both an object of exchange and a prize to be won. Bob's possession of her ("it gave me personal pride to have her for my girl," 10) thus represents a challenge to white men, whom he perceives as also desiring Alice. This homosocial logic of competition works intraracially as well as interracially: Bob is "proud of the way she looked, the appearance she made among white people . . . and [of] her position and prestige among her own people" (10). In this context, even her light complexion becomes coded as another sign of Bob's superiority in relationship to the other African American men and an implicit challenge to white men.

This competitive relationship to other African American men, and the objectification of African American and Anglo-American women that it perpetuates, cuts against the solidarity Bob feels with his fellow black workers, marking the sacrifice of community involved in his narrative of class ascendancy. In this refusal of community and embrace of competition, Bob Jones replays the classic terms of hard-boiled masculinity. To the degree that this competition remains largely intraracial, Bob can function like any other hard-boiled male. But when the competition crosses the racial divide, the systematic threat that white supremacy poses to him, or any other African American who challenges its terms, becomes manifest.

This threat changes the terms of homosocial violence that characterizes the hard-boiled genre. For Bob cannot kill with impunity. While private detectives like the Op or Marlowe can employ "justified" violence in the pursuit of their objectives, Bob cannot do this, especially if the object of his violence is white. While his violence might be random, functioning via the seemingly abstract logic of competitive homosociality, the response to his violence would be systematic and lethal. He knows that any violence on his part is also effectively a suicide. Thus, in order to survive, he must work out a fundamentally different relationship to violence than the one that typically characterizes hard-boiled masculinity.

This different relationship to homosocial violence emerges most clearly in a sequence in which Bob plans to kill one of his white co-workers, begins to execute his plan, and then desists from carrying it through. Bob decides to kill the co-worker after the latter calls him a "nigger" and beats Bob up after a crap game that he has just won. Bob joins the crap game to let off some steam because he has just been fired from his job as a leaderman after his verbal interchange with Madge. The male co-worker becomes symbolic of all the forms of systematic and incidental racism Bob has experienced during the day. Immediately after the fight, Bob goes to where the man works with a knife and fantasizes stabbing him to death: "I could see the blond boy's bloody body lying half across his machine, blood all over the floor, all over the shapes; blood on my hands; his face all cut to pieces, one eye hanging out and wrinkled like an empty grape skin" (36). After conjuring this vivid murder fantasy, Bob decides to spare the man's life for now:

> It was then I decided to murder him cold-bloodedly, without giving
> him a chance. What the hell was the matter with me, running in there
> to fight him? I thought. What the hell did I want to fight him for? I
> wanted to kill the son of a bitch and keep on living myself. I wanted to
> kill him so he'd know I was killing him and in such a way that he'd
> know he didn't have a chance. I wanted him to feel as scared and
> powerless and unprotected as I felt every goddamned morning I woke
> up. I wanted him to know how it felt to die without a chance, how it felt
> to look death in the face and know it was coming and know there wasn't
> anything he could do but sit there and take it like I had to take it from
> Kelly and Hank and Mac [his immediate superiors] and the cracker bitch
> because nobody was going to help him or stop it or do anything about
> it at all. (37)

We can see from this how homosocial relations are transformed by the racial divide. Unlike that of the Op, Bob's violence cannot appear as merely abstract and instrumental. Instead, it is charged with explicit affect and grounded in collective forms of social antagonism. Thus the white worker comes to stand in, synecdochically, for all white people. Similarly, the response to this individual act of rebellion against white supremacy would be swift, collective, and lethal. While Bob fantasizes about killing the white worker in such a way that would allow him to continue living, he finally knows that if he were caught, he would hang for it (38).

This transformation in the organization and effects of homosocial violence produces a parallel transformation in the representation of violence in the hard-boiled narrative. Bob experiences this objectified status in his encounters with the homosocial organization of white supremacy, a status he attempts to contest through the fantasized killing of the white worker. However, this positioning as object of the gaze and the forms of affect it produces also enable Bob to have a more mediated and finally a more ethical relationship to his potential for violence. For while Bob's conscious thoughts are much more violent than those of his hard-boiled brethren, his actions are finally much less so. While his actions throughout the narrative are hardly pristine or unambiguous, they finally are more ethical than those of other hard-boiled protagonists.

The pairing of violent thoughts and ethical action is not coincidental. It suggests that Bob has a fundamentally different relationship to symbolizing affect and fantasy than do the white hard-boiled characters on which he is modeled. Whereas the white hard-boiled characters enact what they don't symbolize, Bob symbolizes, indeed fantasizes, rather than acting out. In symbolizing and narrativizing his affective investments in the murder fantasies related above, Bob is able to work through the violent impulses that other hard-boiled characters merely act out. The symbolization, or bringing to consciousness, of repressed wishes is foregrounded in the passage itself through the repetition of the phrase "I wanted . . ." (which can be read as a past-tense correlate to "I wish"). This symbolizing of these repressed wishes enables Bob to refrain from acting on them: while he follows the worker home and points his gun at him, making his face go "stiff white" with fear, he does not pull the trigger. In refraining from violence, especially disorganized violence that furthers no direct political end, Bob Jones represents a significant mutation in the iconography of hard-boiled masculinity. For he symbolizes a potentially more ethical masculinity, one that can recognize and work through the fantasy investments that constitute it and thus gain more freedom within the sphere of action.

The Disjunction between Fantasy and Action

Bob's murder fantasies about the white male worker are merely a prelude to the violent fantasies that structure his relationship to Madge. In working through his phantasmatic relationship to Madge, Bob simultaneously works through two iconic and intertwined figurations of male/female relationships in the mid-twentieth-century United States: the relationship of the hard-boiled male to the femme fatale and the relationship of the "black rapist" to the "virtuous white woman."

Madge is Himes's figuration of the femme fatale—but a figuration with a difference. As I demonstrate in my reading of *Red Harvest* in chapter 2, the femme fatale functions allegorically in the conventional hard-boiled narrative. She embodies all the forms of connection—national, economic, sexual, racial—that the hard-boiled male both desires and repudiates. Madge's function in the narrative is similarly allegorical, but unlike the conventional femme fatale, her allegorical significance is underwritten by a literal prohibition: the taboo against miscegenation. This prohibition is intimately tied to the logic of manhood that organizes the workings of white supremacy. While theoretically all forms of interracial sex were prohibited by antimiscegenation laws, the laws were conceived as and interpreted to be a prohibition on sex between black men and white women. Indeed, white manhood and its privileges were defined in part through the masculinist privilege of interracial sexual access and an exclusive access to white women, a form of sexual access that was rigorously denied to African American men. In this context, the allegorical dimensions of the femme fatale become, to a certain extent, concretized. While she still represents, in her fallen state, the failure of various economic, national, racial, and sexual promises, these promises become partly materialized as the forms of exclusion that are symbolically linked to the prohibition against miscegenation.

The codes that construct the relationships between the hard-boiled male and the femme fatale as well as the black rapist and the virtuous white woman are evident in Bob's first description of Madge:

> She was a peroxide blonde with a large-featured, overly made up face, and she had a large, bright-painted, fleshy mouth, kidney-shaped, thinner in the middle than at the ends. Her big blue babyish eyes were mascaraed like a burlesque queen's and there were tiny wrinkles in their corners and about the flare of her nostrils, calipering down about the edges of her mouth. She looked thirty and well-sexed, ripe but not quite rotten. She looked as if she might have worked half those years in a cat house, and if she hadn't she must have given a lot of it away. We stood there for an instant, our eyes locked, before either of us moved; then she deliberately put on a frightened, wide-eyed look and backed away from me as if she was scared stiff, as if she was a naked virgin and I was King Kong. (21)

Bob's description of Madge initially echoes the Op's description of Dinah Brand. Madge is represented as both "ripe" and potentially "rotten," both sexually desirable and dangerously and unattractively corrupt. As with the Op, Bob's alternation between desire and repudiation in his description of Madge suggests the ambivalence that structures the relationship of the hard-boiled male to the femme fatale. She represents the forms of connection that he desires and the broken promises that he repudiates. However, in the second part of the description, the relationship between the femme fatale and the hard-boiled male is transformed by its combination with the myth of the black rapist. Bob goes from unambiguously being the desiring subject of the masculinist sexual narrative of the hard-boiled novel to being the simultaneously objectified and hypersexualized black rapist, the mythic proportions of which are hyperbolically embodied in the pop culture icon King Kong. Madge is similarly transformed from fallen femme fatale to naked virgin. These transformations demystify the ideology of both phantasmatic narratives to a certain extent even as the combination of the two produces a new phantasmatic relationship. The combination of the femme fatale with the endangered virgin partially undoes the oppositions between innocence and experience, virtue and corruption that both narratives depend on. Similarly, the combination of the hard-boiled male with the black rapist undoes the oppositions between subject and object, protagonist and antagonist that are central to both narratives.

These contradictions open up a space for Bob to transform his relationship to these narratives, but in order to do so, he must work through the new phantasmatic context organized by this conflation of narratives. This new phantasmatic context is evident in Bob's next encounter with Madge. He runs into her after being humiliated by a racist joke told by his boss, Kelly:

> I knew where I was going. I didn't want to go. My body just carried me and my mind just pushed me along. I didn't feel rash nor reckless, nothing like that. I felt low, dispirited, black as I've ever felt. Really a black boy now.
>
> But I knew I was going to have to say something to Madge if I got shot on the spot. Not to rack her back or to cuss her out. That wasn't going to be enough. Not now. Not after having been tricked into listening to that bastard tell that joke. I was going to have to have her. I was going to have to make her as low as a white whore in a Negro slum—a scummy two dollar whore . . . I was going to so I could keep looking white folks in the face . . .
>
> So I started over where she was working. She was over to one side by herself, leaning against some staging. There were a lot of other workers around, but I didn't see them; all I could see was her standing there between me and my manhood. (116)

The compulsion that directs Bob's steps suggests that he is in the thrall of cultural fantasy: while he consciously resists going to Madge, the fantasy narrative being played out by his unconscious insists that he confront her. While the encounter Bob fantasizes in this passage cannot unproblematically be described as rape, it conflates race, power and sexuality in a way that conforms to the basic coordinates of the myth of the black rapist. Bob imagines destroying Madge's ability to define herself as a virtuous white woman by having sex with her and this act is imagined as an act of revenge. And indeed, a few pages later this act becomes explicitly renamed as rape: "What I ought to do is rape her, I thought. That's what she wanted" (118). Bob is not the only one caught in the phantasmatic machinery of the myth of the black rapist. Madge is also portrayed as being invested in the myth: "So it wasn't that Madge was white; it was the way she used it. She had a sign up in front of her as big as Civic Centre—KEEP AWAY NIGGER, I'M WHITE! And without having to say one word she could keep all the white men in the world feeling they had to protect her from black rapists" (118). While this description participates in the ideological displacement that blames white women for the workings of white supremacy, a system maintained largely by and for the benefit of white men, it also suggests the way in which the myth of the black rapist structures the fantasy investments of white women as well as white and black men.

In marking both Bob's and Madge's phantasmatic investments in this myth, the passage demonstrates how the relationship between the hard-boiled male and the femme fatale is transformed by the myth of the black rapist. Most important, the temporality of the fantasy shifts. The classic relationship between the hard-boiled male and the femme fatale is organized around a melancholia in which the hard-boiled male perpetually and unconsciously mourns the loss of the promise of social connection, a promise that is represented as irrevocably located in a (mythic) past. In the relationship between Bob and Madge, however, the promise is located in the present and is actively withheld through a logic of exclusion. This latter promise is that of manhood and citizenship—or, more precisely, manhood as citizenship—a promise that is withheld via the workings of white supremacy. Part of Bob's fantasy investment in desiring to embody the figure of the black rapist, then, is a desire to forcefully gain access to the same privileges that are accorded to white men: privileges that are coded within the myth as sexual, but which are also civic and gendered. All these meanings are condensed into Bob's statement: "all I could see was her standing there between me and my manhood." They are also inscribed in his claim that "I was going to have to [degrade Madge] so I could keep looking the white folks in the face." However, the intermixing of these present meanings with the irrecoverable promises that conventionally organize the hard-boiled narrative suggests the unattainability and hollowness of the former, replaying Himes's critique of the possibilities of even the most inclusive aspects of FDR liberalism.

It is in the context of this complex intermixing of phantasmatic cultural narratives that Bob must negotiate his own subjective relationship to the workings of cultural fantasy. Initially he opts to literalize his rape fantasy and thus the larger cultural fantasy of the black rapist. This fantasy begins to be played out in a scene that takes place in Madge's apartment. Bob initially wrestles with Madge, pinning her down and holding her beneath him on the bed. But rather than pressing on, he loosens his grip: "I relaxed my hold and she snatched a hand loose and hit me in the face" (137). After this, the scene shifts from one of rape to one of a consensual sexual struggle that never develops beyond its opening moments: "She kicked off her shoes and ran across the room, big, gawky, awkward, and grotesque, but with a certain wild grace in her every awkward motion. 'You can't have none unless you catch me,' she teased" (138). This play ceases when Madge uses the word "rape": "'All right, rape me then, nigger!' Her voice was excited, thick, with threads in her throat. I let her loose and bounced to my feet. *Rape*—just the sound of the word scared me, took everything out of me, my desire, my determination, my whole build up" (138). As with his murder fantasy, Bob symbolizes his rape fantasy rather than fully acting it out. The opposition that the novel presents between symbolization and action is underscored by the de-escalating effect that Madge's use of the word "rape" has. Madge's utterance of the word not only emphasizes this distinction and the possibility for ethics that it opens up but also underscores the way in which Bob, like Madge herself, is objectified within the myth of the black rapist. For part of what makes Madge's comment so de-escalating is the fact that Bob realizes the lethal consequences of being accused of rape: "I was taut, poised, ready to light out and run a crooked mile. The only thing she had to do to make me stop was just say the word" (138). The implications of the intimate relationship between Bob's subjective ethics and his objectification is further developed by the novel's ironic conclusion—a conclusion that marks the limit of individual ethics as a mode of subjectively working through the modalities of cultural fantasy.

An Ethics Forged by Necessity

The disjunction between Bob's thoughts and his actions opens up a space for the emergence of a form of subjective ethics predicated on the psychoanalytic distinction between symbolization and acting out. By bringing to consciousness and narrativizing the unconscious cultural fantasies that organize and materialize his subjectivity, Bob is able to gain a modicum of subjective agency around their relationship to his actions. This agency distinguishes the form of masculinity Bob embodies from the one that characterizes the conventional hard-boiled protagonist who acts out what he refuses to symbolize. In place of the homosocial violence that characterizes the hard-boiled male's relationship to other men, Bob has murder fantasies but does not act them out. Similarly, in place of the lethal relationship between the hard-boiled male and the femme fatale, Bob has rape fantasies but does not materialize them. His ability to recognize, and thus work through, his fantasy investments stands in stark contrast to the disavowed yet determining (determining because disavowed) character of the conventional hard-boiled male's fantasy investments. This ability to recognize and work through his fantasy investments in turn suggests that his subjectivity represents an important ethical mutation in the literary evolution of hard-boiled masculinity—one that potentially has extraliterary significance.

I will address this extraliterary significance more fully in the conclusion. Before doing so, however, I need to acknowledge the limits that Himes places on this subjective agency. Bob's subjective agency is ironically produced, in part, out of the forms of cultural, political, and economic constraint that circumscribe the material and symbolic terms of his existence. It is Himes's attempt to represent the constraints on black male subjectivity in the mid-twentieth century that produces a transformation in the form and content of the hard-boiled novel—a transformation that, in turn, enables the emergence of a potentially more ethical protagonist. This protagonist emerges as more potentially ethical because his actions are more constrained and because he must address the affect produced by objectification. The forms of ethical agency that Bob embodies emerge paradoxically out of necessity and out of his attempt to strategically negotiate larger forms of cultural constraint. While this agency has the ability to transform Bob's relationship to the cultural fantasies that organize and materialize his subjectivity, it does not have the ability to alter others' investments in these same fantasies or the larger forms of cultural and material power to which they are bound. Thus while Bob does not rape Madge, he still winds up being accused of it. This accusation, in turn, precipitates his brutalization at the hands of a group of white men and his forced entrance into the army. The latter, which occurs because there is not enough evidence to make the charge against him stick, is represented throughout much of the narrative as a fate close to death. Although Bob ethically refrains from homosocial and sexual violence, he becomes accused of the latter and the victim of the former.

This conclusion seems to negate the possibility for cultural change suggested by the form of subjective agency embodied by Bob. While Bob changes his relationship to cultural fantasy, the world around him does not. However, I want to suggest that the limits on Bob's agency are the product of its individual character. Himes's narrative does not so much negate the possibility of cultural change being produced through a subjective working through of fantasy as negate that such a transformation can happen on the individual level. The novel leaves open the possibility that such a cultural praxis of phantasmatic working through is achievable on a collective rather than individual level. It also suggests that such a praxis needs to be accompanied by collective forms of struggle and transformation on the material level. Similarly, as the novel's dystopian representation of wartime Los Angeles asserts, material transformation without a concomitant change on the level of cultural fantasy does little to alter the forms of violent intersectionality that form the stuff of everyday life in the United States.

In asserting the value of phantasmatic change to material change and vice versa, Himes's novel poses an important challenge to even the most progressive forms of contemporary scholarship on American culture in the mid-twentieth century. To Michael Denning's and Nikhil Pal Singh's salutary materialist histories of counterhegemonic struggle in the period, Himes's novel suggests the necessity of adding a parallel account of intersubjective forms of fantasy and their relationship to social negativity and antagonism. Without such an account, these histories threaten to reproduce an overly positive representation of the social field, one that runs the risk of reanimating the incorporative and de-politicizing social imaginary of the ostensible object of their critique: American liberalism.[26] Himes's novel thus shows the value of tarrying with the negativity embedded in noir (and in noir-inflected forms such as the hard-boiled narrative) for thinking through and working through the limits of liberalism.

Of course in reading Himes's negative representation of the social field as the basis for constructing a positive ethics, I too run this risk of reproducing the terms of liberalist discourse. Yet by underscoring Himes's critique of the political efficacy of individual agency, my analysis rejects one of the central categories of liberal thought. Moreover, this positive ethics does not exclude the use of negation or even the use of violence to achieve a more just social order.[27] An ethics of working through does, however, insist on recognizing the way in which the value and efficacy of negation is often limited by the unconscious libidinal investments that overdetermine its expression.

Thus, if we are to read Himes's novel as more than an early version of what Alan Nadel terms a containment narrative (2–3), we must find the positive political potential buried in the rigorous negativity of Himes's aesthetic. As I have argued, this positive potential is linked to the very power of negative representation itself. This power resides in negative representation's ability to provide a site of transference for a cultural praxis of collective working through, one that has the potential to produce new forms of political agency and more politically efficacious uses of the forms of negativity that haunt the American cultural landscape. In the conclusion that follows, I attempt to outline the possibility of just such a practice.

Conclusion
Pulp Magazine Readership
and the Politics of
Collective Fantasy

Collective Fantasy and Everyday Life

A politics that is at once material and phantasmatic—this is the radical promise simultaneously offered and negated by Chester Himes's *If He Hollers Let Him Go*. While the novel suggests the powerful potential of such a politics, it also asserts the impotence of individual ethical and political agency in attempting to realize such a politics. Individual agency is presented as severely limited in relationship to the broad workings of cultural fantasy and to the forms of political-economic power that organized American society in the twentieth century. On the possibility of a collective version of such a politics, the novel remains stubbornly mute. This silence is not unique to Himes's novel but characterizes all the novels considered in this book. The shared inability to imagine a collective politics of fantasy in texts that consistently engage the subject of cultural fantasy suggests that this oversight is intimately bound up with the epistemological and formal structure of the hard-boiled form itself. The hard-boiled narrative, in spite of its political and cultural malleability, is almost always organized around an opposition between the individual and the collective that epistemologically privileges the former in relation to the latter. This opposition is a positivizing of one pole of the allegory of the negative relationship between the subject and the law that, as we saw in chapter 1, resides at the heart of the noir form. By positivizing one term of this negative relationship, that is, by transforming the noir subject into the hard-boiled male, the hard-boiled form also places a limit on the former's allegorical resonances. The hard-boiled male, as relatively positive and stable site of reader identification, becomes celebrated for his rugged individualism and his opposition to all forms of collectivity, whether existing or imaginary. It is this epistemological limit that we encounter again and again in hard-boiled novels and modernist works grounded in the hard-boiled aesthetic.

Yet if the organization of the hard-boiled form marks the epistemological horizon of the forms of fantasy work undertaken by the novels I have examined, the status of the hard-boiled text as an object of mass— or collective—fantasy points beyond this epistemological horizon, suggesting a more productive dialectic between the individual and the collective in relationship to the dynamics of cultural fantasy. While cultural historians have long commented on the bourgeois and privatized nature of novel reading, the pulp magazine and paperback suggest a different understanding of the relationship between aesthetic object and reading public. As Sean McCann and Erin Smith have differently documented, the pulp magazine enabled the emergence of a sense of community in its working-class readership.[1] The letters to the editor pages of pulp magazines represent one of the key sites where this reading community can be reconstructed. In this conclusion I undertake such a reconstruction, examining the letters to the editors pages in *Clues* and *Black Mask* in order to glean what they can tell us not only about the reading community that formed around detective pulps but also about the possibilities for political community formation in the present.

This historical reconstruction is itself an exercise in cultural fantasy, a phantasmatic reanimation of a certain moment in the past shaped by the libidinal investments of the present, specifically those of the present study. As such, what I produce here is a metahistory of the reception of hard-boiled fiction in the pulp magazine. This metahistory works to be attentive not only to the historical record and what it has to teach us about the present but also to the historical roads not taken, unrealized historical possibilities that remain frozen in the record of what was and that perhaps can suggest possibilities for transforming what is.[2]

This metahistorical approach is motivated by both a theoretical concern with thinking through a politics for the present and by the exigencies of the historical archive itself. As Erin Smith has noted, the letters to the editor sections of the pulp magazines are simultaneously an invaluable source of material for reconstructing readers' responses to the fiction featured in the pulp magazines and a notoriously unreliable one (9). While many of the letters were written by real readers, some were written by the editors and writers themselves to produce the responses they wanted or, in the case of pulps with flagging readerships, to produce any response at all. In her meticulous historical reconstruction, Smith overcomes this obstacle by supplementing her analysis of readers' letters with an account of other historical indexes of pulp magazine readership, such as magazine advertisements and library surveys of working-class readership. I am less concerned in this conclusion with attempting to produce a meticulous reconstruction of the demographics of pulp magazine readership, something Smith has already done quite convincingly, than with producing a metahistory about the forms of collective fantasy that shaped the reception of hard-boiled fiction.

In reconstructing the significance of the letters to the editor that I examine below, I draw on work done under the rubric of "reception theory" as it has been theorized by cultural studies practitioners such as Constance Penley, Janice Radway, and Ien Ang. Central to the work of all three theorists is the conception of readers or viewers as a potential imagined community of reception.[3] Reception theory thus challenges the bourgeois notion of reading or viewing as a solitary activity, arguing that such a notion is particularly misplaced when understanding the reception of popular cultural materials. Such an approach is particularly promising in the case of the pulps, which, as I have already noted, produced a sense of community in their readership.

Reception Theory and the Commodity Form

Reception theory is particularly attentive to the workings of fantasy as its shapes the reception of popular texts. As such, it lines up nicely with the conception of cultural fantasy that is central to this book. While the understanding of fantasy is different in the work of Penley, Radway, and Ang, all three suggest that fantasy has the potential to organize a political relationship between the popular cultural object and a given community of readers or consumers. Central to this understanding of the fantasy that bonds reader and text is the idea, as Fredric Jameson has also argued, that such a relationship can function in a utopian as well as an ideological register, imagining forms of community that transcend the commodity form itself.[4] As Constance Penley has asserted, this understanding of fantasy, "with its ability to describe how the subject participates in and restages a scenario in which crucial questions about desire, knowledge and identity can be posed, and in which the subject can hold a number of identificatory positions," opens up the text to multiple political meanings, ones determined in part by the construction of the text within the interpretive community itself ("Feminism" 480). Popular readers are thus active and semiautonomous participants in the production of the meaning of a given text. Moreover, this act of producing meaning can function critically, producing forms of readerly disidentification as well as identification or readings that subversively recode the dominant codes of popular narrative.

Of course, the conception of readerly agency that comes out of reception theory is only half the story. Before turning to my analysis of reader responses, I need to restore the other half of the dialectic between agency and constraint that shapes the practice of popular cultural reading and consumption. This other half of the dialectic is the political and conceptual limitations imposed by the commodity form itself. As Marx demonstrated in *Capital*, the political limitations of the commodity form inhere in the exploitative socioeconomic relations that enable its production.[5] Moreover, these relations are masked by the logic of commodity fetishism, which transforms an exploitative relation among people into an abstract relation of equivalence among things. These constraints set limits on the forms of phantasmatic agency posited by reception theory and, indeed, mark the limits of many of the forms of agency posited by cultural studies in general when it does not articulate a theory of the commodity form.

To suggest that the commodity form exerts a constraint on readerly agency does not mean that it is an insurmountable one. For as Slavoj Žižek has demonstrated, the logic of commodity fetishism is itself dependent on fantasy, though a more determining conception of fantasy than is at work in the forms of fantasy theorized by the reception theorists:

> So now we have made a decisive step forward; we have established a
> new way to read the Marxian formula "they do not know it, but they are
> doing it": the illusion is not on the side of knowledge, it is already on
> the side of reality itself, of what the people are doing. What they do
> not know is that their social reality itself, their activity, is guided by
> an illusion, by a fetishistic inversion. What they overlook, what they
> misrecognize, is not the reality but the illusion which is structuring
> their reality, their real social activity. They know very well how things
> really are, but still they are doing it as if they didn't know. The illusion
> is therefore double: it consists in overlooking the illusion which is
> structuring our real, effective relationship to reality. And this
> overlooked, unconscious illusion is what may be called the ideological
> fantasy.[6]

The key point in this very complex passage is that what is materialized in both the commodity form and the actions of consumers is a form of collective fantasy. This fantasy does not take place on the level of conscious belief but manifests as an unconscious belief that materializes on the level of action. In this way, it takes the form of a fetishistic disavowal, one for which we can rewrite the Freudian formula for disavowal ("I know very well . . . but nevertheless") in the following manner: "I know very well that the commodity is just an object with use value that is the product of social labor, but nevertheless I believe that it is a sublime object that has a transcendental value, one that can only be understood in relation to other objects with similarly transcendental values." The commodity is thus a fetish in the Freudian as well as the Marxian sense. The key example for Žižek of such a fetishized object is the money form. We consciously know that money has no inherent value—that it is paper, or, in our contemporary world, that it is digits on a computer screen with no reference to any kind of international monetary standard. Yet we unconsciously believe that it has value, and this belief, because it is collective, becomes materialized as an essential part of the workings of the capitalist world-economy, one that embodies value beyond the conscious belief or disbelief of any given individual. The popular cultural object partakes, as a commodity, of this structure of fantasy.[7]

How do we understand the relationship between the differing conceptions of fantasy proffered by reception theory and Žižek? The most productive way, and one that also aligns them with my conception of cultural fantasy, is to see them as mutually constitutive and determining. In the introduction, I posited a conception of cultural fantasy that is both idealizing and materializing; fantasy not only is a way of imagining beyond the material contradictions of the present but it also can have the effect of inscribing and instantiating material contradictions. This double relationship is evident in the two conceptions of fantasy coming out of reception theory and Žižek. In theorizing both the limits and the possibilities of readerly agency, what is most important about this double relationship is its dialectical character. Not only does the form of fantasy central to commodity fetishism place material limits on the forms of agency celebrated by reception theory but the heterodox forms of readerly investment articulated by the latter also have the potential to make conscious and thus to critically interrogate the fantasy relation that Žižek posits as central to the commodity form. Such investments are able not only to construct utopian imaginings of a collectivity outside or situated strategically against the commodified world of consumer capitalism but they can also metacritically interrogate the ideological fantasy elementary to the commodity form that makes this imagining possible. In other words, the popular text *because of its very status as a popular commodity* is uniquely situated to employ the kinds of fantasy work described by reception theorists to metacritically engage the fantasy work posited by Žižek as central to the functioning of the commodity form.

Communities of Pulp Readership

The model I have just elaborated, then, enables me to begin the work of producing an account of reception that grants a modicum of critical and cultural agency to the popular culture reader or consumer while still situating the reader within the larger forms of phantasmatic and material constraint that place initial limits on this agency. The letters to the editor columns in the detective pulp magazines are one place where the possibility of this agency and its limits can begin to be perceived. Only a few detective pulp magazines had letters to the editor columns. *Clues*, which published a mix of hard-boiled and classical detective fiction, had a column that ran throughout the magazine's fifteen-year existence. *Black Mask*, the magazine that oversaw the birth of hard-boiled fiction and published the most notable of the hard-boiled writers, also had a letters column—or, actually, a few different ones—in its early years. My thorough, if not exhaustive, survey of the letters that appeared in these two magazines reveals a reader culture with an active sense of identity derived from the magazine and a concomitant sense of proprietorship over the magazine and the stories it published. This active sense of identity and proprietorship are, to take just one example, evident in the letter written by one G. C. B. in the December 1922 issue of *Black Mask:*

> The October number of *Black Mask* is exceptionally good. "The Sand Devil" and "A Gold Digger's Man" have weak spots. Detectives who amount to anything do not go about unarmed as "Prentice" did in the garden the night when the six shots were fired. Detectives have enemies and they never know when a weapon will be needed. How comes it that "Anders" did not smell the "dreadful" odor in his hair tonic and refuse to use it? . . .
>
> You have now a magazine that stands in a class by itself, so far as I know. But please do not sacrifice plausibility to the bizarre or unreal. Unusual stories are probably hard to get, but it pays to get them in order to keep your publication up to a certain standard.[8]

The reader's identification with the magazine is evident everywhere from his declaration of its superlative status to his comfortable assertion that the "October number" is exceptionally good. A proprietary sense is also everywhere in evidence, especially in the letter writer's detailing of various stories' shortcomings. Implicit in this catalogue of mistakes is a fantasy of the reader as writer, accompanied by the belief that the reader could be a better writer than those paid to produce the stories.

Of course on one level this sense of proprietorship is thoroughly ideological. It is precisely such consumerist fantasies of choice and ownership that Adorno and Horkheimer warn about in the famous mass culture section of *Dialectic of Enlightenment* and that is part of the structure of disavowal that Žižek articulates as central to the commodity form.[9] But on another level, this sense of proprietorship and identity form the basis for the possibility of readers defining a more active and empowered relationship to the ideology and meanings of the culture they consume. This sense of empowerment is captured by the fantasy of the reader as writer. Rather than cowering before the pen of the master artist, the reader assumes that he or she can do a better job than the writers the magazine employs. This active sense of reading leads me to posit the relationship between popular reader and text as one of cultural fantasy rather than simply one of ideology, for the former term contains the idea of the reader as active participant as well as passive receptor while complicating any direct or unmediated theory of agency that theories of reader response or consumerist agency usually entail.

This distinctive relationship of reader to text produced its own set of responses to the hard-boiled fiction that appeared in the magazine. The letters I examined seemed equally split between letters like one I just read that measure the detective story against a standard of ostensible reality and ones that discussed the detective story in terms of its conventions as an intellectual game or a self-consciously literary artifact. On one level the notion of the text's "realism" merely replays the fantasy of the one-to-one correspondence between life and art that, as we saw in the introduction, was central to the cultural fantasy of hard-boiled masculinity. The text's "realness" ensured that the masculinity in fiction could be duplicated in life and vice versa; any recognition of the phantasmatic genesis and basis of this duplication was disavowed. This disavowal of fantasy is not only central to the reading of hard-boiled fiction but, as we've seen throughout *Hard-Boiled Masculinities*, to the construction of hard-boiled masculinity itself. This emphasis on realism thus initially seems to merely reinforce the phantasmatic parameters of hard-boiled masculinity.

However, this emphasis on realism also had a more critical dimension. While the readers who approached the stories through the lens of the first vantage didn't use terms like "socioeconomic mapping" or, for the most part, even terms like "mimesis" or "verisimilitude," their understanding of the "realness" or unreality of a text was not entirely unconnected to the qualities celebrated by the most famous theories of realism.[10] Indeed, ideas of mimesis or verisimilitude are very much in line with the kinds of "realism" demanded by G. C. B. in the letter cited above. While on one level this emphasis on mimesis reinforces the fantasy of the story's "realness," on another level it indicates the reader's critical awareness about the production of "realness" as a specific literary effect.

This critical awareness could be developed into an awareness of the story's representation of social or economic division. Letter writers often indicated their taste in the kinds of "realistic" story by undertaking a form of social mapping and indicating which social perspective they preferred. For example, in the March 10, 1929, issue of *Clues*, a Thomas R. Thompson of 4965 Knox Court, Denver, Colorado, asserts: "I am not particularly keen on the 'crook' story, not even when the *poor devil* gets what is coming to him. I would much rather read a story told from the detective or law standpoint."[11] This attention to the fundamental divide that structures the noir and hard-boiled narrative, the divide between law and criminality, and the forms of economic and social division that it narrates, suggests that the tradition of allegorical reading that Michael Denning associates with dime-novel narratives of social banditry persists in the reading of pulp magazine narratives.[12] This tradition reads the opposition between the law and criminality as allegorizing the class antagonisms in a given society and, as we saw in chapter 1, forms one of the precursors to the forms of social negativity embedded in the noir and hard-boiled narrative. While Thomas Thompson clearly identifies with the law and enjoys seeing the criminals get their comeuppance, the letter suggests that the allegorical dimensions of the crime narrative are just as open to the opposite reading.

Another group of readers read the stories in the pulp narrative as literary games or as the products of a self-conscious literary artifice. On one level, this type of reading suggests the influence of classical detective fiction, with its construction of the story as a game between author and reader with an established set of rules. These readers tended to dismiss the narrative as mere amusement. Yet within this tendency, another impulse is discernible. The readers who read the story as self-consciously playful or literary often replicated a modernist understanding of the text as a linguistic artifact, one more concerned with the artfulness of the telling and the language employed. This last impulse is evident in a letter written by a G. C. H. in the December 1922 issue of *Black Mask*. He writes: "'The Concrete Facts About Thomas Hancock' could have been made a fine story, but the author depended so entirely upon the one

(124)(124)(124)(124)(124)(124)(124)(124)(124)(124)(124)(124)(124)(124)(124)(124)(124)(124)(124)(124)(124)(124)(124)(124)(124)(124)(124)(124)(124)(124)(124)(124)(124)

the ideology of postmodern cynicism toward cultural narratives—I want to propose a third possibility for popular interpretation: reading the text as a culturally produced fantasy about the social world and the forms of subjectivity that inhabit it (Žižek, *Sublime* 28–30). This approach would, in other words, take seriously both the popular cultural text and the act of reading that text as the work of cultural fantasy. Such an approach to reading the popular cultural text would attend to the allegorical social meanings of the text as libidinally charged fantasies about the social, and at the same time it would see these meanings as bound up with the production of certain phantasmatic constructions of subjectivity. This approach would move the understanding of the text beyond either the notion of representation as an objective index of reality or as a subjective construction that has no bearing on the material world. It would also provide a more complicated understanding of the work of critically engaging the popular cultural text. As we have seen, readers of the pulp magazines were savvy in their engagement with the magazines' fiction, some insisting on a critical distance between themselves as readers and the depiction of everyday life in hard-boiled fiction. However, even this mode of critical distance remains bound to an entirely rationalist understanding of subjectivity. It leaves untouched the phantasmatic and libidinal investments that overdetermine the reader's relationship to the mass cultural commodity. Without a critical engagement with fantasy, this conscious distance functions as part of the structure of disavowal that Žižek articulates as central to the workings of commodity fetishism. It is only by engaging the reader's phantasmatic investments as well as the story itself as a form of cultural fantasy, that a critical relationship to these phantasmatic materials can begin to be produced.

Fantasy never became a key term in reader responses to the hard-boiled fiction published by magazines such as *Clues* and *Black Mask*. Indeed, the latter magazine actively encouraged the conflation of the stories and the forms of masculinity narrated within them with everyday life. The one exception to this was a short-lived reader's column in *Black Mask* entitled "Our Dreams" and written by the psychoanalyst Gregory Stragnell. The column ran for about nine months, in late 1923 and early 1924, precisely the period when Carroll John Daly and Dashiell Hammett were first constructing the hard-boiled detective hero by reworking the earlier genre of noir crime fiction that appeared in the magazine. In the column, the intrepid Dr. Stragnell provided an explicitly psychoanalytic interpretation of dreams submitted by readers. The pedagogical model of the column was clearly a top-down one, in which the master psychoanalyst explicated the dreams to the unknowing readers, and as such discouraged the active sense of proprietorship that readers felt toward the stories that appeared in the magazine (which might help to explain the short existence of the column).

Still, this column coexisted side by side with the letters to the editor column, and it is interesting to speculate what might have happened if readers had appropriated the language of fantasy in the one and applied it to their readings of stories appearing in the other. Perhaps it would have provided the language that would have mediated between the understanding of a story as mimesis and the understanding of it as purely literary artifact in order to begin to produce an understanding of a story as a fantasy about the material and historical world, one that functions as neither an unmediated representation of this world nor a purely subjective construction of it but rather is formed in the dialectical relationship between the writing/reading subject and the social world. Such an understanding might have lead to a very different interpretive community than the one that finally did form around the detective pulps. The kinds of reading practiced by this other community might have begun to enable the kinds of collective phantasmatic politics that would transcend the individualist politics that the hard-boiled form marks as its epistemological limit. Of course, this is a metahistorical speculation, and perhaps a seemingly far-fetched one at that, but as Walter Benjamin reminds us, it is important to "brush history against the grain" in order to reveal what the dominant narrative of history has suppressed (*Illuminations* 259). Implicit in Bejamin's formulation is also the injunction to trace the alternate routes history might have taken if circumstances had been different.

Out of the different historical possibilities for collective interpretations, a particularly crude understanding of the realist aesthetic, one that proposed a one-to-one correspondence between literature and life, increasingly gained ascendancy throughout the 1920s and 1930s as the authorized discourse of the detective pulps. For example, in the first three years of *Black Mask's* existence the magazine seemed to move between touting the realistic action of its stories and celebrating their unconventional and extraordinary character. The latter terms were especially used in describing the magazine's "daytime" stories, which appeared in the magazine between 1920 and 1923 and were so called because they were supposedly too scary to read at night. However, already by February 1923, even as the letters columns were still generating different kinds of interpretation and the dream column was about to begin, *Black Mask* was advertising its stories in the following manner: "We believe—in fact, know absolutely—that the American public wants strong stories—real people, with real emotions, involved in real plots with unusual endings"

(23). By December 1927 the magazine was advertising itself as "the he-man's magazine" and suggesting a collapse of the line between fiction and reality by describing the activities of its writers in an almost parodic imitation of the masculine heroes found within the magazine: "And it would seem that all at once the thing [i.e., the writer's composing of the story] has started, with renewed life, with reawakened interest, with increased virility" (107). Strikingly, at this time the readers' letters column was also abandoned, as if analysis of the stories might somehow detract from the illusion of their utter realness and virility (and it is instructive to note the increasing conjunction of the two concepts at this point). The detective pulps instead began featuring "true life" columns written by various ex–law enforcement officials and ex-criminals, such as those by "Convict No. 12627," a prisoner in an Oregon penitentiary, and Lemuel De Bra, a former secret service agent. Moreover, *Clues* began running a column in the back of the magazine that demonstrated the ways in which its stories paralleled events in real life.

The ascendancy of this emphasis on the realness of the stories paralleled the rise of hard-boiled detective fiction and set the terms of the latter's interpretation. It is interesting to speculate how the authorization of a different interpretive discourse, or even a set of interpretive discourses as was present in the early days of *Black Mask*, might have produced a different popular understanding of both the hard-boiled story's social critique and the image of masculinity it helped to construct. This, in turn, might have produced a different set of cultural fantasies about the relationship between masculinity and economic and social life than the ones that animated not only popular culture but significant aspects of everyday life in the 1920s and 1930s.

Transforming the Present

It is this possibility of a collective politics of fantasy, a possibility produced by the forms of popular fantasy elicited by the commodity form itself, that suggests the antidote to the limits of individual agency and individual ethics indicated by *If He Hollers Let Him Go*. The possibility of these forms of collective politics is precipitated by the commodity form and the forms of collective readership and consumption that it produces. However, if cultural fantasy is to become the ground for a truly collective politics, one that moves beyond the forms of consumerist agitation that often pass for politics in our late capitalist world, it must work through its relationship to the commodity and the structure of phantasmatic disavowal that the commodity underwrites, in order to recognize the forms of material and symbolic inequality that enable its production. In some of the most radical moments of the fiction I have considered in the preceding pages, such as the metacritical meditation on consumption in *Light in August,* or the intentional disruption of the seemingly stable line between fantasy and "reality" in Ashton Crowell's "The Prison Clock Strikes Nine," or the dream sequences in *Red Harvest* and *If He Hollers Let Him Go,* the popular text itself seems itself to invite the reader to do this work of interrogating its status as a commodity.

As a privileged site of collective phantasmatic investment, then, popular culture has the potential to become a locus of transformation. It has the potential to contribute to the transformation not only of gendered fantasy and forms of gendered subjectivity but also of the forms of economic, racial, sexual, and national fantasy that underwrite the inequitable social order in which we live. However, as I demonstrated in my readings of the social negativity that structures the noir narrative and the forms of negative intersectionality engaged by *If He Hollers Let Him Go,* popular culture's power to transform is not exclusively embedded in its power to produce positive images, a power that is, moreover, often indistinguishable from its function as ideology. Himes's novel suggests instead that popular culture's capacity to symbolize forms of social antagonism and negativity enable it to elicit a transferential relationship with its audience that holds the promise of working through rather than merely repeating the forms of cultural inequality and violence underwritten by this negativity.

In order for this possibility to be realized, we need to have a different understanding of both the cultural object and the cultural consumer than the one that circulates throughout much discourse—both popular and academic—on popular culture. Throughout *Hard-Boiled Masculinities* I have tried to create such a different understanding. In place of popular and academic conceptions of popular culture as solely a locus of positive or negative discourse—discourse that produces that which it represents—I have offered an alternative understanding of popular culture as a locus of cultural fantasy, one that has a complex, reciprocal, and at times contradictory relationship to the consumer and to the forms of material life and production in which it is embedded. Similarly, in place of the representation of mass cultural consumers as either passive or freely choosing, I have advanced an understanding of them as subjects situated in fantasy—forms of fantasy that have the potential to produce both constraint and agency, repetition and transformation.

In order for transformation to be possible, this understating of the phantasmatic relationship of subjectivity to culture must be recognized and made a part of cultural analysis and political praxis. In this book, I have attempted to demonstrate the value such an understanding holds for rethinking the constitution of modern masculinity in the United States. I would suggest that it holds a similar value for rethinking masculinity in our own postmodern moment. While forms of hegemonic masculinity have changed in ways both subtle and obvious in the shift from a Fordist to a post-Fordist political economy and in the concomitant shift from a modernist to a postmodernist cultural logic, the legacy of hard-boiled masculinity is still very much with us.[13] As Fred Pfeil has demonstrated, the forms of masculinity represented in contemporary detective fiction may have acquired a "soft-boiled" exterior, but this merely serves as a more palatable coating for their continuing adherence to hard-boiled gender politics.[14] Similarly, the fundamental structures of male privilege that contributed to the emergence of hard-boiled masculinity have unfortunately altered very little in the shift from the modern to the postmodern era. As R. W. Connell argues, the change in gender relations in the last fifty years has not been "the crumbling of the material and institutional structures of patriarchy" but the crumbling of "the legitimation of patriarchy" in certain sectors of industrial countries.[15] To Connell's analysis of discursive challenge and material persistence, I would add a similar picture of discursive challenge and *phantasmatic* persistence.

The phantasmatic significance of the hard-boiled male is thus still very much with us. It is evident in various forms of popular nostalgia that have emerged in recent years—from the neo-swing and lounge movements to mainstream reprintings of classic hard-boiled and noir novels to the revival of the noir aesthetic in cinema. But its persistence is even more significant in present-oriented forms of popular culture: from the tough guys of action films and cop shows to that most compelling contemporary version of the social bandit, the gangsta rapper. The image of unemotive violent masculinity thus persists, suggesting that if we are to imagine real change in the material and discursive construction of gender in the United States and around the globe, we must imagine ways of producing phantasmatic change as well. It has been the argument of *Hard-Boiled Masculinities* that such change is possible only by working through the very logic of popular fantasy itself, unmooring its productively critical and libidinally charged negativity from the forms of racial and gendered violence to which it has for too long been bound. Only by working through this logic can a subject's affective relationship to his or her culture be altered. Such an alteration is necessary if we truly want to transform the unequal material and symbolic structures that currently organize the world in which we live.

Acknowledgments

As with any book, when one looks past the name on the title page one begins to perceive the irreducibly collective endeavor that enables its production. Accordingly, I want to acknowledge the different communities and conversations that were integral to the genesis of *Hard-Boiled Masculinities*.

First and foremost I want to thank the University of Minnesota Press and my editor, Richard Morrison, for faith in and unswerving support of this project. One rarely thinks of publishers as providing a community for their authors, but this is precisely what Minnesota has done. No one was more important in establishing this sense of community than Richard; his support and unerring judgment have made this a much stronger book than when I first submitted it. These improvements must also be credited to the two outside reviewers, Catherine Nickerson and the reviewer who remains anonymous. Nickerson's suggestions in particular are responsible for a much improved final version of the manuscript. Finally, I thank Heather Burns, editorial assistant at the Press, and Lynn Walterick, copy editor for the Press.

I thank my home institution, Illinois State University, which has provided much-needed support for this project, both financial and intellectual. I was the recipient of a New Faculty Initiative Grant, which enabled me to do original archival research in the pulp magazine special collections at the University of California, Los Angeles. I received a subvention from the English department at ISU to acquire the artwork and illustrations for the book. I also wish to acknowledge the intellectual community that has sustained me and the pedagogical opportunities that have energized me while working at ISU. Its integrated vision of English studies challenges me on a daily level to rethink my research and teaching in interdisciplinary ways. My intellectual endeavors have also been sustained by a remarkable community of scholars at ISU, many of whom have given me excellent readings on different parts of the book manuscript. Accordingly, I wish to thank Joe Amato, Karen Coats, Patricia Dunn, Kristin Dykstra, Kass Fleisher, Ronald Fortune, Gabriel Gudding, David Hammontree, Waïl Hassan, Susan Kalter, Susan Kim, Katarzyna Jakubiak, Hilary Justice, Kenneth Lindblom, Jeffrey Ludwig (who also did a wonderful initial copy edit of the manuscript), Christopher McGee, Nathalie Op de Beeck, Cherie Rankin, James Reid, Rebecca Saunders, Gerald Savage, Ronald Strickland, and Curtis White.

I thank the Charles E. Young Research Library at UCLA for granting me permission to access the library's remarkable pulp magazine archive and the special collections staff for their invaluable assistance with this research and with obtaining the pictures for the book's illustrations. Librarians Simon Elliott, Octavio Olvera, Genie Geurard, and Daniel Slive deserve special mention for going well beyond the call of duty in their assistance. Without their assistance and the research I was able to do at UCLA, this book would be a mere shadow of its present form.

Hard-Boiled Masculinities began its life as a dissertation project at the University of California, Santa Cruz. I will forever value the intellectual and political camaraderie I discovered there; it continues to be the standard by which I measure all other academic communities. The support and inspiration I received at Santa Cruz came from a number of sources, both official and unofficial. Susan Gillman was an ideal dissertation director, carefully nurturing the project's core insights, casting a judicious eye on some of its stylistic and intellectual excesses, and serving, at all times, as an intellectual inspiration and a professional role model. I thank her and another invaluable dissertation committee member, Michael Cowan, for sharing with me their knowledge of the discipline of American studies and the debates that shape its "field imaginary." Richard Terdiman and José David Saldívar, in different ways, far transcended the typical role of dissertation committee member. For the past ten years, Richard has been a central intellectual interlocutor and a constant source of inspiration. To the degree that my thinking displays any dialectical suppleness, it is directly attributable to his teaching. I thank him not only for this formidable intellectual training but also for continuing to be a great mentor, supporter, and friend. José was a similarly foundational intellectual influence. Not only did he first introduce me to cultural studies and the work of Marx and Hegel but he, along with Susan, challenged me to think outside the constraints of the narrowly national. If this project fails fully to do so, it is through no fault of theirs. Carla Freccero and Earl Jackson Jr., while not official committee members, were also foundational intellectual influences. I owe almost everything I know about psychoanalysis, gender theory, and queer theory to them, and many of their teachings shape the core claims of this book.

Other people at UCSC, friends, graduate student colleagues, and mentors, contributed to the realization of this project. I thank the core group of colleagues from my graduate cohort who continue to be the closest of friends and intellectual partners-in-arms: Valerie Kaussen, without whose friendship and intellectual comradeship my life would be immeasurably impoverished; Scott Davis, who read repeated versions of the manuscript and was perhaps my primary theoretical interlocutor (usually over drinks in a bar); and Robin Baldridge, who, besides being a great friend and intellectual comrade, lent me my first hard-boiled novel, *The Big Sleep*, in our first year of graduate school and thus started me off on this strange obsession. I also thank Louis Chude-Sokei and Kirsten Silva Gruesz, who provided invaluable intellectual support to my project and who as friends and mentors taught me what being both a professional and an intellectual is all about. I also received critical feedback on my work and intellectual support from an array of other people at UCSC: Gordon Bigelow, Troy Boone, Christopher Connery, Valerie Forman, Michelle Habell-Pallán, Tyrus Miller, Keta Miranda, Scott Mobley, Ray Nayler, Catherine Newman, Becky Roberts, Marc Schachter, and Rob Wilson.

Another community that has played an integral role in catalyzing the arguments of this book is the group of scholars and friends with whom I repeatedly attended the Futures of American Studies Summer Institute at Dartmouth University. These institutes, which were organized by Donald Pease and Robyn Wiegman, were hotbeds of intellectual activity and theoretical engagement. It is hard to overstate the influence the institute and the intellectual friendships I forged there have had on my thinking. Accordingly, I not only want to thank Don and Robyn for organizing the institutes but also the following friends and colleagues: Rachel Adams, Renee Bergland, Leigh Edwards, Jennifer Fleissner, Kevin Floyd, Elizabeth Freeman, Gregory Jackson, Leerom Medovoi, Pamela Thoma, and Sasha Torres.

I thank my parents, Joseph and Giovanna Breu, and my sister, Eugenia Breu. My family provided the best possible upbringing for a future academic: I was raised in a home filled with art, culture, political debate, and philosophical questioning. The debt I owe them for this upbringing is immeasurable. I also want to thank my parents for their financial support throughout the lean years of graduate school; without their help, this book would not exist. Joseph Breu also gave copy-editing support at various stages throughout the production of this manuscript. I owe as well a debt of thanks to the following friends whose support during this long project has been invaluable: Catherine Harley, Philip Hatmaker, Jan Hatmaker, Robin Hendershot, Megan Lewis, Tim Marks, and Max Rovner.

If I had space enough, my thanks would go to all the artists whose music I listened to while composing this book; the list would range from Derrick May and Sonic Youth through Miles Davis and Sun Ra to Steve Reich and Gustav Mahler. I also thank my two constant feline companions, Annabel "Tiny" Hatmaker and Striped Breu.

Finally, my greatest gratitude goes to my wife, Elizabeth Hatmaker. To say that we are soulmates is almost to understate the ways in which our minds work as one strange organism that portions itself into separate entities as we work on our different writing projects and theoretical trajectories. She enriches my life in every way imaginable. I dedicate this book to her.

Notes

Introduction

1. On the psychoanalytic dynamics that underpin both the constitution and dissolution of the hard-boiled male's shell-like exterior, see Greg Forter's *Murdering Masculinities: Fantasies of Gender and Violence in the American Crime Novel* (New York: New York University Press, 2000), 1–45.

2. The concept of instrumentalization (or instrumental rationality) is central to the writings of Max Horkheimer and Theodor Adorno, appearing both in their jointly authored *Dialectic of Enlightenment* and in many of their individually authored works. Like all the formulations of these two thinkers, the concept was submitted to an ongoing process of dialectical revision over the course of their two careers. Max Horkheimer provides an early definition of the term in his essay "The End of Reason": "Its features can be summarized as the optimum adaptation of means to ends" (28). In later writings, Adorno and Horkheimer add an important dialectical twist to this initial formulation, asserting that instrumental reasoning is the adaptation of means to ends in which the ends have finally given way to the primacy and autonomy of the means. As Fredric Jameson nicely puts it in "Reification and Utopia in Mass Culture": "At this point, then, the quality of the various forms of human activity, their unique and distinct 'ends' or values, has effectively been bracketed or suspended by the market system, leaving all these activities free to be ruthlessly reorganized in efficiency terms, as sheer means or instrumentality" (10). It is this later definition that I will use in my discussion of Dashiell Hammett's *Red Harvest*. While it is nowhere explicitly formulated, this later definition of instrumental rationality is already clearly at work in the *Dialectic of Enlightenment*'s account of the modern instrumentalization of the rational ethos of the Enlightenment which finds its logical conclusion in the culture of mass destruction represented by the Holocaust and World War II. See Horkheimer, "The End of Reason," in *The Essential Frankfurt School Reader*, ed. Andrew Arato and Eike Gebhardt (New York: Continuum, 1993), 26–48; Horkheimer and Adorno, *Dialectic of Enlightenment*, trans. John Cumming (New York: Continuum, 1999); Jameson, "Reification and Utopia in Mass Culture," in *Signatures of the Visible* (New York: Routledge, 1990), 9–34.

3. See Erin Smith, *Hard-Boiled: Working-Class Readers and Pulp Magazines* (Philadelphia: Temple University Press, 2000), 1–14, 79–102. For the relationship between hard-boiled fiction and individualism, see Christopher Metress, "Dashiell Hammett and the Challenge of the New Individualism," in *The Critical Response to Dashiell Hammett*, ed. Christopher Metress (Westport, Conn.: Greenwood Press, 1994); and Sean McCann, *Gumshoe America: Hard-Boiled Crime*

Fiction and the Rise and Fall of New Deal Liberalism (Durham, N.C.: Duke University Press, 2000),1–86. For a history of the pulp magazines, see Ron Goulart, *The Dime Detectives* (New York: Mysterious Press, 1988); and Lee Server, *Danger Is My Business: An Illustrated History of the Fabulous Pulp Magazines, 1896–1953* (San Francisco: Chronicle Books, 1993). On the relationship of hard-boiled fiction both to modernism and to film noir, see James Naremore's *More than Night: Film Noir in its Contexts* (Berkeley: University of California Press, 1998); and William Marling's *The American Roman Noir: Hammett, Chandler, Cain* (Athens: University of Georgia Press, 1994). On the relationship between hard-boiled and classical detective fiction, see Ernest Mandel, *Delightful Murder: A Social History of the Crime Story* (Minneapolis: University of Minnesota Press, 1984), 1–52; John Cawelti, *Adventure, Mystery, and Romance: Formula Stories as Art and Popular Culture* (Chicago: University of Chicago Press, 1976); and Edward Margolies, *Which Way Did He Go?: The Private Eye in Dashiell Hammett, Raymond Chandler, Chester Himes, and Ross MacDonald* (New York: Holmes and Meier, 1982), 1–16.

4. In discussing hard-boiled masculinity in terms of male identity, I do not mean to reproduce the conflation of masculinity exclusively with male identity that Judith Halberstam rightly criticizes in *Female Masculinity*. What I am critiquing in *Hard-Boiled Masculinities* is a dominant ideological construction of masculinity that itself conflates masculinity with male bodies (or with bodies marked as male). I choose to focus on this ideology because I find the work of interrogating and dismantling dominant ideological, phantasmatic, and cultural formations a necessary precondition to constructing socially powerful and broadly meaningful alternative ones. Thus I hope this book is read as making a parallel, if differently focused, contribution to undoing the dominant understandings and embodiments of masculinity. See Halberstam, *Female Masculinity* (Durham, N.C.: Duke University Press, 1998), esp. 1–43.

5. Frank Krutnik, *In a Lonely Street: Film Noir, Genre, Masculinity* (London: Routledge, 1991), 56–91.

6. The texts I'm thinking of here are the following: Krutnik; Robert Corber, *Homosexuality in Cold War America: Resistance and the Crisis of Masculinity* (Durham, N.C.: Duke University Press, 1997); Kaja Silverman, *Male Subjectivity at the Margins* (New York: Routledge, 1992), 52–121; and Steven Cohan, *Masked Men: Masculinity and the Movies in the Fifties* (Bloomington: Indiana University Press, 1997).

7. See Forter, *Murdering Masculinities*; McCann, *Gumshoe America*; Smith, *Hard-Boiled*.

8. The one exception to this divide between the social and the subjective in recent theorizations of masculinity in hard-boiled fiction is Megan E. Abbott's excellent *The Street Was Mine: White Hard-Boiled Fiction and Film Noir* (New York: Palgrave, 2002). However, while I share Abbott's interest in historicizing the forms of racialized masculine subjectivity that appeared in hard-boiled fiction, both my methodology and my conclusions differ significantly from hers. Methodologically, her poststructuralist-influenced approach differs from

my own investments in a psychoanalytic theorization of subjectivity and a Marxian account of political economy. Moreover, I am more interested in theorizing hard-boiled masculinity in relationship to the larger dynamics of twentieth-century hegemonic and counterhegemonic social formations.

9. Bryce Traister, "Academic Viagra: The Rise of American Masculinity Studies," *American Quarterly* 52, no. 2 (2000): 274–304.

10. Dana D. Nelson, *National Manhood: Capitalist Citizenship and the Imagined Fraternity of White Men* (Durham, N.C.: Duke University Press, 1998), 1–28.

11. *Homosexuality in Cold War America*, 23–54. In treating hard-boiled masculinity as a postwar phenomenon, Corber takes his lead from a whole tradition of film theory that has dismissed or downplayed the ideological and formal continuities between the hard-boiled and noir fiction of the twenties and thirties and film noir of the forties and fifties. For two recent, representative examples of this tendency, see Marc Vernet, "*Film Noir* on the Edge of Doom," in *Shades of Noir*, ed. Joan Copjec (London: Verso, 1993), 1–31; and Alain Silver's introduction to *The Film Noir Reader*, ed. Alain Silver and James Ursini (New York: Limelight, 1996), 3–15.

12. For a brief account of the shift from entrepreneurial to corporate capitalism, see Martin Sklar, *The United States as a Developing Country: Studies in U.S. History in the Progressive Era and the 1920s* (Cambridge: Cambridge University Press, 1992), 20–30. This transformation is also the subject of his book-length study *The Corporate Reconstruction of American Capitalism, 1890–1916: The Market, the Law, and Politics* (Cambridge: Cambridge University Press, 1988). On the emergence of a Fordist political economy and its relationship to modernism, see David Harvey, *The Condition of Postmodernity: An Enquiry into the Origin of Cultural Change* (Cambridge: Blackwell, 1989), 10–38, 121–40. My own understanding of the relationship between Fordism and the representation of masculinity in hard-boiled texts has been influenced by Fred Pfeil's brief but suggestive comments on this relationship in *White Guys: Studies in Postmodern Domination and Difference* (London: Verso, 1995), 120–21.

13. Catherine Ross Nickerson has pointed out that this aggressive reassertion of male hegemony is central to the emergence of the hard-boiled aesthetic itself. In the conclusion to her study of forms of nineteenth-century detective fiction by women, *The Web of Iniquity*, Nickerson charts the way in which the hard-boiled form emerged in part as a rejection of the earlier aesthetic of the female detective story. See *The Web of Iniquity: Early Detective Fiction by American Women* (Durham, N.C.: Duke University Press, 1998), 179–217.

14. For an account of the relationship between the frontier hero and the hard-boiled male, see Richard Slotkin's *Gunfighter Nation: The Myth of the Frontier in Twentieth-Century America* (New York: Harper Collins, 1992), 194–228; and Cynthia Hamilton's *Western and Hard-Boiled Detective Fiction in America: From High Noon to Midnight* (London: Macmillan, 1987). For an account of the difference between the gentleman detective and the hard-boiled protagonist, see David Geheren, *The American Private Eye: The Image in Fiction* (New York: Ungar, 1985),

1–16; and Sinda Gregory, *Private Investigations: The Novels of Dashiell Hammett* (Carbondale: Southern Illinois University Press, 1985), 1–28.

15. See Gail Bederman, *Manliness and Civilization: A Cultural History of Gender and Race in the United States, 1880–1917* (Chicago: University of Chicago Press, 1995), 1–44; and Michael Kimmel, *Manhood in America: A Cultural History* (New York: Free Press, 1996), 117–221.

16. The word "antimodernism" comes from the cultural historian T. J. Jackson Lears, who uses it to describe the various forms of cultural protest against modernization in the turn-of-the-century United States. See *No Place of Grace: Antimodernism and the Transformation of American Culture, 1880–1920* (New York: Pantheon, 1981), 4–58.

17. *Black Mask* (June 1, 1923): 3.

18. The term "great divide" to describe the relationship between high and popular culture in the modernist period comes, of course, from Andreas Huyssen. See *After the Great Divide: Modernism, Mass Culture, Postmodernism* (Bloomington: Indiana University Press, 1986), vii–xii, 3–15; and also Lawrence Levine's *Highbrow/Lowbrow: The Emergence of Cultural Hierarchy in America* (Cambridge, Mass.: Harvard University Press, 1988). See also Huyssen's recent revision of his earlier argument, "High/Low in an Expanded Field," *Modernism/Modernity* 9, no. 3 (2002): 363–74.

19. See Huyssen, *After the Great Divide*, and Jameson, "Reification and Utopia in Mass Culture."

20. See the essays in Kevin J. H. Dettmar, ed., *Rereading the New: A Backward Glance at Modernism* (Ann Arbor: University of Michigan Press, 1992); and Dettmar and Stephen Watt, *Marketing Modernisms: Self-Promotion, Canonization, and Rereading* (Ann Arbor: University of Michigan Press, 1996). See also David Chinitz, "T. S. Eliot and the Cultural Divide," *PMLA* 110, no. 2 (March 1995): 236–47; Michael North, *The Dialect of Modernism: Race, Language, and Twentieth-Century Literature* (Oxford: Oxford University Press, 1994); and Thomas Strychacz, *Modernism, Mass Culture, Professionalism* (Cambridge: Cambridge University Press, 1993).

21. My understanding of the class-based address of modernism and other self-consciously "aesthetic" forms of cultural production has been influenced by the work of Pierre Bourdieu. See Bourdieu, *Distinction: A Social Critique of the Judgment of Taste*, trans. Richard Nice (Cambridge, Mass.: Harvard University Press, 1987), 1–96; and Bordieu, *The Rules of Art: Genesis and Structure of the Literary Field*, trans. Susan Emanuel (Stanford, Calif.: Stanford University Press, 1996), 47–112.

22. The work I am thinking of here includes the following: David Roediger, *The Wages of Whiteness: Race and the Making of the American Working Class* (London: Verso, 1991); Robyn Wiegman, *American Anatomies: Theorizing Race and Gender* (Durham, N.C.: Duke University Press, 1995); Eric Lott, *Love and Theft: Blackface Minstrelsy and the American Working Class* (New York: Oxford University Press, 1993); Lott, "Racial Cross-Dressing and the Construction of American

Whiteness," in *The Cultural Studies Reader*, 2d ed., ed. Simon During (New York: Routledge, 1999), 241–55; and the essays in *Critical Race Theory: The Key Writings That Formed the Movement*, ed. Kimberlé Crenshaw, Neil Gotonda, Gary Peller, and Kendall Thomas (New York: New York University Press, 1995).

23. See Walter Benjamin, *Charles Baudelaire: A Lyric Poet in the Era of High Capitalism* (London: New Left, 1973), 36–73.

24. J. Laplanche and J. B. Pontalis, *The Language of Psycho-Analysis*, trans. Donald Nicholson-Smith (New York: Norton, 1973), 314.

25. Jean Laplanche, *Seduction, Translation, Drives*, trans. Martin Stanon (London: ICA, 1992), 9–10.

26. Karl Marx, "The German Ideology: Part 1," in *The Marx-Engels Reader*, ed. Robert C. Tucker (New York: Norton, 1978), 176.

27. Karl Marx, *Capital*, vol. 1, trans. Ben Fowkes (New York: Random House, 1976), 163–64.

28. In addition to the theorists cited in the body of the text above, my understanding of cultural fantasy has been deeply influenced by the work of Lauren Berlant. See her discussion of national fantasy in *The Anatomy of National Fantasy: Hawthorne, Utopia, and Everyday Life* (Chicago: University of Chicago Press, 1991) and *The Queen of America Goes to Washington City: Essays on Sex and Citizenship* (Durham, N.C.: Duke University Press, 1997).

29. This is a very quick summary of a very complex argument. For a full account of this argument, see Fredric Jameson, *The Political Unconscious: Narrative as a Socially Symbolic Act* (Ithaca: N.Y.: Cornell University Press, 1981), 9–102 and 281–99.

30. Given this definition, it might seem to make more sense to describe the category as "social fantasy" rather than cultural fantasy—since it provides a phantasmatic map of relationships such as the political-economic that are not simply cultural but more broadly social. Changing the name in this way would also go part of the way toward meeting the objections Rosemary Hennessy astutely raises about the limitations of cultural theory and cultural materialism in dealing with issues of class and the political-economic. However, in spite of these arguments I have decided to keep the term as "cultural fantasy," largely because the fantasies that I am discussing, while they phantasmatically extend beyond the sphere of the cultural, are born of and bound to cultural and commodified forms such as pulp fiction and the forms of masculinity it encouraged. So I want to leave the term "cultural" as a mark of one of the central concerns of this book: the ways in which the cultural imagines and represents the social to itself. See Hennessy, *Profit and Pleasure: Sexual Identities in Late Capitalism* (New York: Routledge, 2000).

31. See Slavoj Žižek, *Enjoy Your Symptom! Jacques Lacan in Hollywood and Out*, 2d ed. (New York: Routledge, 2001), 5–6.

32. Freud articulates a distinction between symbolization and acting out. In order to move beyond mere repetition, the subject must work through his or her fantasy investments by bringing them to consciousness within the transferential

context of the analytic setting. I deploy this distinction more broadly in order to discuss the relationship of individual and collective subjects to the workings of cultural fantasy. See Sigmund Freud, "Remembering, Repeating, and Working-Through," in *The Standard Edition of the Complete Psychological Works of Sigmund Freud*, trans. and ed. James Strachey (London: Hogarth, 1955), 12: 145–56. See also the entries on "Acting Out," "Transference," and "Symbolism" in Laplanche and Pontalis, *The Language of Psycho-Analysis*, 4–6, 442–46, 455–62.

1. Wearing the Black Mask

1. For examples of each of these conceptions of negativity, see Marx, *The Economic and Philosophic Manuscripts of 1844*, trans. Martin Mulligan (New York: International Publishers, 1986); Žižek, *Tarrying with the Negative: Kant, Hegel, and the Critique of Ideology* (Durham, N.C.: Duke University Press, 1993); and Kaja Silverman, *Male Subjectivity at the Margins* (New York: Routledge, 1992).

2. The specific texts I'm thinking of here are Marc Vernet, "*Film Noir* on the Edge of Doom," in *Shades of Noir*, ed. Joan Copjec (London: Verso, 1993), 1–31; Christopher Metress, "Living Degree Zero: Masculinity and the Threat of Desire in the *Roman Noir*," in *Fictions of Masculinity: Crossing Cultures, Crossing Sexualities*, ed. Peter F. Murphy (New York: New York University Press, 1994); and William Marling, *The American Roman Noir* (Athens: University of Georgia Press, 1994).

3. See both introductions to the revised edition of E. Ann Kaplan, ed., *Women in Film Noir* (London: BFI, 1998), 1–19; Alain Silver and James Ursini, "Introduction," and Silver, "Son of Noir," in *Film Noir: A Reader*, ed. Silver and Ursini (New York: Limelight, 1996), 3–17, 331–38; Frank Krutnik, *In a Lonely Street: Film Noir, Genre, Masculinity* (London: Routledge, 1991), esp. 57–62; Robert Corber, *Homosexuality in Cold War America: Resistance and the Crisis of Masculinity* (Durham, N.C.: Duke University Press, 1997); Paula Rabinowitz, *Black and White and Noir* (New York: Columbia University Press, 2003); and David Reid and Jane L. Walker, "Strange Pursuit: Cornell Woolrich and the Abandoned City of the Forties," in *Shades of Noir*, ed. Joan Copjec (London: Verso, 1993), 57–96.

4. See Slavoj Žižek, *Enjoy Your Symptom! Jacques Lacan in Hollywood and Out*, 2d ed. (New York: Routledge, 2001), 149–93; Joan Copjec, "The Phenomenal Nonphenomenal: Private Space in *Film Noir*," in *Shades of Noir*, ed. Copjec, 167–97; and Elizabeth Cowie, "Film Noir and Women," in *Shades of Noir*, 121–65.

5. This noir fiction of the early twenties was not entirely unique to *Black Mask*. An occasional noir by these authors would appear in other magazines such as *Mystery Magazine* and *Detective Story Magazine*. What is striking to me about the appearance of these stories in *Black Mask*, and why I choose to focus on them, is the large number of such stories published by the magazine and the way in which they precede and lead up to the birth of hard-boiled fiction in the magazine. It is this history that I want to trace in the analysis to follow. Biographical research on these authors is beyond the scope of the present chapter.

6. My periodization of the different stages in capitalist production here

comes from David Harvey, *The Condition of Postmodernity: An Enquiry into the Origin of Cultural Change* (Cambridge: Blackwell, 1989); Fredric Jameson, *Postmodernism, or, The Logic of Late Capitalism* (Durham, N.C.: Duke University Press, 1991); and Martin Sklar, *The Corporate Reconstruction of American Capitalism, 1890–1916* (Cambridge: Cambridge University Press, 1988).

7. On the gothic true-crime narrative, see Karen Halttunen, *Murder Most Foul* (Cambridge, Mass.: Harvard University Press, 1998); and on the gothic fictional narrative, see Teresa Goddu, *Gothic America* (New York: Columbia University Press, 1997), 1–12. For accounts of the city mystery and its relationship to the gothic fiction of Edgar Allan Poe, see David S. Reynolds, *Beneath the American Renaissance* (Cambridge, Mass.: Harvard University Press, 1988), 169–248.

8. See Michael Denning, *Mechanic Accents: Dime Novels and Working-Class Culture in America* (London: Verso, 1987), 65–84.

9. For the sources that have shaped my understanding of the emergence of corporate capitalism and the advent of Taylorism and incipient Fordism in this period, see Martin Sklar, *The United States as a Developing Country: Studies in U.S. History in the Progressive Era and the 1920s* (Cambridge: Cambridge University Press, 1992), 20–30; Sklar, *The Corporate Reconstruction of American Capitalism*; and Harvey, *The Condition of Postmodernity*, 10–38, 121–40.

10. For an account of the deskilling of labor in corporate or, as it is also known, monopoly capitalism, see Harry Braverman, *Labor and Monopoly Capital: The Degradation of Work in the Twentieth Century* (New York: Monthly Review Press, 1975). On laborite republicanism and its persistence as an ideological touchstone in twentieth-century popular fiction, see Erin Smith, *Hard-Boiled: Working-Class Readers and Pulp Magazines* (Philadelphia: Temple University Press, 2000), esp. 43–78.

11. See David Roediger, *The Wages of Whiteness: Race and the Making of the American Working Class* (London: Verso, 1991); and Dana Nelson, *National Manhood: Capitalist Citizenship and the Imagined Fraternity of White Men* (Durham, N.C.: Duke University Press, 1998), 1–28.

12. See Theodor W. Adorno, *Aesthetic Theory*, trans. Robert Hullot-Kentor (Minneapolis: University of Minnesota Press, 1997); and Adorno, "Commitment," in *The Essential Frankfurt School Reader*, ed. Andrew Arato and Eike Gebhardt (New York: Continuum, 1993), 300–18.

13. On noir's relationship to the Freudian dream work, see Kelly Oliver and Benigno Trigo, *Noir Anxiety* (Minneapolis: University of Minnesota Press, 2003).

14. The texts I am referring to here, in addition to the Halttunen and Goddu already cited, are the following: Eric Hobsbawm, *Bandits* (New York: New Press, 2000); Michael Denning, *Mechanic Accents*, esp. 65–166. For an account of the city mysteries, in addition to Denning, see Reynolds, *Beneath the American Renaissance*, 169–210, and Stephen Knight, *Form and Ideology in Crime Fiction* (London: Macmillan, 1980). On the salacious guidebook genre, see Marcus Klein, *Easterns, Westerns, and Private Eyes* (Madison: University of Wisconsin Press, 1994), 29–52. On the relationship of the gothic to noir, see also Eric Sundquist, "Faulkner,

Race, and the Forms of American Fiction" in *Faulkner and Race: Faulkner and Yok-napatawpha, 1986,* ed. Doreen Fowler and Ann J. Abadie (Jackson: University Press of Mississippi, 1986), 18–22, and Leslie Fiedler, *Love and Death in the American Novel* (New York: Criterion, 1960), 475–78. For an account of the literature of empire and its relationship to racial and class formation as well as an account of the racialized and geopolitical limits of the class-imaginary of the city mystery, see Shelley Streeby, *American Sensations: Class, Empire, and the Production of Popular Culture* (Berkeley: University of California Press, 2002). For an account of the race melodramas of Thomas Dixon and of the form more generally, see Susan Gillman, *Blood Talk: American Race Melodrama and the Culture of the Occult* (Chicago: University of Chicago Press, 2003), esp. 1–31, 73–116.

15. On the *corrido,* see José Limón, *Mexican Ballads, Chicano Poems: History and Influence in Mexican-American Social Poetry* (Berkeley: University of California Press, 1992), 16–77; José David Saldívar, "Chicano Border Narratives as Cultural Critique," in *Criticism in the Borderlands: Studies in Chicano Literature, Culture, and Ideology,* ed. Hector Calderón and Saldívar (Durham, N.C.: Duke University Press, 1991), 167–80; and Streeby, *American Sensations,* 251–90. On the Molly Maguires, see Kevin Kenny, *Making Sense of the Molly Maguires* (Oxford: Oxford University Press, 1998). On bandit stories about Jessie James, Billy the Kid, and Bonnie and Clyde, see Richard Slotkin, *Gunfighter Nation: The Myth of the Frontier in Twentieth-Century America* (New York: Harper Collins, 1992).

16. It is important to note that the representation of the detective in nineteenth-century popular literature was not gender exclusive, as Catherine Nickerson demonstrates in her groundbreaking study of women's detective fiction in the nineteenth century, *The Web of Iniquity: Early Detective Fiction by Women* (Durham, N.C.: Duke University Press, 1998), esp. 4–28.

17. See Richard Hofstadter, "The Paranoid Style in American Politics," in Hofstadter, *The Paranoid Style in American Politics and Other Essays* (New York: Knopf, 1965), 3–40.

18. Halttunen puts it this way: "It was thus the peculiar nature of the Gothic narrative of murder to try *and fail* to come to terms with the shocking revelation that murder had been committed. For Gothic mystery and Gothic horror affirmed the ultimate incomprehensibility of any given crime of murder, in sharp contrast to the execution sermon's unproblematic acceptance of the act and the guilt of the condemned murderer" (*Murder Most Foul,* 4).

19. See, for example, the essays contained in *Romancing the Shadow: Poe and Race,* ed. J. Gerald Kennedy and Liliane Weissberg (New York: Oxford University Press, 2001). See as well Goddu, *Gothic America,* and Toni Morrison, *Playing in the Dark: Whiteness and the Literary Imagination* (Cambridge, Mass.: Harvard University Press, 1992).

20. See Eric Lott, *Love and Theft: Blackface Minstrelsy and the American Working Class* (New York: Oxford University Press, 1993), esp. 3–107.

21. For an account of the image of the black rapist and its relationship to what Susan Gillman has aptly termed the "race melodrama," as well as a range

of other nineteenth- and early-twentieth-century fictional and nonfictional forms, see the following: George Fredrickson, *The Black Image in the White Mind: The Debate on Afro-American Character and Destiny, 1817–1914* (Hanover, N.H.: Wesleyan University Press, 1971), 256–82; Angela Davis, *Women, Race, and Class* (New York: Vintage, 1983), 172–201; Robyn Wiegman, *American Anatomies: Theorizing Race and Gender* (Durham, N.C.: Duke University Press, 1995); Susan Gillman, *Blood Talk*, 1–31.

22. See James Naremore, *More than Night: Film Noir in its Contexts* (Berkeley: University of California Press, 1998), 9–39.

23. See Sean McCann, "Constructing Race Williams: The Klan and the Making of Hard-Boiled Crime Fiction," *American Quarterly* 49 (1997): 677–716.

24. For an account of the codification of the color line at the turn of the century, see Siobahn Somerville, *Queering the Color Line: Race and the Invention of Homosexuality in American Culture* (Durham, N.C.: Duke University Press, 2000).

25. For accounts of the gangster narratives, journalism, and film of this era, see David E. Ruth, *Inventing the Public Enemy* (Chicago: University of Chicago Press, 1996); on the political and cultural resonances of Mencken's journalism, see Chip Rhodes, *Structures of the Jazz Age* (London: Verso, 1998), 18–43; for a general discussion of the transformations in popular culture in the era that saw the first emergence of noir, see Lewis A. Erenberg, *Steppin' Out: New York Nightlife and the Transformation of American Culture, 1890–1930* (Westport, Conn.: Greenwood Press, 1981), esp. 233–63.

26. See Pierre Bourdieu *Distinction: A Social Critique of the Judgment of Taste*, trans. Richard Nice (Cambridge, Mass.: Harvard University Press, 1987), 1–96.

27. On the concept of "cultural capital," see Bourdieu, *Distinction*, 1–96, and John Guillory, *Cultural Capital* (Chicago: University of Chicago Press, 1993).

28. For the classic account of this heroic narrative, see William F. Nolan, "History of a Pulp: The Life and Times of *Black Mask*," in *The Black Mask Boys: Masters in the Hard-Boiled School of Detective Fiction* (New York: Morrow, 1985), 19–34.

29. Bertolt Brecht, *The Three-Penny Opera*, in Brecht, *Collected Plays: Two*, trans. Stephan S. Brecht (London: Methuen, 1979), 166.

30. My understanding of interpellation comes of course from Louis Althusser's famous essay "Ideology and Ideological State Apparatuses," in *Lenin and Philosophy and Other Essays*, trans. Ben Brewster (New York: Monthly Review, 2001).

31. On the uncanny, see Freud, "The Uncanny," in *The Standard Edition of the Complete Psychological Works of Sigmund Freud*, trans. and ed. James Strachey (London: Hogarth, 1955) 17: 217–56.

2. Going Blood-Simple in Poisonville

1. For a brief definition of instrumental rationality, see Fredric Jameson, "Reification and Utopia in Mass Culture," in *Signatures of the Visible* (New York: Routledge, 1990), 10.

2. On Taylorism and Fordism, see Martin Sklar, *The United States as a Developing Country: Studies in U.S. History in the Progressive Era and the 1920s* (Cambridge: Cambridge University Press, 1992), 20–30; Sklar, *The Corporate Reconstruction of American Capitalism, 1890–1916: The Market, the Law, and Politics* (Cambridge: Cambridge University Press, 1988); and David Harvey, *The Condition of Postmodernity: An Enquiry into the Origin of Cultural Change* (Cambridge: Blackwell, 1989), 10–38, 121–40. My thinking on Fordism in the American context has also been influenced by Antonio Gramsci, *Prison Notebooks*, ed. and trans. Quintin Hoare and Goeffrey Nowell Smith (New York: International Publishers, 1971), 279–318.

3. See *Écrits: A Selection*, trans. Alan Sheridan (New York: Norton, 1977), 30–113. Greg Forter has recently proposed the similar notion of a "generic unconscious" to talk about certain negative or critical tendencies within the representation of masculinity in hard-boiled detective fiction and noir crime fiction (215). In employing this term, he emphasizes the will to masochism and the negation of mastery (both functioning under an eroticized understanding of the death drive) that form the unconscious or subtextual flip side to the genre's commitment to sadism and mastery (1–45). While my own understanding of *Red Harvest*'s "textual unconscious" bears a number of similarities to Forter's "generic unconscious," it differs both in its understanding of such an unconscious as a site of ideological fantasy as well as subversive desire and in its emphasis on the specifically historical and historicizable character of the materials of this unconscious. See Greg Forter, *Murdering Masculinities: Fantasies of Gender and Violence in the American Crime Novel* (New York: New York University Press, 2000).

4. My understanding of the significance of gaps and silences in a literary text is informed by Pierre Macherey, *A Theory of Literary Production*, trans. Geoffrey Wall (London: Routledge, 1978), 82–101.

5. This split suggests why the cultural politics of hard-boiled fiction has always seemed contradictory. The novels and short stories that make up the genre often combine radical economic and legal critiques with more conflicted, if not reactionary, figurations of gender, sexuality, race, and nation. This split has manifested itself on a critical level as well. Thus, in *City of Quartz* (New York: Vintage, 1992), 36–54, Mike Davis can argue for the hard-boiled narrative (what he calls noir) as a form of populist-Marxist protest, while in "Hard-Boiled Ideology" Bethany Ogdon focuses on the genre's reinscription of gender and racial privilege (*Critical Quarterly* 34 [1992]: 71–87).

6. Unlike his hard-boiled descendants in the twenties and thirties, the gentleman detective had a female counterpart, who could be found in the pages of nineteenth-century women's detective fiction and often challenged the gender and class norms of Victorian-era, middle-class culture. For an account of the female detective in women's detective fiction of the nineteenth century, see Catherine Nickerson, *The Web of Iniquity: Early Detective Fiction by American Women* (Durham, N.C.: Duke University Press, 1998).

7. See Gail Bederman, *Manliness and Civilization: A Cultural History of Gender*

and Race in the United States, 1880–1917 (Chicago: University of Chicago Press, 1995), 1–44; and Michael Kimmel, *Manhood in America: A Cultural History* (New York: Free Press, 1996), 117–221.

8. See Richard Slotkin, *Regeneration through Violence: The Mythology of the American Frontier, 1600–1860* (New York: Harper Collins, 1996), 268–517; and Slotkin, *Gunfighter Nation: The Myth of the Frontier in Twentieth-Century America* (New York: Harper Collins, 1992), 194–228. The genealogical connection between the hard-boiled detective and the adventure hero and more generally between hard-boiled fiction and the western has been made by a number of critics. See especially Cynthia S. Hamilton, *Western and Hard-Boiled Detective Fiction in America: From High Noon to Midnight* (London: Macmillan, 1987); and John G. Cawelti, *Adventure, Mystery, and Romance: Formula Stories as Art and Popular Culture* (Chicago: University of Chicago Press, 1976).

9. For an account of American imperialism and the formation of race and gender privilege in the nineteenth century, see Shelly Streeby, *American Sensations: Class, Empire, and the Production of Popular Culture* (Berkeley: University of California Press, 2002); Amy Kaplan, *The Anarchy of Empire in the Making of U.S. Culture* (Cambridge, Mass.: Harvard University Press, 2002), 1–51; and, of course, Kaplan's now-classic "'Left Alone with America': The Absence of Empire in the Study of American Culture," in *Cultures of United States Imperialism*, ed. Kaplan and Donald E. Pease (Durham, N.C.: Duke University Press, 1993), 3–21.

10. For a discussion of these romances and their relationship to U.S. imperialism and constructions of masculinity, see Kaplan, *The Anarchy of Empire*, 92–120.

11. My understanding of the reification of labor in corporate capitalism comes, of course, from Lukács's famous essay on the subject, "Reification and the Consciousness of the Proletariat," in *History and Class Consciousness: Studies in Marxist Dialectics*, trans. Rodney Livingstone (Cambridge, Mass.: MIT Press, 1971), 83–222.

12. Sean McCann has pointed out that this paradoxical modernized antimodernism of the hard-boiled text is also shaped by the relationship of pulp magazines to the marketplace. The "glossy" magazines radically transformed magazine publishing in the United States by relying primarily on advertising revenue, drastically lowering their purchase price, and boosting their distribution. The pulps, in contrast, while a twentieth-century phenomenon, had more in common with dime novels and the nineteenth-century story papers that the glossies replaced than with the glossies themselves. While also keeping their purchase price low, the pulps employed relatively little advertising and made their money by keeping wages down and using cheap paper. This led pulp writers to disavow the commodified status of pulp magazines and celebrate the pulps as more authentic and less commodified than the glossies, which they often characterized, in a revealing gendering, as "women's magazines." While the more marginal status of pulps in relation to the market clearly enabled pulp writers' critique of capitalism and mass culture, the disavowal central to their celebration

of authenticity repeats on a formal level the disavowal that structures the allegorical gendering of capitalism and mass culture in the hard-boiled text that I
will discuss more fully below. See Sean McCann, "'A Roughneck Reaching for
Higher Things': The Vagaries of Pulp Populism," *Radical History Review* 61
(1995): 4–34.

13. Dashiell Hammett, *Red Harvest* (New York: Vintage, 1989), 43.

14. My understanding of the critique of capitalism advanced in *Red Harvest*
draws on the analysis advanced by Carl Freedman and Christopher Kendrick in
"Forms of Labor in Dashiell Hammett's *Red Harvest*," *PMLA* 106 (1991): 209–21.

15. For a discussion of Wilson's key role in shaping the corporate and managed nature of U.S. capitalism in the twentieth century, see Sklar, *The United
States as a Developing Country*, 102–42. The double letters of Elihu Willsson's last
name (as opposed to the single letters in President Wilson's name) seem to be a
conscious allusion to the two pairs of double letters in Hammett's own name. By
aligning himself with Willsson in this way, Hammett suggests parallels between
the role of the author as the controlling authority over a fictional world and
Willsson's command and ownership of much of Personville.

16. The allegorical reading of Poisonville that follows is influenced by Sinda
Gregory's reading of the "mythic" dimension of the town in *Private Investigations:
The Novels of Dashiell Hammett* (Carbondale: Southern Illinois University Press,
1985), 31.

17. In Hammett's time, this ideal would have been expressed most directly by
the rhetoric of Progressivism. In his reading of *Red Harvest*, William Marling
gives an excellent account of Hammett's ambivalent relationship to Progressive
beliefs (106–12). Marling argues that Hammett both subscribed to certain Progressive ideals and sympathized with the populist critique of Progressivism as
being "assimilated by the power elite" (109). It is clearly the populist critique, as
well as what is perhaps a more radical critique derived from Hammett's soon-to-
be proclaimed socialist affiliations, that wins out in *Red Harvest*. See Marling, *The
American Roman Noir: Hammett, Chandler, Cain* (Athens: University of Georgia
Press, 1994).

18. My reading of the national allegory enacted in *Red Harvest*, both in the
initial distinction between Personville and Poisonville and in the dream sequence
discussed below, has been shaped by a number of texts: most fundamentally, of
course, by Benedict Anderson's *Imagined Communities: Reflections on the Origin
and Spread of Nationalism* (London: Verso, 1983); but also in important ways by
Lauren Berlant's further development and complication of Anderson's thesis in
The Anatomy of National Fantasy: Hawthorne, Utopia, and Everyday Life (Chicago:
University of Chicago Press, 1991), and *The Queen of America Goes to Washington
City: Essays on Sex and Citizenship* (Durham, N.C.: Duke University Press, 1997).
Slavoj Žižek, *Tarrying with the Negative*, has also contributed in important ways
to my understanding of the significance of national allegory in *Red Harvest*. See
Tarrying with the Negative: Kant, Hegel, and the Critique of Ideology (Durham, N.C.:
Duke University Press, 1993), 200–237.

19. My understanding of Hammett's aesthetics of identification and dis-identification in *Red Harvest* is informed by Kaja Silverman's discussion of Fassbinder's "aesthetics of pessimism" in *Male Subjectivity at the Margins* (New York: Routledge, 1992), 125–27. Like Silverman, I am interested in an aesthetics that disrupts the conventionality of masculine identification in literary and filmic texts. However, in talking about a popular aesthetics of identification and dis-identification in Hammett, I want to suggest that negativity in his text relies primarily on a literalization of the fantasies that animate the conventional hard-boiled plot rather than an ironic alienation from it.

20. See Steven Marcus, "Dashiell Hammett," in *The Poetics of Murder: Detective Fiction and Literary Theory*, ed. Glenn Most and William Stowe (New York: Harcourt, 1983), 201–2.

21. See Sean McCann, "Constructing Race Williams: The Klan and the Making of Hard-Boiled Crime Fiction," *American Quarterly* 49 (1997): 677–716.

22. For a discussion of the emergence of sociological and Progressive forms of racism, see George Fredrickson, *The Black Image in the White Mind: The Debate on Afro-American Character and Destiny, 1817–1914* (Hanover, N.H.: Wesleyan University Press, 1971), 283–319; Michael Omi and Howard Winant, *Racial Formation in the United States* (New York: Routledge, 1994), 9–11; and Mark Pittenger, "A World of Difference: Constructing the 'Underclass' in Progressive America," *American Quarterly* 49 (1997): 26–65. For an account of primitivist discourse in early-twentieth-century anthropology, see George W. Stocking, *Race, Culture, and Evolution* (New York: Free Press, 1968), 110–32, 270–307; and Marianna Torgovnick, *Gone Primitive: Savage Intellects, Modern Lives* (Chicago: University of Chicago Press, 1990), 3–41.

23. In *Tarrying with the Negative*, Žižek links enjoyment theft with the formation of national sentiment: "Nationalism thus presents a privileged domain of the eruption of enjoyment into the social field. The national Cause is ultimately nothing but the way subjects of a given ethnic community organize their enjoyment through national myths. What is therefore at stake in ethnic tensions is always the possession of the national Thing. We always impute to the other an excessive enjoyment: he wants to steal our enjoyment (by ruining our way of life) and/or he has access to some sort of secret, perverse enjoyment" (202–3). The national dimensions of the specific fantasy of enjoyment theft that structure the hard-boiled narrative will become clear in my reading of the Op's dream below.

24. See Dennis Porter, *The Pursuit of Crime: Art and Ideology in Detective Fiction* (New Haven, Conn.: Yale University Press, 1981), 146–88.

25. In discussing the romance as an allegorical form open to a number of different codings, I am drawing on Sommer's definition, in *Foundational Fictions: The National Romances of Latin America* (Berkeley: University of California Press, 1991), of the form: "By romance, here, I mean a cross between our contemporary use of the word as a love story and a nineteenth century use that distinguished the genre as more boldly allegorical than the novel. The classic examples in Latin America are almost inevitably stories of star-crossed lovers who represent

particular regions, races, parties, economic interests, and the like" (5). Jameson (whom Sommer reflects in her definition) asserts that the allegorical work done by the resolution of these particularist divisions represents an "imaginary solution" to real socioeconomic contradiction (*Political* 119). While Sommer defines the Latin American romance as a "cross" between contemporary uses of the word to denote a love story and the earlier nineteenth-century definition of the term as elaborated by critics like Richard Chase, it seems to me that in the United States these two definitions only sometimes cohere (with Cooper, for example) and at other times are explicitly opposed. Thus what are often called the canonical romances of Hawthorne and Melville, with their rejection of any sort of marriage plot, have more in common with what I am calling, after Leslie Fiedler, the gothic refusal of the romance plot than with the romance tradition represented by late-nineteenth-century historical romances. Given this alternate genealogy, the hard-boiled narrative can be located all too comfortably in what Donald Pease incisively terms the romance "field imaginary" of American studies as elaborated by critics such as Chase. See Fredric Jameson, *The Political Unconscious: Narrative as a Socially Symbolic Act* (Ithaca, N.Y.: Cornell University Press, 1981); Richard Chase, *The American Novel and Its Tradition* (New York: Doubleday, 1957), 1–28; Leslie Fiedler, *Love and Death in the American Novel* (New York: Criterion, 1960), 149–212; and Donald Pease, "New Americanists," in *Revisionary Interventions into the Americanist Canon*, ed. Donald E. Pease (Durham, N.C.: Duke University Press, 1994), 1–9.

26. In my reading of both the homophobia and the disavowed homoeroticism that structures the gothic form, I am indebted to Eve Sedgwick's discussion of the relationship of "homosexual panic" to the tradition of the male gothic in *Between Men: English Literature and Male Homosocial Desire* (New York: Columbia University Press, 1985), 83–96.

27. While brief, Freud's essay on mourning and melancholia is richly and notoriously convoluted, allowing for a range of possible interpretations. See Sigmund Freud, "Mourning and Melancholia," in *The Standard Edition of the Complete Psychological Works of Sigmund Freud*, trans. and ed. James Strachey (London: Hogarth, 1955), 14: 243–58. My reference to melancholia stems largely from Freud's suggestive remark that melancholia, in contrast to mourning, is "a loss of a more ideal kind" (245). Freud goes on to elaborate: "The object has not perhaps actually died, but has become lost as an object of love (e.g. the case of a betrothed girl who has been jilted). In yet other cases one feels justified in maintaining the belief that a loss of the kind has occurred, but one cannot see clearly what it is that has been lost, and it is all the more reasonable to suppose that the patient too cannot consciously perceive what he has lost either. This, indeed, might be so even if the patient is aware of the loss which has given rise to the melancholia, but only in the sense that he knows whom he has lost but not what he has lost in him. This would suggest that melancholia is in some way related to an object-loss which is withdrawn from consciousness, in contradistinction to mourning, in which there is nothing about the loss that is unconscious" (245).

The ideal nature of this loss suggests its ideological or phantasmatic character. Thus I want to suggest that melancholia is structured in relationship to various forms of idealism such as nationalism and romantic love (and here Freud's example of the deserted bride is particularly telling). Freud himself suggests the significance of melancholia for nationalism elsewhere in the essay where he relates mourning (and by implication melancholia) to "the loss of some abstraction . . . such as fatherland, liberty and ideal, and so on" (164).

28. See Andreas Huyssen's *After the Great Divide: Modernism, Mass Culture, Postmodernism* (Bloomington: Indiana University Press, 1986), 44–62.

29. See Judith Butler, *The Psychic Life of Power* (Stanford, Calif.: Stanford University Press, 1997), 132–98. This is, of course, a reworking and expansion of her earlier analysis of the relationship of melancholia to the construction of gender and sexuality in *Bodies That Matter* (New York: Routledge, 1993), 223–42, and *Gender Trouble* (New York: Routledge, 1990), 57–72. For a provocative Lacanian critique of Butler's understanding of melancholia, though one that also recognizes its value for understanding same-sex desire, see Slavoj Žižek, *The Ticklish Subject: The Absent Center of Political Ontology* (London: Verso, 1999), 247–312.

30. See Henry Nash Smith, *Virgin Land* (Cambridge, Mass.: Harvard University Press, 1950); and Annette Kolodny, *The Lay of the Land* (Chapel Hill: University of North Carolina Press, 1975), for extended discussions of these two tropes.

31. See Michael Kazin, *The Populist Persuasion: An American History* (New York: Basic Books, 1995), 12–14; and Richard Hofstadter, *The Age of Reform: From Bryan to FDR* (Boston: Beacon Press, 1955), 60–93.

32. In the context of this argument, it is important to make a theoretical distinction between the populist and the popular (even while the two forms may productively and/or problematically overlap in practice). *Red Harvest* was published just before the emergence of the broad leftist coalition that Michael Denning terms "the cultural front," and parts of the novel (especially in its relatively sympathetic representation of radical unionism) point beyond the populist politics suggested in this passage and toward the more collective and counter-hegemonic forms of popular struggle that Denning terms the "cultural front." See Denning, *The Cultural Front: The Laboring of American Culture in the Twentieth Century* (London: Verso, 1997), 1–45.

33. My understanding of the dynamics of homosociality and homoeroticism in *Red Harvest* derives, of course, from Eve Sedgwick's groundbreaking definition and historicization of these dynamics in *Between Men* and *Epistemology of the Closet* (Berkeley: University of California Press, 1990). Hard-boiled masculinity emerges after what Sedgwick has described as the formation of (always conflicted and incoherent if still powerful) "twentieth century understandings of homo/heterosexual definition" (*Epistemology* 1), and is haunted by both the imposition of this definition and its incoherence. For a more materialist account of the emergence of this divide, one that locates it in the emergence of industrial and especially corporate capitalism (and thus dovetails with my own understanding

of the attendant shifts in masculinity with the advent of corporate capitalism), see Rosemary Hennessy, *Profit and Pleasure: Sexual Identities in Late Capitalism* (New York: Routledge, 2000), 74–110.

34. In the most radical moments of Raymond Chandler's novels, this longing, and even the possibility of homoerotic fulfillment, become explicit. The most famous example is, perhaps, Marlowe's boat ride with Red in *Farewell, My Lovely*, in which, for an all too brief spell, sexual desire doesn't seem to need violence as its necessary counterpart. The fraught but loving bond between Marlowe and Terry Lennox in *The Long Goodbye* is another obvious example. Of course, it is important to remember that Chandler's texts could also be characterized by homophobic repudiations of such longing, as in the fight scene with Carol in *The Big Sleep*.

35. For an account of this geopolitically specific dynamic of racialization and its relationship to U.S. imperialism, see Streeby, *American Sensations*, esp. 251–90.

36. As Siobhan Somerville has recently demonstrated, the racialized dimensions of this image of homosociality are far from accidental or arbitrary but are linked to the twin and interrelated emergences of the divide between homosexuality and heterosexuality and the legal and social codification of the color line at the turn of the century. See Somerville, *Queering the Color Line: Race and the Invention of Homosexuality in American Culture* (Durham, N.C.: Duke University Press, 2000), 1–38.

37. See Roland Barthes, *S/Z*, trans. Richard Miller (New York: Farrar, Straus and Giroux, 1974), 19.

38. In developing my reading of gendered violence in *Red Harvest*, I am indebted to Carla Freccero's analysis of the political stakes of the representation of gendered violence in "Historical Violence, Censorship, and the Serial Killer: The Case of *American Psycho*," *diacritics* 27 (1997): 44–58. This chapter attempts to define the representation of a violent form of masculine subjectivity without falling into what she rightly describes as right-wing discourse of the "serial killer," which serves the purpose of masking larger forms of social violence. On the discourse of the serial killer and its relationship to larger forms of social violence, also see Mark Seltzer, *Serial Killers* (New York: Routledge, 1998).

39. Here I am drawing on Jacques Lacan's famous dictum that "the unconscious is 'discours de l'Autre' (discourse of the Other)" (*Écrits* 312).

40. For this insight I want to thank John Hilgart, one of my readers at *Men and Masculinities* for the article version of this chapter, who saw the implications of my argument about this final scene more clearly than I saw them myself.

41. See "The Interpretation of Dreams," in *The Standard Edition of the Complete Psychological Works of Sigmund Freud*, 4: 277–338.

3. The Hard-Boiled Male Travels Abroad

1. Ernest Hemingway, *The Sun Also Rises* (New York: Macmillan, 1986), 34.

2. *A Dictionary of Americanisms* locates the first modern use of the term "hard-boiled" in 1919. It goes on to distinguish between the modern usage of the

term, denoting "hard-headed, callous, shrewd," from the earlier meanings of "rigid, narrow and pedantic" and "denoting stiff articles of clothing, especially a derby hat" (776). The modern definition clearly corresponds not only to the use of the term in the twenties to describe the tough-guy hero of the newly emergent form of detective fiction but also to Jake's use of the term. The second edition of the *Oxford English Dictionary* gives the same definitions and much of the same genealogy for the term but doesn't distinguish clearly between modern and older uses (6:1109–110). The term "hard-boiled" was employed by Joseph "Cap" Shaw, the editor of *Black Mask* in the late twenties and thirties, to describe a standard of masculine and critical toughness: speaking of a story by J. Paul Suter in the January 1927 issue of the magazine, he asserts that the story has a style that will satisfy the "most hard-boiled critic" (107). Shaw used the same standard of toughness in the August 1926 edition of the magazine to celebrate the fiction appearing in the magazine as "real, honest to Jasper, red-blooded, he-man stories" (3). It is thus not too much of a stretch to think that Hemingway, ever the cultural insider and scrupulously attentive to the fluctuations of popular culture (especially in the 1920s), would be familiar with the term and its significance for the form of masculine toughness advanced in the pages of *Black Mask*. See Mitford M. Matthews, *A Dictionary of Americanisms* (Chicago: University of Chicago Press, 1951); and *Oxford English Dictionary* 2d ed., ed. T. A. Simpson and E. S. C. Weiner (Oxford: Clarendon Press, 1989).

3. For the history of the emergence of hard-boiled fiction in the pages of *Black Mask*, see Ron Goulart, *The Dime Detectives* (New York: Mysterious Press, 1988), 21–50; *The Black Mask Boys: Masters in the Hard-Boiled School of Detective Fiction*, ed. William F. Nolan (New York: Morrow, 1985),19–33; and Lee Server, *Danger Is My Business: An Illustrated History of the Fabulous Pulp Magazines, 1896–1953* (San Francisco: Chronicle Books, 1993), 61–76.

4. While there is no direct evidence that Hemingway read *Black Mask* or other detective pulps, he was, during his Paris years and throughout the rest of his life, an avid reader of detective fiction. As Michael Reynolds puts it in his monumental bibliographical study, *Hemingway's Reading, 1910–1940* (Princeton, N.J.: Princeton University Press, 1981): "Were this book complete, there would be more murder mysteries on the list. Ernest began reading them in Paris" (24). Moreover, according to Reynolds's inventory, Hemingway purchased Hammett's last two novels, *The Glass Key* and *The Thin Man*, immediately upon publication in 1931 and 1934 respectively (134). These were the only two of Hammett's novels that were not first serialized in pulp form, and his immediate purchase of them suggests that Hemingway may have been acquainted with the pulp versions of Hammett's other novels and short stories.

5. See, for example, Sheldon Norman Grebstein, "The Tough Hemingway and His Hard-Boiled Children," in *Tough Guy Writers of the Thirties*, ed. David Madden (Carbondale: Southern Illinois University Press, 1968), 18–41.

6. Thus, rather than simply reversing these histories to argue for the primacy of the hard-boiled story as a site of origin, I want to suggest that the literary

production of hard-boiled masculinity has a number of sources in both popular and high culture.

7. Andreas Huyssen, *After the Great Divide: Modernism, Mass Culture, Post-modernism* (Bloomington: Indiana University Press, 1986), viii.

8. See Rena Sanderson, "Hemingway and Gender History," in *The Cambridge Companion to Hemingway*, ed. Scott Donaldson (Cambridge: Cambridge University Press, 1996), 170–96.

9. In addressing the representation of masculinity in *The Sun Also Rises*, my analysis is in dialogue with a number of important recent treatments of this subject: Ira Elliot, "Performance Art: Jake Barnes and 'Masculine' Signification in *The Sun Also Rises*," *American Literature* 67, no. 1 (1995): 77–94; Richard Fatina, "Hemingway's Masochism, Sodomy, and the Dominant Woman," *Hemingway Review* 23, no. 1 (2003): 94–105; Jacob Michael Leland, "Yes That Is a Roll of Bills in My Pocket: The Economy of Masculinity in *The Sun Also Rises*," *Hemingway Review* 23, no. 2 (2004): 37–46; Thomas Strychacz, "Dramatizations of Manhood in Hemingway's *In Our Time* and *The Sun Also Rises*," *American Literature* 61, no. 2 (1989): 245–60; Carl Eby, *Hemingway's Fetishism* (New York: State University of New York Press, 1999); Nancy Comley and Robert Scholes, *Hemingway's Genders* (New Haven, Conn.: Yale University Press, 1994); and Mark Spilka's pioneering study, *Hemingway's Quarrel with Androgyny* (Lincoln: University of Nebraska Press, 1990).

10. See Kennedy's elegiac, elegant "Hemingway, Hadley, and Paris: The Persistence of Desire," in *The Cambridge Companion to Hemingway*, 197–221. His essay nicely attends to the relationship between subjective desire and the mapping of social space in the Hemingway corpus, a project that, in very different ways, informs the present chapter.

11. The Victorian roots of Hemingway's preoccupations with gender and sexuality have been traced by Mark Spilka in *Hemingway's Quarrel with Androgyny*, esp. 15–174, 197–222.

12. My understanding of the increasing visibility or emergence of these desires in the modernist period is influenced by a number of sources. A partial list includes the following: on the coding of desires and more specifically identities as explicitly "homosexual" (as well as "heterosexual") in the early twentieth century, see Michel Foucault, *The History of Sexuality*, vol. 1, trans. Robert Hurley (New York: Vintage Books, 1990); Eve Kosofsky Sedgwick, *Epistemology of the Closet* (Berkeley: University of California Press, 1990); George Chauncy, *Gay New York: Gender, Urban Culture, and the Making of the Gay Male World, 1890–1940* (New York: Basic Books, 1994); and Rosemary Hennessy, *Profit and Pleasure: Sexual Identities in Late Capitalism* (New York: Routledge, 2000). On the emergence of the desires and identities associated with the (1920s version of) "new woman," see Ellen Wiley Todd, "Art, the 'New Woman,' and Consumer Culture," in *Gender and American History since 1890*, ed. Barbara Melosh (London: Routledge, 1993); and Wendy Martin, "Brett Ashley as New Woman in *The Sun Also Rises*," in *New Essays on "The Sun Also Rises*," ed. Linda Wagner Martin (New

York: Cambridge University Press, 1987), 65–82. On miscegenous desire in this period, see Marianna Torgovnick, *Gone Primitive: Savage Intellects, Modern Lives* (Chicago: University of Chicago Press, 1990); and Gail Bederman, *Manliness and Civilization: A Cultural History of Gender and Race in the United States, 1880–1917* (Chicago: University of Chicago Press, 1995). On commodification and commodity desire in this period, see Fredric Jameson, "Reification and Utopia in Mass Culture," in *Signatures of the Visible* (New York: Routledge, 1990), 9–34; Huyssen, *After the Great Divide*; and David Harvey, *The Condition of Postmodernity: An Enquiry into the Origin of Cultural Change* (Cambridge: Blackwell, 1989).

13. The Adorno quote I am paraphrasing here reads as follows: "Just as the overwhelming power of high capitalism forms myths that tower above the collective conscious [*sic*], in the same way the mythic region in which the modern consciousness seeks refuge bears the marks of that capitalism: what subjectively is the dream of dreams is objectively a nightmare." See Adorno, *In Search of Wagner,* trans. Rodney Livingstone (London: New Left Books, 1981), 123.

14. In this way, the question of masculinity in *The Sun Also Rises* returns us to the novel's much-discussed representation of the expatriate lifestyle. It suggests the doubleness of this lifestyle. The expatriate lifestyle is at once a space of national disidentification and a site of the imperialist extension of American cultural forms.

15. See Allen Tate, "Hard-Boiled," in *Critical Essays on Ernest Hemingway's "The Sun Also Rises,"* ed. James Nagel (New York: G. K. Hall, 1995), 42–43.

16. See Arnold E. and Cathy N. Davidson, "Decoding the Hemingway Hero in *The Sun Also Rises*," in *New Essays on "The Sun Also Rises,"* ed. Wagner-Martin, 91.

17. For an interpretation of the wound, and by extension the novel, as a symbol of the impotence of the lost generation, see Mark Spilka's early essay "The Death of Love in The Sun Also Rises," in *Modern Critical Interpretations: Ernest Hemingway's "The Sun Also Rises,"* ed. Harold Bloom (New York: Chelsea House, 1987), 25–37. For a reading of the wound that links it to Hemingway's career, see Philip Young's (in)famous *Ernest Hemingway: A Reconsideration* (University Park: Pennsylvania State University Press, 1966). For an essay that implicitly aligns Jake's wound with the impotence of "modern man," see Allen Josephs, "Toreo: The Moral Axis of *The Sun Also Rises*," in *Modern Critical Interpretations*, ed. Bloom, 151–67. See Michael Reynolds, *"The Sun Also Rises": A Novel of the Twenties* (Boston: Twayne, 1988) for an account of the wound that reads it merely in terms of Jake's "impotence."

18. My reading of the symbolic cultural values ideologically conflated with the male sex organ draws, of course, on Jacques Lacan's famous distinction between the penis as sex organ and the phallus as "the privileged signifier of that mark in which the role of the logos is joined with the advent of desire," and particularly on feminist and queer theoretical reworkings of this distinction. See Jacques Lacan, "The Signification of the Phallus," in *Écrits: A Selection,* trans. Alan Sheridan (New York: Norton, 1977), 281–91; Elizabeth Grosz, *Jacques*

Lacan: A Feminist Introduction (New York: Routledge, 1990), 115–26; Judith Butler, *Bodies That Matter: On the Discursive Limits of "Sex"* (New York: Routledge, 1993), 57–121; Earl Jackson Jr., *Strategies of Deviance: Studies in Gay Male Representation* (Bloomington: Indiana University Press, 1995), 1–52; and especially Kaja Silverman, *Male Subjectivity at the Margins* (New York: Routledge, 1992), 1–51. Silverman's reading of the cultural valorization of the phallus as "central to the maintenance of classic masculinity" and to the "dominant fiction" of modern patriarchal and capitalist societies has particularly shaped my reading of the significance of Jake's wound (15–16).

19. My rereading of Freud's *Three Essays* here and in my discussion of "polymorphous perversity" in what follows has been influenced by Herbert Marcuse, *Eros and Civilization* (Boston: Beacon, 1966). See Sigmund Freud, "Three Essays on the Theory of Sexuality," in *The Standard Edition of the Complete Psychological Works of Sigmund Freud*, trans. and ed. James Strachey (London: Hogarth, 1955), 18: 1–64.

20. The terms "decoding" and "recoding" come from Gilles Deleuze and Félix Guattari, *Anti-Oedipus: Capitalism and Schizophrenia*, trans. Hurley, Seem, and Lane (Minneapolis: University of Minnesota Press, 1983), 222–62. They describe (in the sense I am using them here) the authors' understanding of the transformative and circumscribing effects produced by the constant reorganization of desire under capitalism.

21. For a classic account of the reification of the labor process in this period, one that appeared almost contemporaneously with *The Sun Also Rises*, see Georg Lukács, "Reification and the Consciousness of the Proletariat," in *History and Class Consciousness: Studies in Marxist Dialectics*, trans. Rodney Livingstone (Cambridge, Mass.: MIT Press, 1971), 83–222.

22. My reading here is informed by Fredric Jameson's incisive analysis of the act of writing for Hemingway as an "ideology of technique" that attempts to resist the "great industrial transformation of America after World War I," by reconciling the Protestant work ethic with the pursuit of leisure. While my understanding of Jake's fantasy of unalienated work corresponds in large part to Jameson's reading of Hemingway's "instinctive and intransigent refusal of what suddenly turns out to have ceased to be real living," my reading stresses that Jake's (and perhaps Hemingway's) conception of real living can only be understood as a retrospective and nostalgic fantasy construction. See Jameson, *Marxism and Form* (Princeton, N.J.: Princeton University Press, 1971), 409–12.

23. For an account of the ideological role of the Protestant work ethic in both American society and American historiography, see Herbert Gutman's classic essay "Work, Culture and Society in Industrializing America, 1815–1919," in *Work, Culture, and Society in Industrializing America: Essays in American Working-Class and Social History* (New York: Knopf, 1976), 3–78. Gutman persuasively argues that, far from a national given, the Protestant work ethic was a central term in the ideological justification of the new regime of rationalized capitalism in the nineteenth and early twentieth centuries. As such, it was strongly

contested by workers and artisans steeped in pre-industrial work habits. Thus the work ethic of Jake and other hard-boiled males emerges at the end of this long period of contestation, when, as David Brody puts it, the "door closed" on premodern artisanal traditions and the modern industrial order structured in large part by a standardized "work ethic" had emerged as victorious, partially subsuming the ideology of the heroic artisan within it (3). See Brody, *Workers in Industrial America: Essays on the Twentieth-Century Struggle* (New York: Oxford University Press, 1993).

24. Karl Marx, *Capital, vol. 1*, trans. Ben Fowkes (New York: Random House, 1976), 125–77.

25. For two insightful treatments of the function of humor in *The Sun Also Rises*, see Scott Donaldson, "Humor in *The Sun Also Rises*," in *New Essays on "The Sun Also Rises*," ed. Wagner-Martin, 19–41, and James Hinkle, "What's Funny in *The Sun Also Rises*," in *Modern Critical Interpretations*, ed. Bloom 151–67. Hinkle, in particular, links the novel's irony to its serious message, paralleling my own analysis (134).

26. Jacob Leland has rightly pointed out the way in which Jake's performance of modern masculinity and his performance of consumption are linked. Leland calls attention to the way in which Barnes embodies a newer conception of masculinity as tied to public expenditure rather than "Franklinian thriftiness" (42). While I agree with and draw on Leland's account, I also read Jake as a more thoroughly ambivalent representation of modern masculinity, one that casts ideologically back to older codes even as it conforms and participates in present ones.

27. In relationship to the emergence of sites of resistance in the metropole, Georg Lukács saw the very possibility of class consciousness developing out of the reification and commodification of the labor process. My own understanding of how this Lukácsian dynamic might apply to gender and sexuality is indebted to Kevin Floyd's "Making History: Marxism, Queer Theory, and Contradiction in the Future of American Studies," *Cultural Critique, Special Issue: The Futures of American Studies* 40 (1998): 167–202, which employs Lukács to theorize the contradictory relationship between class consciousness and the emergence of a homosexual identity in the twentieth-century United States.

28. See Bederman, *Manliness and Civilization*, 1–44 and 217–39, for an account of this fantasy of racial borrowing.

29. While a touristic discourse in the novel, this transformation of space into time is also characteristic of colonial travel narratives and functions to fix the colonized population in an always lapsed temporality. For an analysis of this dynamic, see Renato Rosaldo's discussion of "imperialist nostalgia" in *Culture and Truth: The Remaking of Social Analysis* (Boston: Beacon Press, 1989), 68–87, and Mary Louise Pratt's "Scratches on the Face of the Country; or, What Mr. Barrow Saw in the Land of the Bushmen," in *"Race," Writing, and Difference*, ed. Henry Louis Gates Jr. (Chicago: University of Chicago Press, 1985), 138–62.

30. This scene is suggestively replayed in *Green Hills of Africa* when Hemingway and a group of other hunters drive though an unhunted part of East Africa

214 | NOTES TO CHAPTER 4

and are surrounded by a group of Masai villagers, who are fascinated with the automobile and run beside it for a number of miles. The similarity between the two scenes suggests the colonialist fantasy that underpins both narratives.

31. See Richard Hovey, *Hemingway: The Inward Terrain* (Seattle: University of Washington Press, 1960), 71–72. In "Decoding the Hemingway Hero," Arnold and Cathy Davidson also call attention to these pages in Hovey's text.

32. My analysis here is, of course, a gloss on Lacan's "The Signification of the Phallus."

33. In addressing the triangulation of desire in this scene, I am indebted to, even as I slightly rework, Eve Sedgwick's classic discussion of the triangular structure of male homosocial desire. See Sedgwick, *Between Men: English Literature and Male Homosocial Desire* (New York: Columbia University Press, 1985), 1–27.

34. William Adair has helpfully traced these and other allusions to World War I in the novel (of which there are many) in "Cafés and Food: Allusions to the Great War in *The Sun Also Rises*," *Journal of Modern Literature* 25, no. 1 (2001): 127–33.

35. Both possibilities are, of course, evident in the great inheritor of Hemingway's reworking of the hard-boiled style, Raymond Chandler.

36. See, for example, Donald Morton, "Birth of the Cyberqueer," *PMLA* 110 (1995): 369–81, and Mas'ud Zavarzadeh, "Post-ality," *Transformation* 1 (1995): 1–75, to cite but two influential examples. The vulgar Marxist pronouncements of Zavarzadeh and Morton find their unlikely libidinal echo in liberal movements that are based around "progressive" consumption, which are often structured by a fantasy of the purity of individual acts of consumption, as if consumption were a political act proper. What both types of "left" fantasy miss is, of course, that the work of political-economic transformation is inevitably impure, often contingent, and necessarily structured by contradiction.

37. See, for example, Marx's discussion of "the end of capitalism" in *The Grunrisse*, in *The Marx-Engels Reader*, ed. Robert C. Tucker (New York: Norton, 1978), 291–92.

4. Not Your Average Joe

1. In citing *Light in August*, I have been faithful to the peculiarities of Faulkner's spelling and punctuation. Thus, in the epigraph above, the word "Negro" remains as it appears in the text, uncapitalized.

2. William Faulkner, *Light in August* (New York: Vintage, 1985), 111.

3. For a history of the pulps, see Ron Goulart, *The Dime Detectives* (New York: Mysterious Press, 1988); and Lee Server, *Danger Is My Business: An Illustrated History of the Fabulous Pulp Magazines, 1896–1953* (San Francisco: Chronicle Books, 1993). For an account of the art produced for pulp covers, see Robert Lesser, *Pulp Art* (New York: Gramercy Books, 1997), and for a brief history of *Black Mask*, see William F. Nolan, "Introduction," *The Black Mask Boys: Masters in the Hard-Boiled School of Detective Fiction* (New York: Morrow, 1985).

4. See Faulkner's introduction to the original edition of *Sanctuary* (New York: Modern Library, 1932), v-vii. The introduction is striking for a number of reasons. Ostensibly written as an apology for the commercial and sensationalistic nature of the novel, it also reveals a writer deeply, if ambivalently, invested in reaching a popular audience. Describing the novel as being "deliberately conceived to make money," Faulkner recounts how he came to the decision to write in a commercial manner only after having a couple of his stories rejected by magazines and being told by his publisher that *Sartoris* would never sell (v-vi). Deciding to write a commercial novel, he "speculated what a person in Mississippi would believe to be the current trends, chose what I thought was the right answer and invented the most horrific tale I could imagine and wrote it in about three weeks" (vi). If this story of the novel's genesis is even partly to be believed, it is striking that what emerges from this attempt to write in a quick and explicitly commercial manner is a story about a corrupt world inhabited by amoral gangsters, "fallen" women, and an ineffective detective that would be right at home in the pages of *Black Mask*. While Faulkner's borrowings from the hard-boiled and noir traditions are not directly acknowledged in the introduction, hard-boiled phrases and assertions show up symptomatically throughout its four pages. Faulkner claims to have turned to commercial fiction only after having become soft, losing his "hard-bellied" and "hard-gutted" commitment to art (v). This weakness is only temporary, however, and he quickly decides to tighten his belt, accept a job as a coal passer, and write art for art's sake again. Rife with anxiety, these passages attempt to use the language of pulp fiction against itself. Inverting the claims of many pulp writers who celebrated their craft as masculine labor in contrast to the effeminate musings of the artistic writer, Faulkner asserts that writing art is the truly masculine vocation, one comparable to shoveling coal. While this claim seems to clearly, if anxiously, reaffirm the value of high art by defining it in relationship to the standards of masculine toughness affirmed by hard-boiled fiction, it does so only by deconstructing the opposition between the two forms of writing and asserting the ghostly presence of the hard-boiled aesthetic within the seemingly pure domain of art. Given the complications the introduction presents for maintaining a pure divide between high and popular culture, it is interesting to note that it has been dropped from the most recent Vintage edition of the novel, an elision that speaks simultaneously to the attempt to elevate *Sanctuary* to the status of an art novel (an attempt that has been underway at least since the publication of Cleanth Brooks's *William Faulkner: The Yoknapatawpha Country* [New Haven, Conn.: Yale University Press, 1963]) and to the desire to be rid of the cultural boundary crossings that the introduction enacts. As I argue at length below, these boundary crossings become one of the central preoccupations of *Light in August*. For an account of the significance of this introduction for shaping the critical understanding of Faulkner's relationship to popular culture, see Doreen Fowler, "Introduction," in *Faulkner and Popular Culture*, ed. Doreen Fowler and Ann J. Abadie (Jackson: University Press of Mississippi, 1990), ix-xiv. For an account of the relationship between the

hard-boiled/noir aesthetic and Faulkner's fiction, see Eric Sundquist, "Faulkner, Race, and the Forms of American Fiction," in *Faulkner and Race*, ed. Doreen Fowler and Ann J. Abadie (Jackson: University Press of Mississippi, 1986), 1–34.

5. Following the lead of John N. Duvall's "Murder and the Communities," in *Modern Critical Interpretations: William Faulkner's "Light in August,"* ed. Harold Bloom (New York: Chelsea House, 1988), 135–57, I describe Joe's act of taking Joanna's life (an act we crucially do not witness) as a "killing" rather than a murder. Duvall persuasively argues that to describe the ambiguous act as murder is to accede to the ideological account of the act provided by the community, which it constructs in order to justify its continuing investment in discourses of white supremacy and gender inequality.

6. This divide is such a commonplace in Faulkner criticism that it repeats itself even in many of the essays contained in *Faulkner and Popular Culture*, a volume that is expressly dedicated to thinking beyond the divide.

7. The Edmund Wilson quote that adorns the back of the current Vintage edition of Faulkner's novels is exemplary in this regard: "Faulkner . . . belongs to the full-dressed post-Flaubert group of Conrad, Joyce and Proust." One wonders in what state of dress this leaves other writers usually grouped under the banner of modernism. For two relatively recent texts that situate Faulkner's writing largely, if not exclusively, in relationship to "high modernism," see Richard C. Moreland's *Faulkner and Modernism: Rereading and Rewriting* (Madison: University of Wisconsin Press, 1990); and Daniel J. Singal's *William Faulkner: The Making of a Modernist* (Chapel Hill: University of North Carolina Press, 1997). Moreland's text, while remaining largely within the "high art" discourse that characterizes much work on Faulkner and modernism, also indicates the elements in Faulkner that point beyond this discourse, what he terms "postmodern" elements.

8. See Virginia V. James Hlavsa's *Faulkner and the Thoroughly Modern Novel* (Charlottesville: University Press of Virginia, 1991).

9. See, for example, Greg Forter, *Murdering Masculinities: Fantasies of Gender and Violence in the American Crime Novel* (New York: New York University Press, 2000), 85–125.

10. In summarizing in this way, I am, of course, speaking of general tendencies within each school, ones to which there were significant exceptions. While such generalizations are inevitably reductive, I would argue that they also carry a certain kind of analytic force, one that enables me to map the larger ideological coordinates of modernist criticism and suggest their phantasmatic power even as I move toward challenging those coordinates. For a relatively succinct statement of what has come to be understood as the dominant Frankfurt School position on modernism and mass culture, see Theodor W. Adorno, "Commitment," in *The Essential Frankfurt School Reader*, ed. Andrew Arato and Eike Gebhardt (New York: Continuum, 1993), 300–18. For a more fully developed treatment, see Adorno, *Aesthetic Theory*, trans. Robert Hullot-Kentor (Minneapolis: University of Minnesota Press, 1997). For an account of the Southern Agrarians' attitude

toward industrialism, see John Crowe Ransom et al., *I'll Take My Stand* (New York: Peter Smith, 1951), esp. ix–xx, 1–27. See Alfred Kazin, *On Native Grounds: An Interpretation of Modern American Prose Literature* (New York: Harcourt Brace Jovanovich, 1942), for an account of the moral imperative that subtends the best modern literature and that distinguishes it from mass cultural forms of entertainment. For a good account of the New Criticism and the New York Intellectuals that treats them convincingly as relatively coherent "schools" of criticism, see Vincent B. Leitch's *American Literary Criticism from the Thirties to the Eighties* (New York: Columbia University Press, 1988), 24–59, 81–114. For a similar, if much more fully developed, account of the Frankfurt School, see Martin Jay's *The Dialectical Imagination* (Berkeley: University of California Press, 1996).

11. See Andreas Huyssen, *After the Great Divide: Modernism, Mass Culture, Postmodernism* (Bloomington: Indiana University Press, 1986), esp. vii–62; and Fredric Jameson, "Reification and Utopia in Mass Culture," in *Signatures of the Visible* (New York: Routledge, 1990), 9–34.

12. A partial survey of this recent trend in modernist criticism, what has been termed the "new modernist studies," might include the essays in *Marketing Modernisms: Self-Promotion, Canonization, and Rereading*, ed. Kevin J. H. Dettmar and Stephen Watt (Ann Arbor: University of Michigan Press, 1996); those in *Rereading the New*, ed. Kevin J. H. Dettmar (Ann Arbor: University of Michigan Press, 1992); Bonnie Kime Scott, "Introduction," *The Gender of Modernism* (Bloomington: Indiana University Press, 1990), 1–18; George Hutchinson, *The Harlem Renaissance in Black and White* (Cambridge, Mass.: Harvard University Press, 1995); Walter Benn Michaels, *Our America* (Durham, N.C.: Duke University Press, 1995); Ann Douglas, *Terrible Honesty* (New York: Farrar, Straus and Giroux, 1995); Michael North, *The Dialect of Modernism: Race, Language, and Twentieth-Century Literature* (Oxford: Oxford University Press, 1994); Thomas Strychacz, *Modernism, Mass Culture, Professionalism* (Cambridge: Cambridge University Press, 1993); and Michael Denning, *The Cultural Front: The Laboring of American Culture in the Twentieth Century* (London: Verso, 1997). An interesting corollary to this argument that is suggestive for my consideration of the relationship between hard-boiled writing and modernism is James Naremore's recent rehistoricization of film noir within the context of European and American modernism, in *More than Night: Film Noir in its Contexts* (Berkeley: University of California Press, 1998), 40–96.

13. Alfred Kazin, one of the few critics to attend to the mixed cultural character of much of Faulkner's literary output, describes this lack of fit as Faulkner's "inability to choose between Dostoevsky and Hollywood Boulevard" (426). Of course, Kazin only calls attention to the mixed nature of Faulkner's literary output in order to denigrate it and to further inscribe the very boundary between high and mass culture that Faulkner's work troubles.

14. Another popular genre that *Light in August* can be read in relationship to is the race melodrama. For an account of this genre and its ideological implications for constructions of race in the United States, see Susan Gillman, *Blood*

Talk: American Race Melodrama and the Culture of the Occult (Chicago: University of Chicago Press, 2003).

15. On Faulkner's relationship to orality, see Richard Gray's *The Life of William Faulkner* (Cambridge: Blackwell, 1994), 48–52. Alwyn Berland also touches on Faulkner's relationship to oral forms of storytelling in Light in August: *A Study in Black and White* (New York: Twayne-Macmillan, 1992), 12.

16. For an account of the relationship of Faulkner's fiction to mass culture and more generally to modernization, see John T. Matthews, *"As I Lay Dying in the Machine Age,"* in *National Identities and Post-Americanist Narratives*, ed. Donald E. Pease (Durham, N.C.: Duke University Press, 1994), 69–94.

17. My understanding of the metacritical dimensions of *Light in August* has been shaped by Peter Brooks's groundbreaking account of the metacritical preoccupations with narrative and epistemology in *Absalom, Absalom!* See Brooks, *Reading for the Plot: Design and Intention in Narrative* (Cambridge, Mass.: Harvard University Press, 1984), 286–312.

18. For an account of the relationship of modernist aesthetics to forms of cultural memory, see Richard Terdiman, *Present Past: Modernity and the Memory Crisis* (Ithaca, N.Y.: Cornell University Press, 1993). For a brief account of the relationship of modernist writing practices to transformations in scientific and cultural understandings of perception, see James McFarlane, "The Mind of Modernism," in *Modernism: A Guide to European Literature, 1890–1930*, ed. Malcolm Bradbury and James McFarlane (New York: Penguin, 1991).

19. This understanding of the separation and distinctiveness of the two spheres is, of course, deeply enmeshed in what I have been calling the dynamics of cultural fantasy. Indeed, the division of culture into discrete and seemingly autonomous spheres functions, in part, by a logic of disavowal, in which the irreducible heterogeneity of any cultural object or space becomes defined as homogeneous through an act of selective interpretation. From the point of view of canon formation, this logic of disavowal functions retrospectively, fixing a diverse set of texts into a set of definable and discrete categories. Yet, while it is important to attend to the retrospective dimensions of canon formation, I also do not want to dismiss the distinction between high and popular culture as entirely the product of retrospective fantasy. For, as Lawrence Levine and others have demonstrated, this divide had already emerged as fully formed by the turn of the century, taking shape not only in the domain of cultural fantasy but also within various institutional and material contexts. Indeed, the presence of this divide is clearly visible in the formal miscegenations of a text like *Light in August*. For an account of the emergence of the divide between high and popular culture, see Lawrence Levine, *Highbrow/Lowbrow: The Emergence of Cultural Hierarchy in America* (Cambridge, Mass.: Harvard University Press, 1988); and Stychacz, *Modernism, Mass Culture, Professionalism*.

20. On the race melodrama, see Gilman, *Blood Talk*, 1–31, 73–116.

21. See Joseph Reed, *"Light in August,"* in *William Faulkner: Modern Critical Views*, ed. Harold Bloom (New York: Chelsea, 1986), 77–81.

22. In theorizing the intersections between questions of race and questions of masculinity, this chapter takes part of its inspiration from Michael Uebel's call, in *Race and the Subject of Masculinities*, ed. Harry Stecopoulos and Michael Uebel (Durham, N.C.: Duke University Press, 1997), for a "dialectical constructionist view of racial and gender subjectivities" that would "understand men at the (construction) site of specific power relations, each relation mediating the reproduction and transformation of another" (2–4). While sharing their dialectical and, to a certain extent, their social constructionist aims, my chapter attempts to demonstrate the necessity of supplementing a materialist understanding of culture and the political economy and a theory of individual and collective fantasy to their dialectical understanding of social construction. It has also been shaped by Laura Doyle's brilliant analysis of subjectification and the phenomenological experience of embodiment in *Light in August*. See Doyle, "The Body against Itself in Faulkner's Phenomenology of Race," *American Literature* 73, no. 2 (2001): 339–64.

23. This shift has been theorized in different ways. In his Jamesonian analysis of the effects of this shift on Faulkner's writings, Richard Gray characterizes it as one from a semifeudal mode of production to an industrial-capitalist mode (*Life*, 12–60). Carolyn Porter, in *Seeing and Being: The Plight of the Participant Observer in Emerson, James, Adams, and Faulkner* (Middletown, Conn.: Wesleyan University Press, 1981), on the other hand, implicitly defines the shift as a movement from one phase of capitalism to another by arguing that the conception of the South as "un-American and non-capitalist in the ante-bellum period" is a cultural myth—one that does conservative ideological work (211). While essentially corroborating this latter view, the economist Gavin Wright, in *Old South, New South: Revolutions in the Southern Economy since the Civil War* (Baton Rouge: Louisiana State University Press, 1986), argues that the question itself is badly posed; that, while capitalist, the slave-owning class was distinct from other capitalist classes and thus its situation and the economic organization of the South contributed to the formation of a distinct regional culture and labor pool. Wright goes on to argue that, contrary to conventional accounts, this regional culture and labor pool remained largely intact during the great migrations and modernizations of the twenties and thirties and was only truly transformed after the Second World War. Yet he also situates the process of the nationalization of the Southern economy as an ongoing one that begins in the Reconstruction period and continues up through the Second World War and beyond. While I see modernization as having a greater impact on Southern life in the twenties and thirties than does Wright, this is primarily because I focus on the growth of mass culture and technology rather than on the relative autonomy versus integration of the Southern labor market. In my analysis of the shift between different forms of economic organization, I side with Wright and Porter. As Immanuel Wallerstein has argued, it is important to understand slavery and the imperial conquest of the Americas as part of the emergence of the capitalist world system and not as an archaic holdover from the persistence of semifeudal

modes of production. To do otherwise is to mystify the violence underwritten by
capitalism as a mode of production. Thus I would see the transition as a major
shift, but one between different forms of capitalism within a single capitalist mode
of production rather than as a shift in modes of production. For Wallerstein's
theorization of this issue, see Wallerstein, "American Slavery and the Capitalist
World-Economy," in *The Capitalist World-Economy* (Cambridge: Cambridge University Press, 1979), 202–21; and Wallerstein and Anibal Quijano, "Americanity
as a Concept, or the Americas in the Modern World-System," *International Social
Science Journal* 44, no. 4 (1992): 549–57.

24. I am using the term "antimodernism" in the sense articulated by T. J.
Jackson Lears in *No Place of Grace: Antimodernism and the Transformation of American Culture, 1880–1920* (New York: Pantheon, 1981).

25. While the idea of the New South had been around since the 1880s, it
gained new currency in the late twenties and early thirties with the controversy
around the possibility of federal investment in Mussel Shoals and what would
become the Tennessee Valley Authority in 1933. Both the Ku Klux Klan and
evangelical Protestantism grew exponentially in the twenties, emerging as dominant political forces in whole sections of the South and Southwest and influ-
encing national politics. For a synoptic account of this opposition between
modernist and antimodernist tendencies in the South, see Dewey W. Grantham,
The South in Modern America: A Region at Odds (New York: Harper Collins, 1994),
88–115.

26. See Angela Davis, *Women, Race, and Class* (New York: Vintage, 1983), 172–
202. For recent critical takes on *Light in August* that emphasize the relationship
of Joe Christmas to the figure of the black rapist, see Eric Sundquist, *House
Divided* (Baltimore: Johns Hopkins University Press, 1983), 63–95; and Robyn
Wiegman, *American Anatomies: Theorizing Race and Gender* (Durham, N.C.: Duke
University Press, 1995), 90. For additional accounts of the "myth of the black
rapist" and the more general discourse of Negro-as-savage, see George Fredrickson, *The Black Image in the White Mind: The Debate on Afro-American Character
and Destiny, 1817–1914* (Hanover, N.H.: Wesleyan University Press, 1971), 256–
82; and Gail Bederman, *Manliness and Civilization: A Cultural History of Gender
and Race in the United States, 1880–1917* (Chicago: University of Chicago Press,
1995), 1–77.

27. See Wiegman, *American Anatomies*, 81–113.

28. See Sundquist, *House Divided*, 63–95.

29. See, for example, the epistemological anxiety evident in Cleanth Brooks's
insistence that Joe's tragedy is that "he doesn't know what he is" (51). While critical of the ideals of traditional community celebrated by Brooks, Irving Howe
takes the same view of the tragic dimensions of interracial identity. See Howe,
William Faulkner: A Critical Study (New York: Random House, 1952), 85. And for
an indication of how little has changed in terms of critical anxiety around racial
definition, see Philip Weinstein, "Postmodern Intimations: Musings on Invisi-
bility: William Faulkner, Richard Wright, and Ralph Ellison," in *Faulkner and*

Postmodernism, ed. John N. Duvall and Ann J. Abadie (Jackson: University Press of Mississippi, 2002), 19–38. For a recent discussion of miscegenation in literature that focuses on it as a positive, if conflicted, site of cultural productivity rather than as a social problem in need of solution, see Werner Sollors, *Neither Black nor White yet Both: Thematic Explorations of Interracial Literature* (Oxford: Oxford University Press, 1997).

30. For an account of the way in which the thematics of miscegenation in *Light in August* apply to the novel's engagement with temporality, see Krister Friday, "Miscegenated Time: The Spectral Body, Race, and Temporality in *Light in August*," *Faulkner Journal* 16, no. 3 (2001): 41–63.

31. Freud discusses the dynamics of *nachtraglichkeit*, which has been variously translated as "retroactive meaning" or "deferred action," in the "Wolf Man" case history. See, "From the History of an Infantile Neurosis," in *The Standard Edition of the Complete Psychological Works of Sigmund Freud*, trans. and ed. James Strachey (London: Hogarth, 1955), 17: 29–47. See also the entry on "Deferred Action" in J. Laplanche and J. B. Pontalis, *The Language of Psycho-Analysis*, trans. Donald Nicholson-Smith (New York: Norton, 1973), 111–14.

32. See John T. Irwin, *Doubling and Incest, Repetition and Revenge* (Baltimore: Johns Hopkins University Press, 1975), 8–9.

33. See Sigmund Freud, "The Uncanny," in *The Standard Edition of the Complete Psychological Works of Sigmund Freud*, 17: 217–56. For a suggestive reading of Freud's uncanny in relation to questions of racial and national identity, see Priscilla Wald, *Constituting Americans: Cultural Anxiety and Narrative Form* (Durham, N.C.: Duke University Press, 1995), 1–13.

34. The adjective "lonely" suggests merely the negative recasting of the hard-boiled male's prized individualism, one that has its roots in the noir stories that preceded the hard-boiled genre and became increasingly central to the noir fiction and film noir of the thirties, forties, and fifties. The emphasis on loneliness enabled both French and American critics to read the genre in terms of existentialism.

35. For a discussion of the logic of condensation in the psychoanalytic account of dreams, see Freud, "The Interpretation of Dreams," in *The Standard Edition of the Complete Psychological Works of Sigmund Freud*, 4: 279–304.

36. See David Harvey, *The Condition of Postmodernity: An Enquiry into the Origin of Cultural Change* (Cambridge: Blackwell, 1989), 16–17, for a discussion of this ambivalent promise.

37. It is important to note the retrospective dimension of this representation of the men in the house of prostitution; this section is narrated in flashback and is structured by the complex condensations and displacements that organize Joe's reconstruction of the past. Thus this representation of the presence of hard-boiled masculinity in the years just before 1920 (given that this takes place fifteen years earlier) may be as much a product of Joe's retrospective construction as it is an indication of the ways in which the forms of masculinity found in early-twentieth-century crime fiction functioned as the immediate precursor

of hard-boiled masculinity. In this context Joe's memory here can be read as what Freud terms a "screen memory," one that is employed to provide a useable past for the form of masculinity embodied by the adult Joe. See Freud, "Screen Memories," in *The Standard Edition of the Complete Psychological Works of Sigmund Freud*, 3: 299–322.

38. See George Fredrickson, *The Black Image in the White Mind*, 256–319, and Wiegman, *American Anatomies*, 81–113.

39. My use of the term "abjection" comes from the use of this term by Judith Butler and Lauren Berlant to describe the material and discursive violence produced by phobic ideologies of repudiation, such as homophobia or negrophobia. Central to Butler's theorization of this term is the assertion that it works by a logic of foreclosure, in which that which is repudiated in the individual subject is projected onto and punished in the space of the other. See Butler, *Bodies That Matter: On the Discursive Limits of "Sex"* (New York: Routledge, 1993), 93–119. Berlant emphasizes the "political specificity of abjection's double process: as a kind of social identity and as a kind of effect some people have on others." See Berlant, *The Queen of America Goes to Washington City: Essays on Sex and Citizenship* (Durham, N.C.: Duke University Press, 1997), 286. Both theorists are influenced by Julia Kristeva's pioneering discussion of abjection in *The Powers of Horror*, trans. Léon Roudiez (New York: Columbia University Press, 1982).

5. Freudian Knot or Gordian Knot?

1. See, for example, Wanda Coleman's comments on Himes: "And on my Top Ten list of black writers he [Iceberg Slim] would not appear—neither would Chester Himes, whom I don't like because of all of his shame; all his bootlicking; all of his catering to white racist conceptions about blacks. . . Even though the language and some of the descriptions may be interesting, nevertheless all that hatred is there and it's sick—from my point of view it's very unhealthy." See Coleman, "Wanda Coleman, " in *Angry Women*, ed. Andrea Juno and V. Vale (San Francisco: Re/Search, 1991), 126.

2. See Henry Louis Gates Jr., *Figures in Black: Words, Signs, and the "Racial" Self* (New York: Oxford University Press, 1987), 3–58.

3. See Gilbert H. Muller's *Chester Himes* (Boston: G. K. Hall, 1989), 28–29, for a nice discussion of the absurd dimensions of Himes's fiction and the challenge it poses for the tradition of social protest fiction. My thinking about the postmodern dimensions of Himes's fiction has been influenced by Stephanie Brown's "The Black Joke in Chester Himes' *The End of a Primitive*," which she delivered as part of the "Understanding and Locating Chester Himes" panel at the 1998 meeting of the American Studies Association in Seattle.

4. See Edward Margolies and Michel Fabre, *The Several Lives of Chester Himes* (Jackson: University Press of Mississippi, 1997); James Sallis, *Chester Himes: A Life* (New York: Walker, 2001); and Robert Polito, ed., *Crime Novels: American Noir of the 1950s* (New York: Library of America, 1997). In the last ten

years there have been more than ninety-four separate listings on Chester Himes in the MLA database. The panel is the one mentioned above in note 3.

5. Kimberlé Williams Crenshaw, "Mapping the Margins: Intersectionality, Identity Politics, and Violence against Women of Color," in *Critical Race Theory: The Key Writings That Formed the Movement*, ed. Kimberlé Crenshaw, Neil Gotonda, Gary Peller, and Kendall Thomas (New York: New York University Press, 1995), 357–83.

6. Frantz Fanon, *Black Skin, White Masks*, trans. Charles Lam Markmann (New York: Grove Press, 1967), 109.

7. Lubiano's brilliant critique of the dangers of positive representation emerges in the context of an analysis of gender and national politics in Tupac Shakur's "Keep Ya Head Up": "Why subject such a song to criticism? Because this kind of positive rap, which comes out of conventional Madonna-whore narratives, beautifully plays out the black equivalent of family-values discourse and is therefore more disturbing than gangsta rap. It is more disturbing precisely because it is so easily accommodated, so easily routinized in ways that reproduce the problematic status quo. It does this in large part because it is beautiful. It is because it is not transgressive, not dramatic and sensational, that it doesn't draw our attention to its ideological content. Its contrast to the rhetoric of gangsta rap—a form explicitly and deliberately situated outside civil mores—lulls our critical faculties as it helps contribute aesthetically to the pleasure of consuming family values, differently styled." See Waneema Lubiano, "Black Nationalism and Black Common Sense: Policing Ourselves and Others," in *The House That Race Built: Original Essays by Toni Morrison, Angela Y. Davis, Cornel West, and Others on Black Americans and Politics in America Today*, ed. Lubiano and Arnold Rampersad (New York: Vintage, 1998), 247. Lubiano's critique of positive representation and her defense of transgressive aesthetics have helped to shape my thinking about the value of the transgressive and the negative in Himes's fiction for challenging the repressive dimensions of American liberalism. In my reading of *If He Hollers Let Him Go*, my understanding of the political work done by Himes's fiction challenges Sean McCann's recent account, which situates Himes's texts within the broad purview of American liberalism. See McCann, *Gumshoe America: Hard-Boiled Crime Fiction and the Rise and Fall of New Deal Liberalism* (Durham, N.C.: Duke University Press, 2000), 251–305.

8. The phrase "tarrying with the negative" comes of course from Slavoj Žižek's book of the same name, *Tarrying with the Negative: Kant, Hegel, and the Critique of Ideology* (Durham, N.C.: Duke University Press, 1993).

9. While I will generally use the term "hard-boiled" throughout to characterize the generic borrowings of *If He Hollers Let Him Go*, particularly since the construction of masculinity in the novel is clearly modeled on the forms of male subjectivity found in the hard-boiled novel, it should be understood that this is a hard-boiled text that has been particularly shaped by the generic and phantasmatic deformations that I term "noir" (see chapter 1 for a full theorization of these deformations). And indeed, if one were to attempt to define noir as a genre

(something my own analysis has attempted to resist), the novel could be categorized as a noir novel as much as a hard-boiled one.

10. For accounts of the relationship between Himes's fiction and the hard-
boiled form, see Jay R. Berry Jr., "Chester Himes and the Hard-Boiled Tradition,"
in *The Critical Response to Chester Himes*, ed. Charles L. P. Silet (Westport, Conn.:
Greenwood Press, 1999), 117–26; Fred Pfeil, "Policiers Noirs," in *The Critical
Response to Chester Himes*, 37–40; and George E. Kent, "Rhythms of Black Experience," in *The Critical Response to Chester Himes*, 17–20. For a psychoanalytically
inflected reading of this relationship, see Greg Forter, *Murdering Masculinities:
Fantasies of Gender and Violence in the American Crime Novel* (New York: New York
University Press, 2000), 171–213. While my reading of the phantasmatic logic
that underpins the hard-boiled form differs from Forter's account (he is more
focused on the logic of abjection, while I am more concerned with the broader
political and sexual fantasies that structure the form), our understandings of the
form as libidinally saturated with racial and gendered meanings are quite similar.

11. In an interview with John Williams, Himes himself comments on the
relationship between his representation of the violent intersectionalities of
American life and the hard-boiled detective form: "My French editor says, the
Americans have a style of writing detective stories [i.e., the hard-boiled style]
that no one has been able to imitate, and that's why he has made his *Série Noire*
successful, by using American detective story writers. There is no reason why the
black American, who is also an American, like all other Americans, and brought
up in this sphere of violence which is the main sphere of American detective
stories, there is no reason why he shouldn't write them. It's just plain and simple
violence in narrative form, you know. 'Cause no one, *no one*, writes about violence
the way that Americans do. As a matter of fact for the simple reason that no one
understands or expresses violence like the American civilians do. American violence is public life, it is a public way of life, it became a form, a detective story
form." See Michel Fabre and Robert E. Skinner, *Conversations with Chester Himes*
(Jackson: University Press of Mississippi, 1995), 47–48 (italics in original).

12. My positive use of the term "desublimation" derives from Earl Jackson's
critical rereading of Freud's *Leonardo da Vinci and a Memory of His Childhood* in
Jackson, *Strategies of Deviance: Studies in Gay Male Representation* (Bloomington:
Indiana University Press, 1995). In contrast to Freud's valorization of sublima-
tion as a channeling of libidinal energies and instincts toward the higher ends of
artistic or intellectual production, Jackson constructs it as a specifically phantasmatic form of ideology construction, in which the libidinal investments motivat-
ing forms of representation are occluded and obscured. Jackson instead posits an
ethics and critical practice of desublimation in which the libidinal and phantasmatic investments animating forms of representation and other modes of historiography are foregrounded rather than obscured (53–92).

13. My analysis of the representation of African American masculinity in *If
He Hollers Let Him Go* has been influenced by the following texts: Philip Brian
Harper, *Are We Not Men?* (New York: Oxford University Press, 1996); Hazel V.

Carby, *Race Men* (Cambridge, Mass.: Harvard University Press, 1998); Robyn Wiegman, *American Anatomies: Theorizing Race and Gender* (Durham, N.C.: Duke University Press, 1995); and the essays contained in *Race and the Subject of Masculinities*, ed. Harry Stecopoulos and Michael Uebel (Durham, N.C.: Duke University Press, 1997). Harper's and Carby's analyses of the forms of subjectivity and political representation excluded by dominant constructions of African American masculinity have been particularly valuable in helping me to think through the range of subjectivities embodied by Himes's protagonists in their relationship to dominant constructions of African American masculinity.

14. My understanding of the relationship between the intersubjective gaze and the formation of subjectivity comes out of the work done on the specular constitution of subjectivity in feminist film theory and in the work of Frantz Fanon. See *Black Skin, White Masks*, 109–40, and Laura Mulvey's "Visual Pleasure and Narrative Cinema," in *Feminism and Film Theory*, ed. Constance Penley (New York: Routledge, 1988), as well as Kaja Silverman's important revision of Mulvey's theory in Silverman, *Male Subjectivity at the Margins* (New York: Routledge, 1992), 125–56. Silverman convincingly argues that Lacanian psychoanalysis provides an important corrective to theories such as Mulvey's that seem to equate the possession of the gaze with valorized masculinity. In *The Four Fundamental Concepts of Psycho-Analysis*, trans. Alan Sheridan (New York: Norton, 1981), Lacan provides an account of the specular construction of subjectivity that locates the gaze as necessarily external to the subject. It is that which constitutes subjectivity itself within the visual field. Thus, in the Lacanian schema, no one can possess the gaze; as with the phallus, they can merely appropriate its signification. Masculinist ideology thus works, in part, by conflating the masculine look with the constitutive power of the gaze. While I am persuaded by Silverman's analysis, I have decided to deploy both Mulvey's and Fanon's language, which designates certain subjects as having possession of the gaze. I have opted for this latter language because it describes the way in which the *cultural fantasies* of visual power and visual disempowerment are experienced.

15. The distinctions between symbolization and acting out as well as between repetition and working through come from Freud, "Remembering, Repeating, and Working-Through," in *The Standard Edition of the Complete Psychological Works of Sigmund Freud*, trans. and ed. James Strachey (London: Hogarth, 1955), 12: 145–56. See also the entries on "Acting Out," "Transference," and "Symbolism" in J. Laplanche and J. B. Pontalis, *The Language of Psychoanalysis*, trans. Donald Nicholson-Smith (New York: Norton: 1973), 4–6, 442–45, 455–62.

16. For a very different, Levinasian account of the representation of ethics in *If He Hollers Let Him Go*, see Adam Zachary Newton, "From Exegesis to Ethics: Recognition and its Vicissitudes in Saul Bellow and Chester Himes," *South Atlantic Quarterly* 95, no. 4 (Fall 1996): 979–1007.

17. Himes put it this way: "Well, I would like to see produced a novel that just drains a person's subconscious of all his attitudes and reactions to everything. Because, obviously, if one person has a number of thoughts concerning anything,

there is cohesion. There has to be because they belong to one man. Just let it come out as it is, let it come out in the phrasing of the subconscious and let it become a novel in that form. Of course this has been done, but not purely; there's always been an artificial strain. Since the black American is subject to having millions of thoughts concerning everything, millions of reactions, and his reactions and thoughts will obviously be different from that of the white community, this should obviously create a different structure of the novel" (Fabre and Skinner, *Conversations*, 67).

18. For a full discussion of these two concepts, see Michael Denning, *The Cultural Front: The Laboring of American Culture in the Twentieth Century* (London: Verso, 1997); and Alan Nadel, *Containment Culture: American Narratives, Postmodernism, and the Atomic Age* (Durham, N.C.: Duke University Press, 1995). In addition to the compelling periodizations provided by both these texts, my thinking about politics and culture in the midcentury United States has also been influenced by the following texts: Robert Corber, *Homosexuality in Cold War America: Resistance and the Crisis of Masculinity* (Durham, N.C.: Duke University Press, 1997); Barbara Foley, *Radical Representations* (Durham, N.C.: Duke University Press, 1993); William Maxwell, *New Negro, Old Left* (New York: Columbia University Press, 1999); Nikhil Pal Singh, "Culture/Wars: Recoding Empire in an Age of Democracy," *American Quarterly* 50, no. 3 (1998): 471–522. Maxwell, in particular, provides some important correctives to Denning's occasionally overly optimistic historical narrative. In a similar way, Corber, Singh, and Denning correct Nadel's tendency to see containment everywhere.

19. This disavowal is, of course, a disavowal of the psychological materials inherited from what I termed in chapter 1 the "psychological noir." Thus, while hard-boiled fiction inherited contrasting tendencies from both the psychological and the sociological noir, it worked to disavow the former set of materials. It is these materials that are for the first time critically engaged in the ("psychological") noir narratives of Thompson, Highsmith, and Himes in the 1950s.

20. Chester Himes, *If He Hollers Let Him Go* (New York: New American Library, 1941), 6.

21. Chester Himes, *My Life of Absurdity: The Later Years—The Autobiography of Chester Himes* (New York: Paragon House, 1976), 1.

22. For an account of the failed promise represented by Los Angeles for thousands of African Americans who migrated there during the war and the thematization of this failed promise in Himes's writings, see Bruce A. Glassrud and Laurie Champion, "'No Land of the Free': Chester Himes Confronts California," *CLA Journal* 44, no. 3 (2001): 391–416. For the larger economic and racial contradictions of Los Angeles in this period, see Mike Davis, *City of Quartz: Excavating the Future in Los Angeles* (London: Verso, 1990), 17–97.

23. On the relationship of Himes's fiction to the representation of the black laborer, also see Robert Skinner, "The Black Man in the Literature of Labor: The Early Novels of Chester Himes," in *The Critical Response to Chester Himes*, 187–200.

24. See Steven J. Rosen, "African American Anti-Semitism and Himes' *Lonely Crusade*," in *The Critical Response to Chester Himes*, 221–40, for an account of the relationship of Himes's writings to black anti-Semitism. While I have some quarrels with Rosen's conclusions, he deserves praise for tackling a difficult and important subject.

25. See Eve Kosofsky Sedgwick, *Between Men: English Literature and Male Homosocial Desire* (New York: Columbia University Press, 1985), 1–20.

26. On the power of American liberalism to co-opt even the most seemingly radical political positions, see Sacvan Bercovitch, *Rites of Assent* (New York: Routledge, 1993), 1–67, 307–52. To the degree that Bercovitch's analysis of the resilience of American liberalism is descriptive, I find it an invaluable account of the power of a given ideological and national formation. To the degree that it becomes proscriptive, however, it must be resisted as a manifestation of the very ideology it attempts to critique. See also Louis Hartz's classic account of the terms of American liberalism, *The Liberal Tradition in America* (New York: Harcourt Brace Jovanovich, 1991).

27. Himes was in fact an advocate of violent black revolution for much of his life. His position on this issue remained relatively unchanged, from an early piece written for *The Crisis* in 1944, "Negro Martyrs Are Needed" (in Chester Himes, *Black on Black: Baby Sister and Selected Writings* [New York: Doubleday, 1973]) to the 1970 interview with John Williams, in which he asserts, "It's just an absolute fact that if the blacks in America were to mount a revolution in force, with organized violence to the saturation point, that the entire black problem would be solved" (Fabre and Skinner, *Conversations*, 58). Indeed, one can read Himes's position as it is elaborated in *If He Hollers Let Him Go* as pointing toward the forms of "ethical" revolutionary violence articulated by Frantz Fanon in *The Wretched of the Earth*, trans. Constance Farrington (New York: Grove Press, 1963), 35–106. Like Himes, Fanon denigrated the effects of misplaced and disorganized violence, championing the value of organized violence for colonized peoples. This conception of ethical violence in the service of revolution forms the subject of Himes's final novel, *Plan B*.

Conclusion

1. See Sean McCann, "'A Roughneck Reaching for Higher Things': The Vagaries of Pulp Populism," *Radical History Review* 61 (1995): 4–10; and Erin Smith, *Hard-Boiled: Working-Class Readers and Pulp Magazines* (Philadelphia: Temple University Press, 2000), 1–12, 79–102.

2. The concept of metahistory comes, of course, from the Hayden White volume of the same name. In his practice of metahistory, White emphasizes the tropological and narrative underpinnings of historical narrative. My own use of the concept of metahistory has as much in common with Walter Benjamin's injunction to "brush history against the grain," and my own engagement with cultural fantasy, as it does with White's narratological account of the fictiveness

of historical narrative. See White, *Metahistory: The Historical Imagination in Nineteenth-Century Europe* (Baltimore: Johns Hopkins University Press, 1974), ix-42, and Benjamin, *Illuminations*, trans. Harry Zohn (Bungay, Suffolk: Fontana, 1973), 258–59.

3. The texts I am thinking of here are the following: Janice A. Radway, *Reading the Romance: Women, Patriarchy, and Popular Literature* (Chapel Hill: University of North Carolina Press, 1984); Radway, *A Feeling for Books: The Book-of-the-Month-Club, Literary Taste, and Middle-Class Desire* (Chapel Hill: University of North Carolina Press, 1997); Ien Ang, *Watching "Dallas": Soap Opera and the Melodramatic Imagination*, trans. Della Couling (London: Methuen, 1985); Ang, *Desperately Seeking the Audience* (New York: Routledge, 1991); Constance Penley, "Feminism, Psychoanalysis, and the Study of Popular Culture," in *Cultural Studies*, ed. Lawrence Grossberg, Cary Nelson, and Paula Treichler (New York: Routledge, 1992); Penley, *NASA/TREK: Popular Science and Sex in America* (London: Verso, 1997). For a more complete account of the history of audience/reception studies, especially in the British context, see Graeme Turner, *British Cultural Studies*, 2d ed. (New York: Routledge, 1996), 122–55.

4. See Fredric Jameson, "Reification and Utopia in Mass Culture," in *Signatures of the Visible* (New York: Routledge, 1990), 9–34; and Jameson, *The Political Unconscious: Narrative as a Socially Symbolic Act* (Ithaca, N.Y.: Cornell University Press, 1981), 281–99.

5. See Karl Marx, *Capital, vol. 1*, trans. Ben Fowkes (New York: Random House, 1976).

6. Slavoj Žižek, *The Sublime Object of Ideology* (London: Verso, 1989), 32–33.

7. The commodity status of even the most rarified of high-modernist experiment has been convincingly demonstrated by many of the essays collected in *Marketing Modernisms: Self-Promotion, Canonization, Rereading*, ed. Kevin J. H. Dettmar and Stephen Watt (Ann Arbor: University of Michigan Press, 1996). See especially their introduction to the volume.

8. *Black Mask* 5, no. 8 (December 1922): 123–24.

9. See Max Horkheimer and Theodor W. Adorno, *Dialectic of Enlightenment*, trans. John Cumming (New York: Herder and Herder, 1972), 120–67.

10. I am, of course, thinking here of the definitions of realism proposed by George Lukács in *Studies in European Realism* (New York: Grosset and Dunlap, 1964) (among other places) and Erich Auerbach in *Mimesis*, trans. Willard R. Trask (Princeton, N.J.: Princeton University Press, 1953).

11. *Clues* 9, no. 4 (March 1929): 555–56.

12. Michael Denning, *Mechanic Accents: Dime Novels and Working-Class Culture in America* (London: Verso, 1987), 65–84.

13. See Fredric Jameson, *Postmodernism, or, The Cultural Logic of Late Capitalism* (Durham, N.C.: Duke University Press, 1991), esp. 1–54, for an account of the shift from a modernist to a postmodernist cultural logic. For an account of the shift from Fordism to post-Fordism, see David Harvey, *The Condition of*

Postmodernity: An Enquiry into the Origin of Cultural Change (Cambridge: Blackwell, 1989), 121–200.

14. See Fred Pfeil, *White Guys: Studies in Postmodern Domination and Difference* (London: Verso, 1995), 105–66

15. R. W. Connell, *Masculinities* (Berkeley: University of California Press, 1995), 226.

Index

Abbott, Megan E., 194–95n8
abjection, 140, 154, 163, 222n39, 224n10
Absalom, Absalom! (Faulkner), 116
absurd, the, 145, 151, 153–54, 222n3
acting out, 19, 77, 149, 152, 166, 170–71, 197n32, 225n15. *See also* action
action, 16, 18, 21–22, 89, 120, 150, 153, 155, 161, 165–66, 170–71, 178, 185
Action Detective (magazine), 14, 37
Adair, William, 214n34
Adorno, Theodor W., 27, 43–44, 57, 86, 181, 193n2, 211n13, 216n10
adventure romance. *See* romance
aesthetics, 19, 21, 22, 27, 28, 37–38, 43, 45–46, 58, 63, 68, 70–71, 73, 75, 87–91, 116–18, 126, 133, 143–55, 176, 185, 195n13, 205n19, 218n18
affect, 1, 17–18, 20, 31, 40, 54, 58, 60–61, 68–72, 78, 80, 87–89, 109, 111–12, 149–50, 151, 152–55, 158, 159–60, 162, 163, 165–66, 171, 188
African American hard-boiled writer, 21, 143–73
African American literature, field of, 35, 143, 144–45, 151
African American masculinity, 2, 15, 21–22, 27, 32–36, 51–52, 55, 68, 75, 97–98, 121, 137–38, 143–73, 224–25n13
agency, 21–22, 95, 105, 120, 122, 133, 140–41, 163–64, 170–73, 175, 178–81, 186–87
aggression, 71–72, 106, 144, 149

agrarian capitalism, 28, 122–23
agrarian existence, 124, 126
agricultural capitalism. *See* agrarian capitalism
allegory, 25–27, 43–44, 46, 47, 50, 54, 63, 65–66, 69–72, 74, 111, 130, 135, 143, 163, 166–67, 175–76, 182, 182, 203–4n12, 204n16, 205–6n25. *See also* national allegory
Althusser, Louis, 16, 201n.30
ambivalence, 14, 15, 30, 40, 71, 73, 84–85, 88, 93, 96, 100, 106, 110, 120, 121, 136–37, 151, 167, 213n26, 215n4
American literature, field of, 27, 33, 116, 143, 144–45, 206n25
Anderson, Benedict, 204n18
Anderson, Edward, 25, 46
Ang, Ien, 177, 228n3
animalism, discourse of, 49, 51
antagonism, 135–36, 140, 157, 159, 165, 172, 187
antimodernism, 36, 60, 85, 122–23, 132, 135, 196n16, 203n12, 220n24
anti-passing, 134, 135, 140
antiracist struggle, 156–57, 159. *See also* race
anti-Semitism, 100, 108–9, 158, 227n24
anxiety, 94, 108–9, 118, 220–21n29
artisan, the, 27, 29, 42, 47, 59–60, 91, 213n23
Ashley, Lady Brett, 83–84, 88, 90, 92, 93, 96–97, 99, 101, 105–7, 109, 111
"At the Expense of James Cathew" (Loftus), 41, 43–45
Auerbach, Erich, 228n10

231

everyday life, 1, 2, 22, 45, 58, 62, 86,
90, 116–67, 120, 132, 135, 172,
175–77, 184, 186; hard-boiled
masculinity in, 6–12, 22
excorporation, 139
execution sermon, 31, 200n18
existentialism, 153, 221n34
exteriorization, 58, 61, 93

Fabre, Michel, 222n4
"Fall of the House of Usher, The"
(Poe), 34, 53
"False Burton Combs, The" (Daly), 55
Fanon, Frantz, 146, 154, 162, 163,
225n14, 227n27
fantasy, 1–2, 3, 5, 16–19, 24, 44–46,
58, 68, 71–72, 77–78, 143–44, 152,
175, 176–78, 197–98n32, 224n10,
224n12; collective, 2, 22, 45, 46,
175–79, 185, 186–87, 219n22. See
also cultural fantasy
Farewell My Lovely (Chandler),
208n34
Fatina, Richard, 210n9
Faulkner, William, 13, 19, 21, 37,
115–41, 148, 214n1, 215–16n4,
217n13, 219n23
Faulkner and Popular Culture (Fowler
and Abadie), 215n4, 216n6
Fearing, Kenneth, 25, 37, 46
female sexuality, 32–32, 47–48, 52,
54. See also femininity
femininity, 31–32, 54, 71, 94, 101–2,
124, 136, 137–41
feminist theory, 211n18, 225n14
femme fatale, the, 15, 31, 54–55,
69–75, 78, 166–69, 171
fetish, the, 86, 96, 101, 103, 106–7,
109, 137, 178–99. See also
commodity, the
Fiedler, Leslie, 199n14, 206n25
film noir. See noir
film theory, 2–3, 5, 34–35, 195n11,
225n14

first-person voice, 13, 29, 46–47,
49–51, 58, 60, 68, 79–80, 87–88,
148–50, 152
flaneur, the, 13
Floyd, Kevin, 213n27
Foley, Barbara, 226n18
Fordism, 3, 25, 36, 58, 188, 195n12,
202n2, 228n13
foreclosure, 72, 77, 160, 222n39
Forter, Greg, 1, 193n1, 202n3,
216n9, 224n10
Foucault, Michel, 162, 210n12
Foundational Fictions (Sommer),
205–6, n25
Fowler, Doreen, 215n4
frame narrative, 49
France, 35, 86, 98, 110
Frank, Nino, 34–5
Frankfurt School, 13, 116–17,
216n10
Freccero, Carla, 208n38
Fredrickson, George, 200–1n21,
205n22, 220n26
Freedman, Carl, 204n14
free indirect discourse, 134
Freud, Sigmund, 50, 71–72, 81, 90,
128, 129, 143, 150, 152, 179–80,
197–98n32, 206n27, 212n19,
221n31, 221n33, 221n37, 224n12
Friday, Krister, 221n30
frontier, the, 59–60, 74, 102
frontier hero, 28–29, 47, 59

gangsta rap, 188, 223n7
gangster fiction, 37, 41, 43, 201n25.
See also crime fiction
gangster film, 37
Gardner, Earle Stanley, 38
Gates, Henry Louis, 144–45
gaze, the, 13, 148–49, 165, 225n14
Geheren, David, 195–96n14
gender theory, 4
gendered violence. See violence
genre, noir as, 23–24

Gillman, Susan, 200n14, 200n.21, 217n14, 218n20
Glass Key, The (Hammett), 209n4
Glassrud, Bruce A., 226n22
Goddu, Teresa, 27, 32–33, 199n7, 200n19
golden-era detective fiction, 38. *See also* detective fiction
Goodis, David, 25, 46
Gordian knot, 143, 150, 152
gothic, the, 20, 25–26, 27, 31–34, 47–48, 50–55, 61, 70, 78, 87, 200n18, 206nn25–26
Goulart, Ron, 194n3, 209n3, 214n3
Gramsci, Antonio, 151, 202n2
Grantham, Dewey W., 220n25
Gray, Richard, 218n15, 219n23
Grebstein, Sheldon Norman, 209n5
Green Hills of Africa (Hemingway), 213n30
Gregory, Sinda, 195n14, 204n16
Griffith, D. W., 33
Grifters, The (Thompson), 53
grift plot, 53–54, 55
Grosz, Elizabeth, 211n18
Grundrisse, The (Marx), 214n37
Guattari, Félix, 212n20
Guillory, John, 201n27
Gutman, Herbert, 212n22

Halberstam, Juidth, 194n4
Halttunen, Karen, 27, 31–32, 50, 52, 61, 199n7, 200n18
Hamilton, Cynthia, 195n14, 203n8
Hammett, Dashiell, 12, 19, 20, 25, 38–39, 55–56, 57–81, 88–89, 92, 115, 148, 152, 184, 193n2, 204n15, 205n17, 205n19, 209n4
hard-boiled fiction, 1–2, 3, 5, 11, 13–15, 17, 19–22, 23, 25, 31, 34–36, 37–39, 40–41, 46–48, 51–52, 55–56, 57–58, 63, 65–66, 66–75, 76, 78, 80–81, 84, 92, 98, 115–17, 121, 125, 137, 143, 144, 146, 147–51, 152–55, 165, 172, 175–77, 180–84, 186, 188, 194–95n8, 195n11, 195n13, 198n5, 202n3, 202n5, 203n8, 203n12, 205n19, 206n25, 209n3, 214n35, 215n4, 217n12, 221n34, 223n9, 224n10–11. *See also* detective fiction
Harper, Philip Brian, 224n13
Hartz, Louis, 227n26
Harvey, David, 130, 195n12, 198n6, 199n9, 202n2, 211n12, 228n13
hegemony, 141, 159, 188, 195n8; male, 3, 4–5, 195n13
Hemingway, Ernest, 19, 20–21, 37, 83–113
Hennessy, Rosemary, 197n30, 207n33, 210n12
hermeneutic delay, 76
heterosexuality. *See* sexuality
high culture, 12–13, 84, 87, 117–18, 124–25, 143, 196n18, 209n6, 215n4, 217n13, 218n19
Highsmith, Patricia, 25, 46, 144, 151, 226n19
Hilgart, John, 208n40
Himes, Chester, 19, 21–22, 141, 143–73, 175, 187, 222n1, 222nn3–4, 224n11, 225nn16–17, 226n19, 226n23, 227n27
Hinkle, James, 213n25
historical romance. *See* romance
historicism, 17–18, 24–25, 176, 185, 194n8, 202n3
historiography, 5, 160, 212n23, 224n12
history. *See* historicism
Hlavsa, Virginia V. James, 216n8
hobo, the, 125–26
Hobsbawm, Eric, 27–28, 199n14
Hofstadter, Richard, 74, 200n17
"Hole in the Alibi, The" (Baer), 40–41
Holmes, Sherlock, 59, 65

238 | INDEX

Invisible Man (Ellison), 151
irony, 89, 93, 110–11, 205n.19
Irwin, John T., 127–28
"It" (Hammett), 55

Jackson, Earl, Jr., 211n18, 224n12
Japanese-Americans, 157–58
Jay, Martin, 217n10
Jameson, Fredric, 1, 12, 17–19, 70,
117–18, 177, 193n2, 197n29,
198n6, 201n1, 206n25, 211n12,
212n22, 219n23, 228n13
Jeffersonian republic. *See*
republicanism
Jewishness, 108, 158
Jim Crow, 33, 121, 123, 137
J'irai cracher sur vos tombes (Vian),
35
Jones, Bob, 21–22, 143–73
Josephs, Allen, 84–85, 211n17

Kaplan, Amy, 203n9
Kaplan, E. Ann, 24
Kazin, Alfred, 217n10, 217n13
Kazin, Michael, 74
Kendrick, Christopher, 204n14
Kennedy, J. Gerald, 85, 200n19
Kenny, Kevin, 200n15
Kent, George E., 224n10
Kilman, Julian, 19, 39, 40–43
Kimmel, Michael, 6, 61
Klein, Marcus, 29, 199n14
Knight, Stephen, 30, 199n14
"Knights of the Open Palm" (Daly),
36
Kolodny, Annette, 207n30
Kristeva, Julia, 222n39
Krutnick, Frank, 2–3, 24
Ku Klux Klan, 11, 36, 56, 67, 123,
220n25

Lacan, Jacques, 23, 58, 207n29,
208n39, 211n18, 214n32, 225n14
Lait, Jack, 37, 41

Laplanche, Jean, 16, 198n32, 221n31,
225n15
late capitalism, 25, 186–87
law: psychoanalytic concept of, 25,
27, 54–55, 57, 175; social
representatives of, 11, 14, 25, 27,
59, 29–30, 42–43, 46, 48, 54, 57–
58, 62, 64, 96–97, 104, 112, 126,
137–38, 159, 160, 175, 182, 202n5
Lears, T. J. Jackson, 60, 196n15,
220n24
leisure, 85, 92, 93–94, 212n22
Leitch, Vincent B., 217n11
Leland, Jacob Michael, 210n9, 213n26
Lesser, Robert, 214n3
letters to the editor, 22, 176–77, 180,
185–86
Levine, Lawrence, 196n18, 218n19
liberalism, 116, 147, 157, 169;
American, 3, 160, 172, 223n7,
227n26
libido, 1, 15, 17–18, 54, 77, 123, 144,
152, 161, 162–63, 172, 176, 184,
188, 214n36, 224n10, 224n12
Liederman, Earle, 7, 10
Light in August (Faulkner), 15, 21,
115–41, 148, 187, 214n1
Limón, José, 200n15
Lippard, George, 30, 39–40
Loftus, J. Burton, 41, 43–45
Long Goodbye, The (Chandler), 208n34
Los Angeles, 156–58, 163, 172,
226n22
lost generation, 84, 90, 92, 101, 107,
108, 211n17
Lott, Eric, 13, 33, 196n22
Lubiano, Whaneema, 147, 223n7
Lukács, Georg, 203n11, 212n21,
213n27, 228n10
lynching, 123, 137–38, 154–55, 161

Macherey, Pierre, 202n4
Madge (from *If He Hollers*), 158, 164,
166–70, 171

Christopher Breu is assistant professor of English at Illinois State University, where he teaches American literature and popular culture, literature in a global frame, and cultural and critical theory. He has published articles on Chester Himes, Maryse Condé, Frank Sinatra, and Dashiell Hammett in journals such as *Callaloo*, *Men and Masculinities*, and *Prospects*.